PRACTICE TESTS FOR

COGAT®

FORM 7

GRADE 3

LEVEL 9

By Brian Rhee

2 Full-Length Practice Tests

9 Lessons for each Subtest

Detailed Explanations

Legal Notice

CogAT® Cognitive Abilities Test was not involved in the production of this publication nor endorses this book.

Published by: Solomon Academy
First Edition
ISBN-13: 978-1724030160

Acknowledgements

I wish to acknowledge my deepest appreciation to my wife, Sookyung, who has continuously given me wholehearted support, encouragement, and love. Without you, I could not have completed this book.

Thank you to my sons, Joshua and Jason, who have given me big smiles and inspiration. I love you all.

About The Author

Brian(Yeon) Rhee obtained a Masters of Arts Degree in Statistics at Columbia University, NY. He served as the Mathematical Statistician at the Bureau of Labor Statistics, DC. He is the Head Academic Director at Solomon Academy due to his devotion to the community coupled with his passion for teaching. His mission is to help students of all confidence levels excel in academia to build a strong foundation in character, knowledge, and wisdom. Now, Solomon academy is known as the best academy specialized in Math in Northern Virginia.

Brian Rhee has published more than sixteen books. The titles of his books are 7 full-length practice tests for the AP Calculus AB/BC Multiple choice sections, AP Calculus, SAT 1 Math, SAT 2 Math level 2, 12 full-length practice tests for the SAT 2 Math Level 2, SHSAT/TJHSST Math workbook, and IAAT (Iowa Algebra Aptitude Test) Volume 1 and 2, CogAT form 7 Level 8, and NNAT 2 Level B Grade 1. He's currently working on other math books which will be introduced in the near future.

Brian Rhee has more than twenty years of teaching experience in math. He has been one of the most popular tutors among TJHSST (Thomas Jefferson High School For Science and Technology) students. Currently, he is developing many online math courses with www.masterprep.net for AP Calculus AB and BC, SAT 2 Math level 2 test, and other various math subjects.

SOLOMON ACADEMY

Solomon Academy is a prestigious institution of learning with numerous qualified teachers of various fields of education. Our mission is to thoroughly teach students of all ages and confidence levels, elevate skills to the highest standard of education, and provide them with all the tools and materials to succeed.

5723 Centre Square Drive
Centreville, VA 20120
Tel: 703-988-0019

Email: solomonacademyva@gmail.com
info@solomonacademy.net

CLASSES OFFERED

MATHEMATICS	TESTING	ENGLISH
1st-6th grade math	CogAt	1st-6th Reading
Algebra 1, 2	IAAT and SOL 7	1st-6th Writing
Geometry	TJHSST Prep	Essay Writing
Pre-Calculus	SAT/ACT Prep	SAT Writing
AP Calculus AB BC	SAT 2 Subject Tests	
AP Statistics	MathCounts	
Multivariate Calculus	AMC 10/12	

LEARN FROM THE AUTHOR

Private sessions with Brian Rhee is also available on the following subjects: SAT Math, SAT 2 Subject Math Level 2, Pre-Calculus, AP Calculus AB/BC, AP Statistics, IB SL/HL, Multivariate Calculus, Linear Algebra, AMC 8/10/12, and AIME.

Feel free to contact me at solomonacademyva@gmail.com

About Cognitive Abilities Test

The Cognitive Abilities Test (CogAT®) is published by Riverside Publishing. The CogAT® is a multiple choice test and is used to measure the strength of cognitive development and problem solving skills among students. Many school districts use the CogAT® to identify gifted children for admissions into their gifted and talented programs.

The CogAT® consists of three sections called batteries: The verbal battery, the quantitative battery and the nonverbal battery. Each battery is divided into three subtests with different number of questions as shown below.

Battery	Subtests	Number of questions
Verbal	Verbal Analogies	22
	Sentence Completion	20
	Verbal Classification	20
Quantitative	Number Analogies	18
	Number Puzzles	16
	Number Series	18
Nonverbal	Figure Matrices	20
	Paper Folding	16
	Figure Classification	20

Contents

9 LESSONS

FOR

EACH SUBTEST

LESSON 1 Verbal Analogies

Verbal Analogies

In the verbal analogies section, there are 22 questions. In each question, the first 3 words are given to you.

[1st word] $\rightarrow$ [2nd word] : [3rd word] $\rightarrow$ [4th word]

The 1st and 2nd word, and the 3rd and 4th word are separated by an arrow. There is a colon between the first two words and the last two words. It is read as "the 1st word is to the 2nd word as the 3rd word is to the 4th word. "

The 1st and 2nd word are somehow related, and the 3rd and 4th word are also related in a similar way as the first two words.

The verbal analogies questions are about

- Synonyms or Antonyms
- Purpose
- Cause and effect
- Characteristics in common

The objective of the verbal analogies questions is to choose the 4th word from the answer choices so that the relationship between the 3rd and 4th words are similar to the relationship between the 1st and 2nd words.

EXERCISES

Direction: For each question, find the word that completes the relationship between two pairs of words.

1. Bicycle is to road as ship is to ________________.

2. Orange is to fruits as carrot is to ________________.

3. Fingers is to hand as toes is to ________________.

4. Fork is to eat as straw is to ________________.

5. Picture is to wall as watch is to ________________.

6. Wedding is to marriage as cap is to ________________.

7. Pencil is to write as scissors is to ________________.

8. Gift is to happy as funeral is to ________________.

9. Eyes is to see as ears is to ________________.

10. [Morning] → [breakfast] : [evening] → [__________]

11. [Rose] → [flowers] : [hammer] → [________]

12. [Glasses] → [see] : [cane] → [________]

ANSWERS AND EXPLANATIONS

1. **Water**

   A bicycle travels on a road, and a ship travels on water.

2. **Vegetables**

   An orange belongs to fruits, and a carrot belongs to vegetables.

3. **Foot**

   Fingers are a part of a hand, while toes are a part of a foot.

4. **Drink**

   You use a fork to eat, and use a straw to drink.

5. **Wrist**

   A picture hangs on wall, and a watch is on wrist.

6. **Hat**

   A wedding and a marriage are synonym, and a cap and a hat are synonym, too.

7. **Cut**

   You use a pencil to write, and use scissors to cut.

8. **Sad**

   You will be happy if you receive a gift. Whereas, you will be sad if you attend a funeral.

9. **Hear**

   You use your eyes to see, while you use ears to hear.

10. **Dinner**

    You eat breakfast in the morning, and eat dinner in the evening.

11. **Tools**

    A rose is a kind of flowers, and a hammer is a kind of tools.

12. **Walk**

    You use glasses to see, while you use a cane to walk.

LESSON 2 Sentence Completion

Sentence Completion

In the sentence completion section, there are 20 questions. In each question, a sentence with a missing word is provided. The objective of the sentence completion questions is to choose a word from the answer choices so that the word replaces the blank space in the sentence.

The sentence completion questions are about

- Similarities and differences
- Characteristics
- Action
- Description
- Logic

Some students may feel that the sentence completion questions are very easy if they are familiar with words used in the questions. Otherwise, they may feel that the questions are difficult. Simply doing well on the sentence completion section depends on how much students know vocabulary words. The best way of improving in the sentence completion section is to read as many as books possible.

EXERCISES

Direction: For each question, find the word that best completes the sentence below.

1. Joshua and his friend went to a _________ to buy clothes.

   (A) theater (B) shopping mall (C) school (D) hospital (E) museum

2. In the _________, flowers bloom.

   (A) morning (B) afternoon (C) evening (D) spring (E) winter

3. After running about an hour, Jason was _________.

   (A) exhausted (B) energetic (C) strong (D) happy (E) gloomy

4. A mechanic _________ a car in his shop.

   (A) repaired (B) washed (C) cleaned (D) painted (E) punched

5. Joshua _________ the window because it was a windy day.

   (A) broke (B) opened (C) closed (D) installed (E) entered

6. A bold eagle laid her _________ on a nest.

   (A) feather (B) eggs (C) balloon (D) silhouette (E) duckling

7. During the trip, a car was _________ with gallons of gasoline because it ran out of fuel.

   (A) finished (B) stopped (C) filled (D) poured (E) tossed

8. I could not study because my neighborhood was very _________.

   (A) noisy (B) dirty (C) angry (D) average (E) fun

9. The weather was very _________ because there was ice on the street.

   (A) humid (B) tropic (C) hot (D) warm (E) freezing

10. A model rocket was launched into the _________.

   (A) forest (B) air (C) mountain (D) sea (E) desert

ANSWERS AND EXPLANATIONS

1. **B**
   Joshua and his friend went to a shopping mall to buy clothes.

2. **D**
   In the spring, flowers bloom.

3. **A**
   After running about an hour, Jason was exhausted.

4. **A**
   A mechanic repaired a car in his shop.

5. **C**
   Joshua closed the window because it was a windy day.

6. **B**
   A bold eagle laid her eggs on a nest.

7. **C**
   During the trip, a car was filled with gallons of gasoline because it ran out of fuel.

8. **A**
   I could not study because my neighborhood was very noisy.

9. **E**
   The weather was very freezing because there was ice on the street.

10. **B**
    A model rocket was launched into the air.

LESSON 3 Verbal Classification

Verbal Classification

In the verbal classification section, there are 20 questions. In each question, there are three words given to you. Look closely at the three words and determine how they are related. Choose a word from the answer choices that is most similar to the top three words.

The verbal classification questions are about

- Size and shape
- Purpose
- Characteristics in common

The objective of the verbal classification questions is to choose the word from the answer choices that is most similar to the top three words.

EXERCISES

Direction: For questions 1-10, think about the three words and determine how they are related. Choose a word from the answer choices that is most similar to the three words.

1. Hour Minute Second

   (A) Thermometer (B) Ruler (C) Calendar (D) Clock (E) Calculator

2. Yard Inch Foot

   (A) Ounce (B) Pound (C) Gallon (D) Mile (E) Liter

3. Flood Drought Earthquake

   (A) Disasters (B) Temperature (C) Weather (D) Water (E) Festival

4. Fear Joy Love

   (A) Laughing (B) Shout (C) Sadness (D) Crying (E) Throwing

5. Frog Grasshopper Kangaroo

   (A) Rabbit (B) Snake (C) Snail (D) Crocodile (E) Parrot

6. Pen Crayon Pencil

   (A) Paper Clip (B) Marker (C) Stapler (D) Eraser (E) Paper

7. Orange Cherry Peach

(A) Lettuce (B) Onion (C) Raspberry (D) Potato (E) Carrot

8. Tall Short Narrow

(A) Wide (B) Shiny (C) Dull (D) Dark (E) Heavy

9. Yellow Green Red

(A) Art (B) Colors (C) Flag (D) Sports (E) Flowers

10. Milk Cheese Yogurt

(A) Bacon (B) Eggs (C) Chocolate (D) Sugar (E) Butter

ANSWERS AND EXPLANATIONS

1. **(D)**

   A thermometer is a device that measures temperature. A ruler is a piece of wood or plastic that measures length. A calendar is a series of paper showing days, weeks, and months of a particular year. A clock measures time indicating hours, minutes, and seconds. Therefore, (D) is the correct answer.

2. **(D)**

   Ounce and pound are the units of weight. Gallon and liter are the unit of volume. However, yard, inch, foot, and mile are the units of length. Therefore, (D) is the correct answer.

3. **(A)**

   Flood, drought, and earthquake are natural disasters. Therefore, (A) is the correct answer.

4. **(C)**

   Fear, joy, love, and sadness are natural instinctive state of mind derived from one's feeling or mood. Therefore, (C) is the correct answer.

5. **(A)**

   A frog, a grasshopper, a kangaroo, and a rabbit all hop to move from one place to another. Therefore, (A) is the correct answer.

6. **(B)**

   A pen, a crayon, a pencil, and a marker are used for writing, drawing, or coloring. Therefore, (B) is the correct answer.

7. **(C)**

   A lettuce, an onion, a potato, and a carrot are vegetables. However, an orange, a cherry, a peach, and a raspberry are fruits. Therefore, (C) is the correct answer.

8. **(A)**

   Tall, short, narrow, and wide are words that describe the size or length of an object. Therefore, (A) is the correct answer.

9. **(B)**

   Yellow, green, and red are different types of colors. Therefore, (B) is the correct answer.

10. **(E)**

Milk, cheese, yogurt and butter are dairy products. Therefore, (E) is the correct answer.

LESSON 4 Number Analogies

Number Analogies

In the number analogies section, there are 18 questions. In each question, there are 3 sets of numbers, with the first two sets containing two numbers and the third set containing a question mark as shown below.

$$[2 \rightarrow 3] \qquad [5 \rightarrow 6] \qquad [8 \rightarrow ?]$$

In the example above, the second number in the first two sets is one more than the first number: $3 = 2 + 1$ and $6 = 5 + 1$. Therefore, the question mark in the third set should be $? = 8 + 1 = 9$.

The most common number analogies questions are about

- Addition
- Subtraction
- Multiplication
- Division

The objective of the number analogies questions is to find the numerical relationship between the first two sets of numbers and choose a number that replaces the question mark in the third set that has the same relationship with the first two sets of numbers.

EXERCISES

Direction: For each question, find the missing number that completes the numerical relationship between three sets of numbers.

1. $[5 \rightarrow 2]$ $[10 \rightarrow 7]$ $[7 \rightarrow ?]$

2. $[5 \rightarrow 15]$ $[7 \rightarrow 21]$ $[9 \rightarrow ?]$

3. $[2 \rightarrow 13]$ $[21 \rightarrow 32]$ $[15 \rightarrow ?]$

4. $[137 \rightarrow 3]$ $[378 \rightarrow 7]$ $[915 \rightarrow ?]$

5. $[1:20 \rightarrow 1:25]$ $[3:40 \rightarrow 3:45]$ $[5:55 \rightarrow ?]$

6. $[24 \rightarrow 12]$ $[36 \rightarrow 18]$ $[98 \rightarrow ?]$

7. $[100 \rightarrow 83]$ $[84 \rightarrow 67]$ $[45 \rightarrow ?]$

8. $[64 \rightarrow 4]$ $[17 \rightarrow 7]$ $[70 \rightarrow ?]$

9. $[10 \rightarrow 21]$ $[25 \rightarrow 51]$ $[34 \rightarrow ?]$

10. $[123 \rightarrow 321]$ $[246 \rightarrow 642]$ $[569 \rightarrow ?]$

ANSWERS AND EXPLANATIONS

1. **4; Subtract 3**

   Since $5 - 3 = 2$ and $10 - 3 = 7$, $7 - 3 = 4$.

2. **27; Multiply by 3**

   Since $5 \times 3 = 15$ and $7 \times 3 = 21$, $9 \times 3 = 27$.

3. **26; Add 11**

   Since $2 + 11 = 13$ and $21 + 11 = 32$, $15 + 11 = 26$.

4. **1; Choose the number in the tens digit**

   The tens digits of 137 and 378 are 3 and 7, respectively. Therefore, the tens digit of 915 is 1.

5. **6:00; Add 5 minutes**

   Five minutes after 1:20 and 3:40 are 1:25 and 3:45, respectively. Therefore, five minutes after 5:55 is 6:00.

6. **49; Divide the first number by 2**

   Since $24 \div 2 = 12$ and $36 \div 2 = 18$, $98 \div 2 = 49$.

7. **28; Subtract 17**

   Since $100 - 17 = 83$ and $84 - 17 = 67$, $45 - 17 = 28$.

8. **0; Choose a number in the units digit**

   The units digits of 64 and 17 are 4 and 7, respectively. Therefore, the units digit of 70 is 0. $[64 \rightarrow 4]$ $[17 \rightarrow 7]$ $[70 \rightarrow ?]$

9. **69; One more than the twice the first number**

   Since $2 \times 10 + 1 = 21$ and $2 \times 25 + 1 = 51$, $2 \times 34 + 1 = 69$.

10. **965; Read the number backward**

    If you read 123 and 246 backward, it would be 321 and 642, respectively. Therefore, if you read 569 backward, it would be 965.

LESSON 5 Number Puzzles

Number Puzzles

In the number puzzles section, there are 16 questions. The number puzzles questions are either addition, subtraction, multiplication, or inequality problems.

$$9 - 4 + \boxed{?} = 8$$

In each question, there is a box with a question mark as shown above. In order to find the number that replaces the question mark in the example above, subtract first.

$$\begin{aligned} 9 - 4 + \boxed{?} &= 8 \\ 5 + \boxed{?} &= 8 \\ \boxed{?} &= 3 \end{aligned}$$

The objective of the number puzzles section is to find the number that replaces the question mark so that the equation or inequality is true.

EXERCISES

Direction: For each question, find the missing number that satisfies the equation.

1. $7 - \boxed{?} = 3$

   (A) 1 (B) 2 (C) 3 (D) 4 (E) 5

2. $\boxed{?} + 3 = 12$

   (A) 5 (B) 8 (C) 9 (D) 10 (E) 15

3. $8 + 3 - \boxed{?} = 5$

   (A) 7 (B) 6 (C) 5 (D) 4 (E) 3

4. $12 - \boxed{?} + 7 = 14$

   (A) 9 (B) 7 (C) 6 (D) 5 (E) 2

5. $4 \times \boxed{?} = 4 + 4 + 4$

   (A) 7 (B) 6 (C) 5 (D) 4 (E) 3

6. $5 + 7 = \boxed{?} + 4$

   (A) 8 (B) 7 (C) 6 (D) 5 (E) 4

7. $\boxed{?} < 3 + 7$

   (A) 9 (B) 11 (C) 12 (D) 13 (E) 14

8. $7 + \boxed{?} > 11$

(A) 1 (B) 2 (C) 3 (D) 4 (E) 5

9. $6 + 5 - 2 = 2 + \boxed{?} + 4$

(A) 1 (B) 2 (C) 3 (D) 4 (E) 5

10. $13 - \boxed{?} - 2 = 7 + 3 - 4$

(A) 5 (B) 4 (C) 3 (D) 2 (E) 1

ANSWERS AND EXPLANATIONS

1. **D;** $7 - \boxed{4} = 3$

2. **C;** $\boxed{9} + 3 = 12$

3. **B;** $8 + 3 - \boxed{6} = 5$

4. **D;** $12 - \boxed{5} + 7 = 14$

5. **E;** $4 \times \boxed{3} = 4 + 4 + 4$

6. **A;** $5 + 7 = \boxed{8} + 4$

7. **A;** $\boxed{9} < 3 + 7$

8. **E;** $7 + \boxed{5} > 11$

9. **C;** $6 + 5 - 2 = 2 + \boxed{3} + 4$

10. **A;** $13 - \boxed{5} - 2 = 7 + 3 - 4$

LESSON 6 Number Series

Number Series

In the number series section, there are 18 questions. In each question, a list of numbers including a box with a question mark follows some type of pattern as shown below. The question mark can be either at the end of the list or between numbers.

2 5 8 11 14 17 ?

The example above follows pattern such that the first six numbers in the list are increased by 3. Therefore, the number that replaces the question mark should be $17 + 3 = 20$.

The objective of the number series section is to find the number that replaces the question mark so that a list of numbers follows the same type of pattern.

The common patterns used in the number series questions are as follows:

- Increase or decrease
  The list of numbers either increases or decreases by a certain number. For instance, $\{1, 2, 3, 4, 5, 6\}$ or $\{7, 6, 5, 4, 3, 2\}$.
- Both increase and decrease at the same time
  The list of numbers both increases and decreases by a certain number. For instance, $\{2, 4, 6, 8, 6, 4\}$ or $\{7, 6, 5, 4, 5, 6\}$.
- Multiplication or division
  The list of numbers are either multiplied or divided by a certain number. For instance, $\{1, 3, 9, 27, 81, 243\}$ or $\{128, 64, 32, 16, 8, 4\}$.
- Repeating numbers

The numbers in the list are repeating. For instance, from the list $\{1, 2, 3, 1, 2, 3\}$, the numbers $\{1, 2, 3\}$ are repeating in the list.

- Two patterns in the list
  The list of numbers forms two patterns: all numbers in the odd-numbered positions form one pattern, whereas all numbers in the even-numbered positions form another.

  For instance, from the list $\{1, 5, 2, 3, 3, 1\}$, the numbers in the odd-numbered positions are $\{\mathbf{1}, 5, \mathbf{2}, 3, \mathbf{3}, 1\}$ and they are increased by 1. Whereas, the numbers in the even-numbered positions are $\{1, \mathbf{5}, 2, \mathbf{3}, 3, \mathbf{1}\}$ and they are decreased by 2.

EXERCISES

Direction: For each question, find the missing number that follows a specific pattern.

1. 1, 2, 3, 4, 5, 6, ______

2. 2, 4, 6, 8, 10, 12, ______

3. 19, 16, 13, ______, 7, 4, 1

4. 1, 1, 2, 2, 3, ______, 4, 4

5. 3, 5, 7, 9, 7, ______, 3, 1

6. 2, 4, 6, 2, 4, 6, ______, 4, 6

7. 11, 9, 7, 5, 3, 5, ______, 9

8. 2, 3, ______, 3, 2, 3, 2, 3

9. 1, 5, 25, 125, ______, 3125

10. 256, 128, 64, ______, 16, 8, 4

ANSWERS AND EXPLANATIONS

1. **7; Increase by 1**

   The first six numbers in the list are increased by 1. So, the seventh number in the list is $6 + 1 = 7$. Therefore, the pattern is $\{1, 2, 3, 4, 5, 6, 7\}$.

2. **14; Increase by 2**

   The first six numbers in the list are increased by 2. So, the seventh number in the list is $12 + 2 = 14$. Therefore, the pattern is $\{2, 4, 6, 8, 12, 14\}$.

3. **10; Decrease by 3**

   The numbers in the list are decreased by 3. So, the fourth number in the list is $13 - 3 = 10$. Therefore, the pattern is $\{19, 16, 13, 10, 7, 4, 1\}$.

4. **3: Each number is shown twice**

   Each number in the list is shown twice. There are two 1's, followed by two 2's, followed by two 3's, followed by two 4's. So, the sixth number in the list is 3. Therefore, the pattern is $\{1, 1, 2, 2, 3, 3, 4, 4\}$.

5. **5; Increase by 2 and then decrease by 2**

   Up to 9, the numbers are increased by 2 and then decreased by 2. So, the sixth number in the list is $7 - 2 = 5$. Therefore, the pattern is $\{3, 5, 7, 9, 7, 5, 3, 1\}$.

6. **2; The numbers 2, 4, 6, are repeating**

   The numbers 2, 4, 6 are repeating. So, the seventh number in the list is 2. Therefore, the pattern is $\{2, 4, 6, 2, 4, 6, 2, 4, 6\}$.

7. **7; Decrease by 2 and then increase by 2**

   Up to 5, the numbers are decreased by 2 and then increased by 2. So, the seventh number in the list is $5 + 2 = 7$. Therefore, the pattern is $\{11, 9, 7, 5, 3, 5, 7, 9\}$.

8. **2; The numbers 2, 3 are repeating**

   The numbers 2, 3 are repeating. So, the third number in the list is 2. Therefore, the pattern is $\{2, 3, 2, 3, 2, 3, 2, 3\}$.

9. **625; multiply by 5**

   Each number in the list is multiplied by 5. So, the fifth number in the list is $125 \times 5 = 625$. Therefore, the pattern is $\{1, 5, 25, 125, 625, 3125\}$.

10. **32; divided by 2**

    Each number in the list is divided by 2. So, the fourth number is $64 \div 2 = 32$. Therefore, the pattern is $\{256, 128, 64, 32, 16, 8, 4\}$.

LESSON 7 Figure Matrices

Figure Matrices

In the figure matrices section, there are 20 questions. In each question, there are 4 squares that are given to you: 2 squares on top and 2 squares on the bottom. Below the 4 squares, there are 4 answer choices in a row.

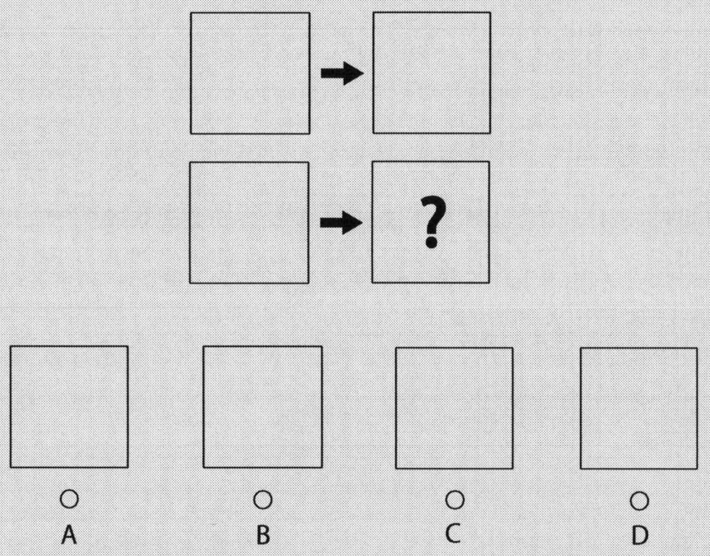

The two figures in the top row are somehow related, and the other two figures in the bottom row are also related in a similar way as shown on the top row.

The figure matrices questions are about

- Shape
- Shading
- Arrangements
- Rotation (clockwise or counterclockwise)

- A line of symmetry
- Dilation (make bigger or smaller)

The objective of the figure matrices questions is to choose the figure from the answer choices that replaces the question mark so that the bottom left figure and the figure that you have chosen are similar as shown on the top row.

EXERCISES

Direction: For each question from 1-4, two conditions on the left and figures on the right are given to you. Change the figures so that it satisfies the given conditions.

1. (a) Turn the figure upside down
   (b) Change the color from white to black

2. (a) Rearrange the figures from right to left
   (b) Rotate each figure 90° clockwise

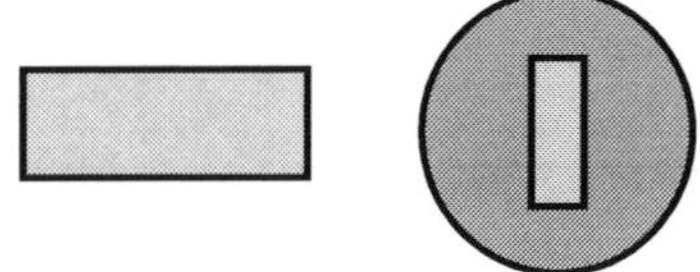

3. (a) Make the figure two times bigger
   (b) Turn inside out

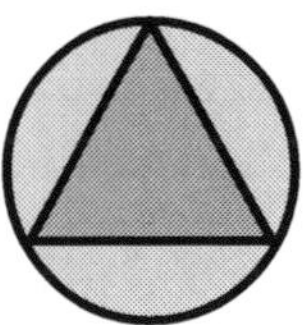

4. (a) Change the color from white to black
   (b) Rotate each figure 90° counterclockwise

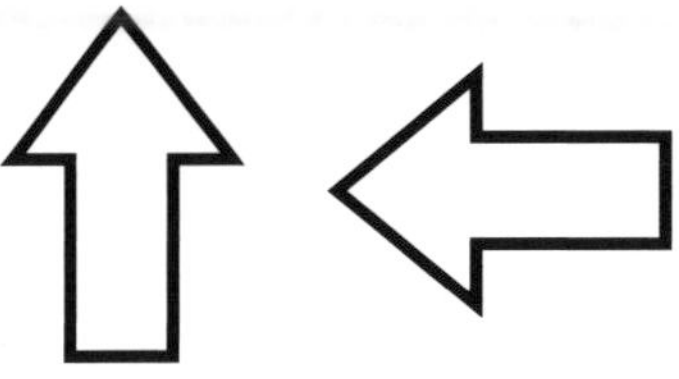

5. Find the figure from the answer choices that goes with the bottom left figure in a similar way as shown on the top row.

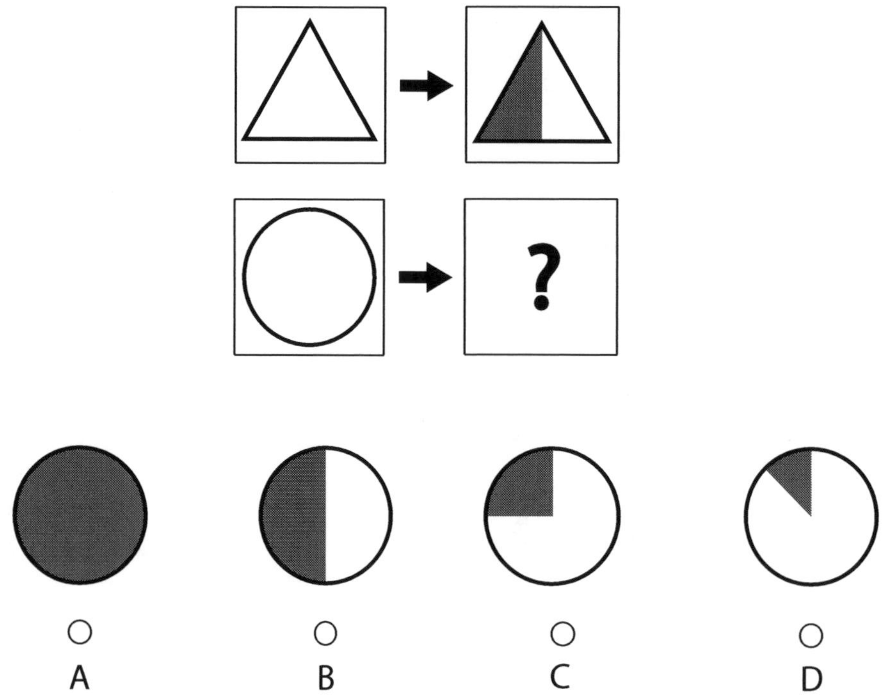

ANSWERS AND EXPLANATIONS

1. Turn the figure upside down, and change the color from white to black.

2. Rearrange the figures from right to left and rotate each figure 90° clockwise.

3. Make the figure two times bigger and turn inside out.

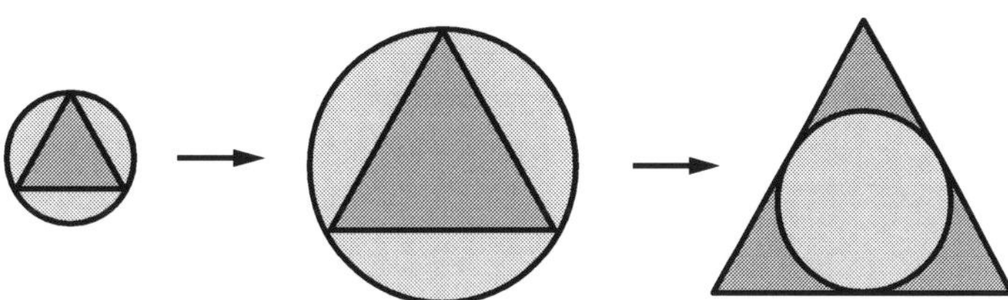

4. Change the color from white to black and rotate each figure 90° counterclockwise .

5. **B**

   The top left figure is a triangle. The top right figure is the same triangle as the top left figure, but half of it is shaded. Since the bottom left figure is a circle, the bottom right figure should be the same circle as the bottom left figure, but half of it should be shaded. Therefore, (B) is the correct answer.

LESSON 8 Paper Folding

Paper Folding

In the paper folding section, there are 14 questions. You are given a square paper. Then the paper is being folded either horizontally, vertically, or diagonally as shown below.

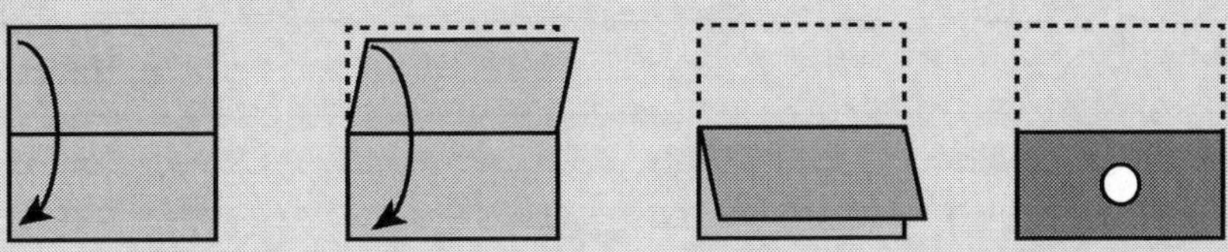

The paper is being folded horizontally

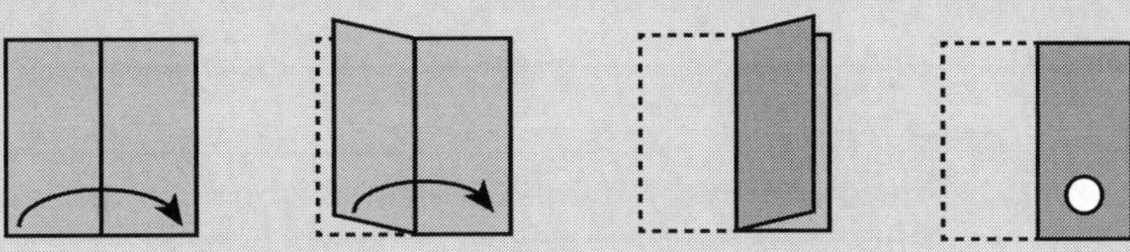

The paper is being folded vertically

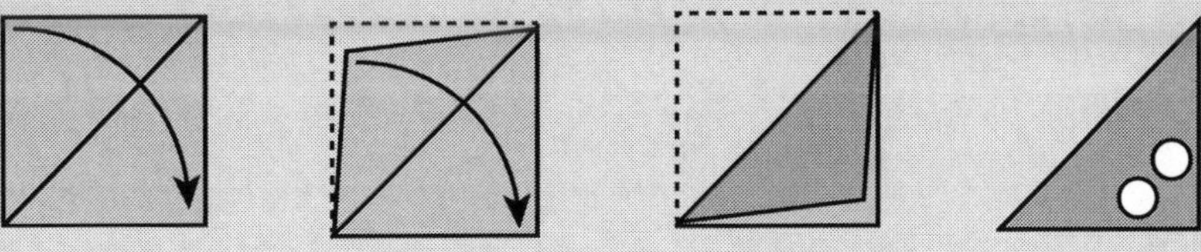

The paper is being folded diagonally

Usually, the paper is being folded either once, twice, or three times. After the paper is being folded completely, one or more holes are punched into the paper.

The objective of paper folding questions is to determine how the paper will look like when it is unfolded completely. In other words, you need to figure out how many holes there are and where they are on the paper.

Here are some some examples shown below.

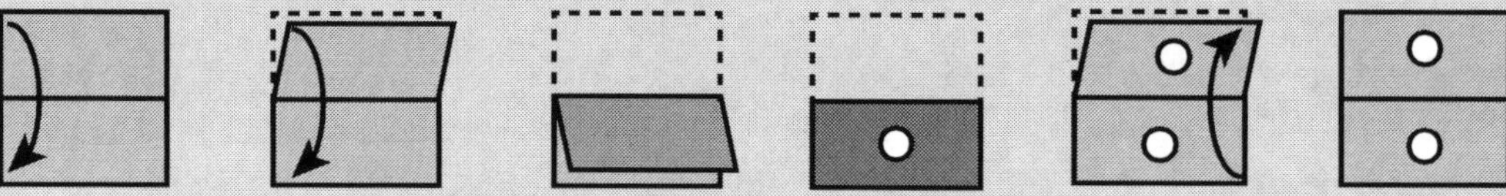

The paper is unfolded horizontally

The paper is unfolded vertically

The paper is unfolded diagonally

EXERCISES

Direction: For questions 1-6, draw a reflection (mirror image) of a figure over the given line.

1.

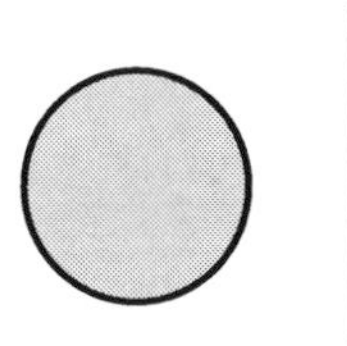

2.

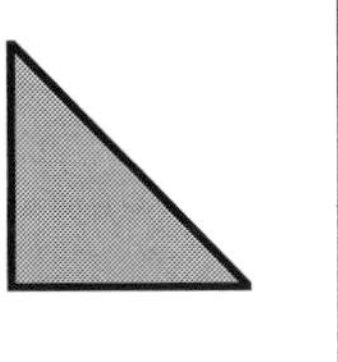

3.

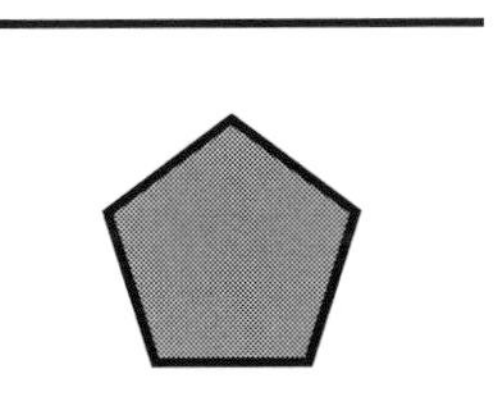

4.

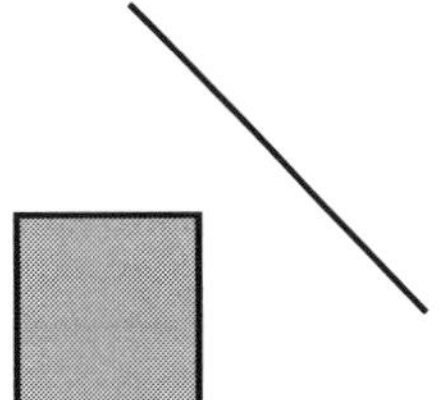

5.

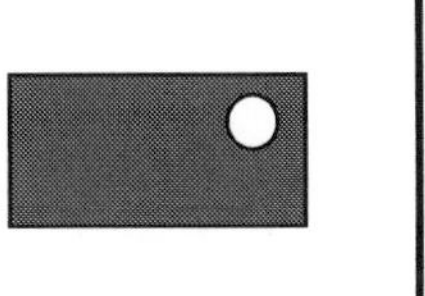

6.

7. Find the picture from the answer choices that shows you how the paper will look like when it is unfolded completely.

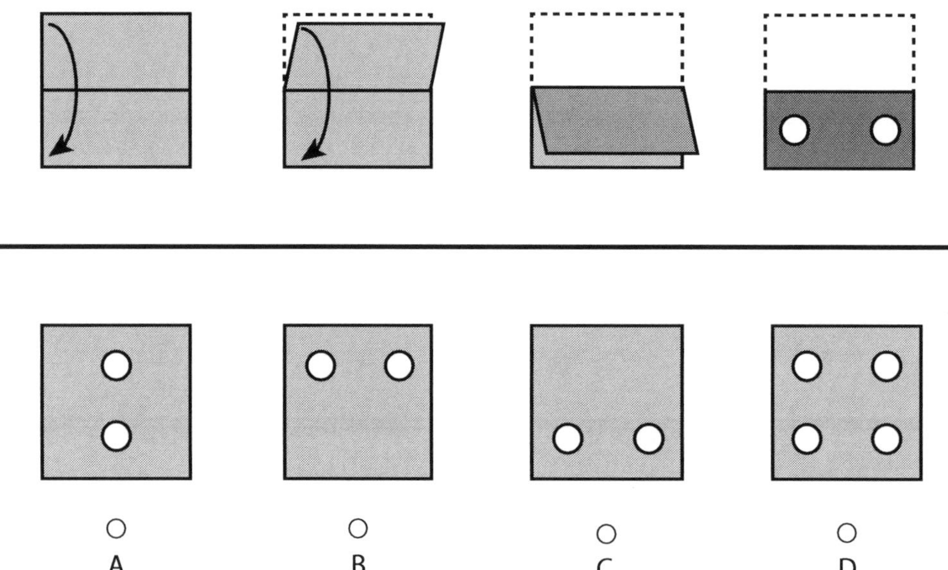

ANSWERS AND EXPLANATIONS

Drawing a mirror image of a figure over a line is called **reflection**. The line that you reflect the figure over is called **a line of symmetry**. The reflection of the figure has the same size as the original figure. Every point on the reflection and the original figures are the same distance from the line of symmetry.

1.

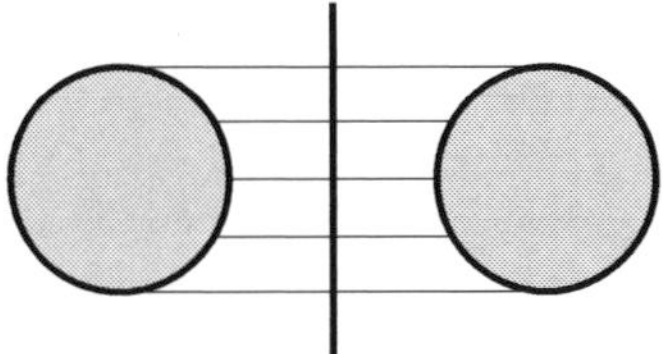

2.

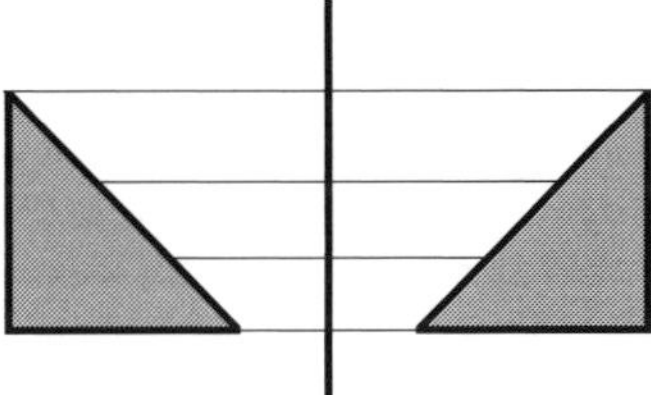

3.

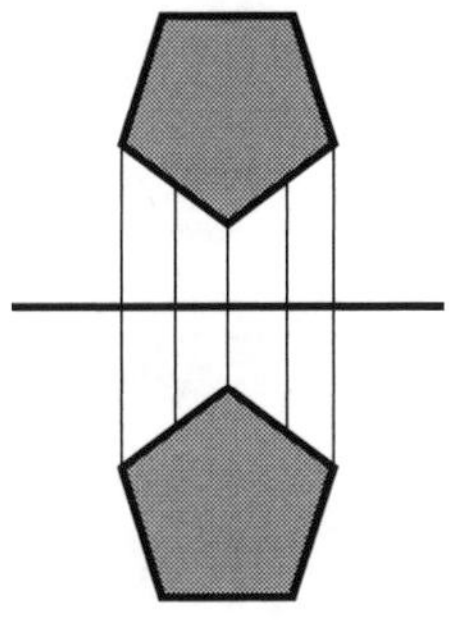

4.

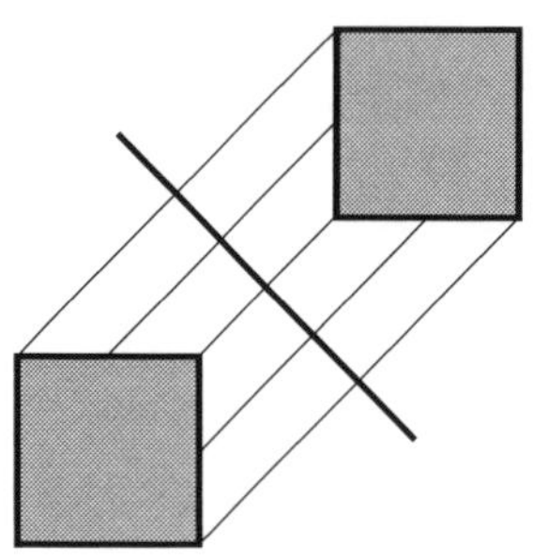

5.

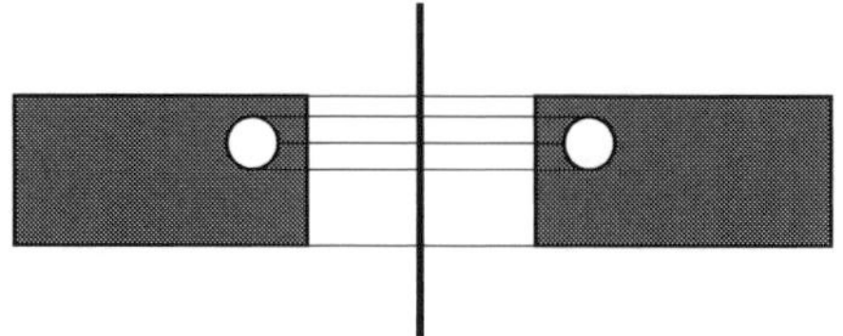

6.

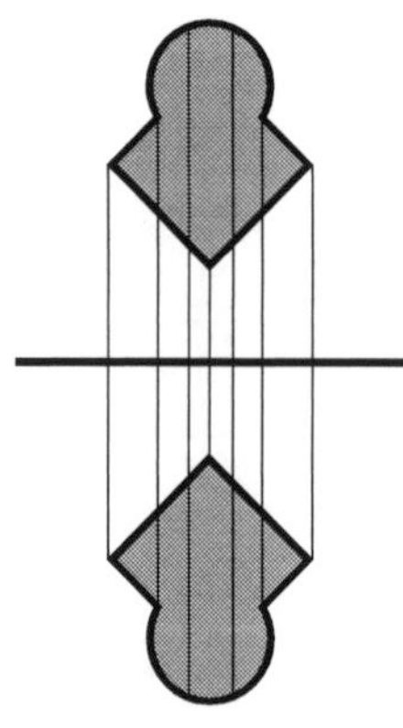

7. **D**; The paper will have 4 holes.

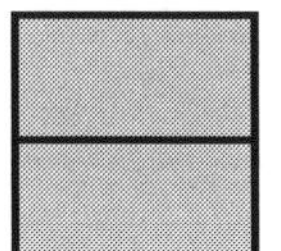

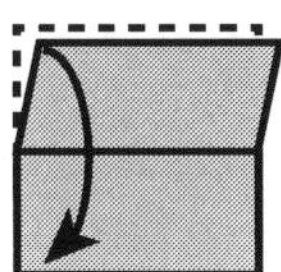

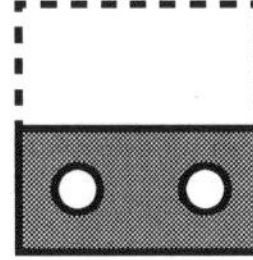

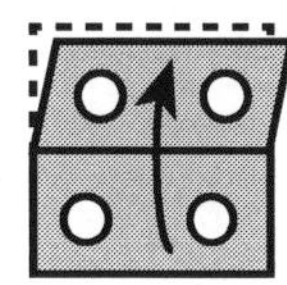

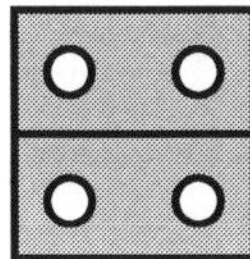

LESSON 9 Figure Classification

Figure Classification

In the figure classification section, there are 18 questions. In each question, the three figures in the top row make up the question, and the four figures in the second row are answer choices as shown below.

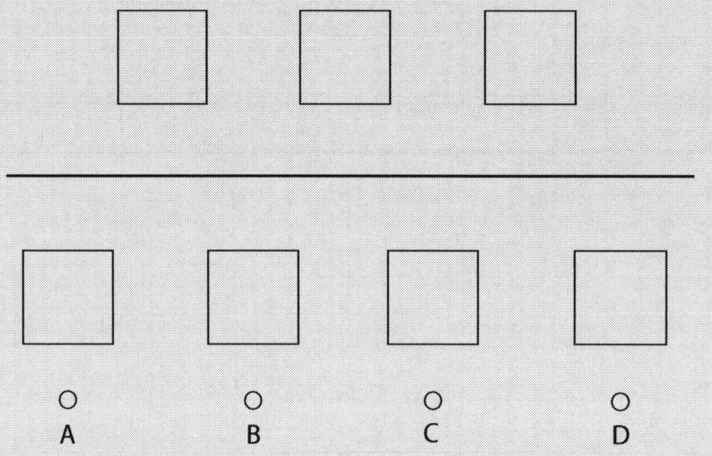

A B C D

Look closely at the three figures in the top row and determine how they are related. Choose the figure from the answer choices that is most similar to the figures on the top row.

The figure classification questions are about

- Shape and color
- Shading
- Arrangement
- Pattern
- Reflection and a line of symmetry

- Characteristics in common

The objective of the figure classification questions is to choose the figure from the answer choices that is most similar to the pictures on the top row.

EXERCISES

Direction: For each question from 1-6, among the 5 figures given, choose the figure that is the "**odd ball**" in the group.

1.

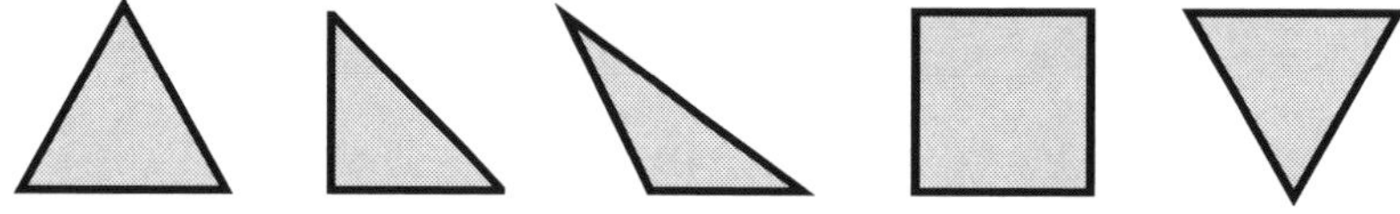

2.

3.

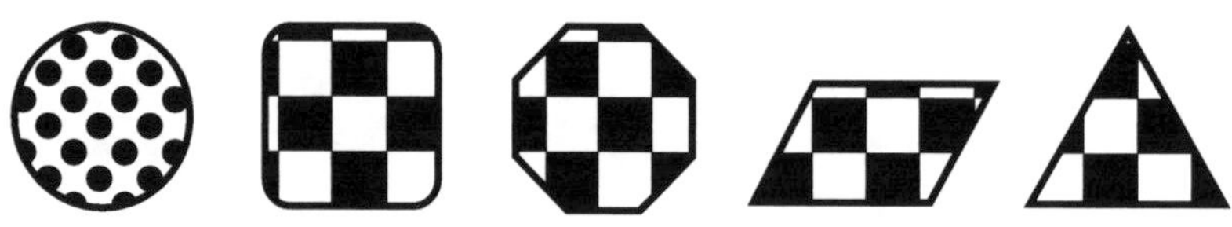

4.

5.

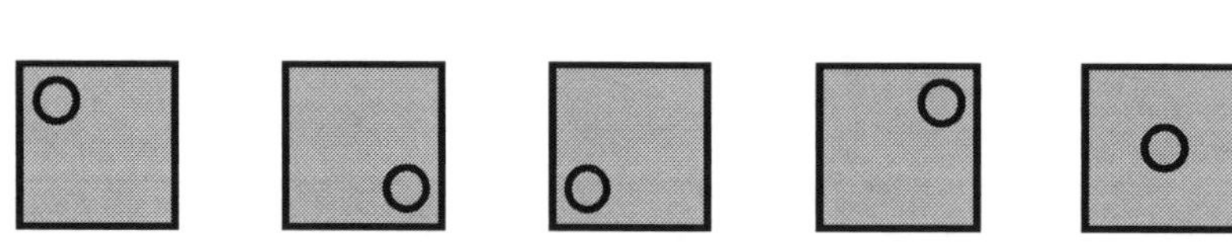

6.

7. Find the figure from the answer choices that is most similar to the figures on the top row.

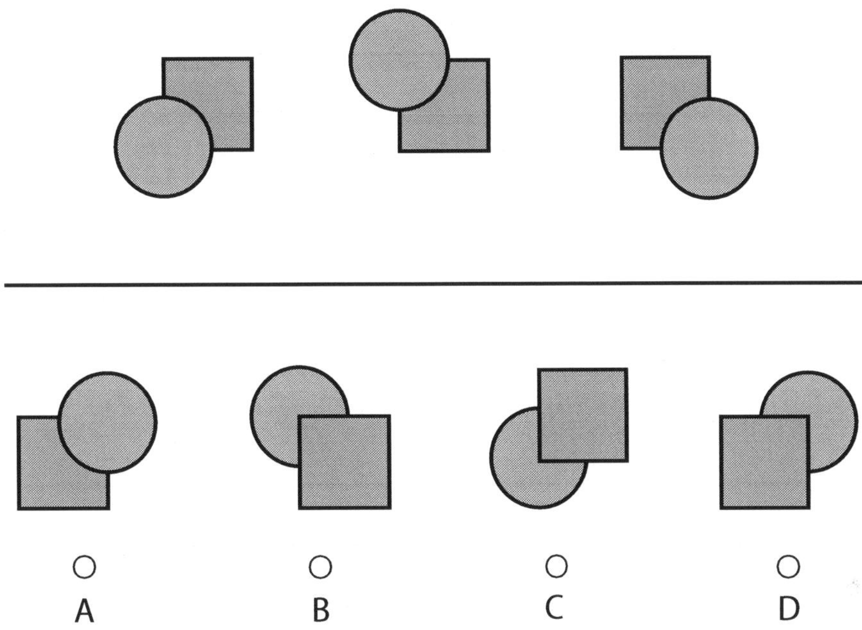

ANSWERS AND EXPLANATIONS

1.

This is the only figure that has four sides.

2.

This is the only figure that has a triangle inside.

3.

This is the only figure that has dots inside.

4.

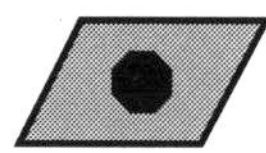

This is the only figure that has a small black figure inside.

5.

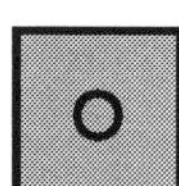

This is the only figure that has a small circle at the center.

6.

This is the only figure that has five sides.

7. **A**
   In each figure in the top row, a circle is on top of a square. Since the figure in (A) has a circle on top of a square, (A) is the correct answer.

PRACTICE TEST 1

VERBAL BATTERY

1. VERBAL ANALOGIES
2. SENTENCE COMPLETION
3. VERBAL CLASSIFICATION

Verbal Analogies

Directions: In each question, three words are given to you. The first two words are somehow related. Find the word that relates to the third word in the same way that the first two words are related.

Below is an example of a verbal analogies question:

Example

diamond → jewelry : pizza →

(A) hamburger (B) soda (C) ketchup (D) food (E) exercise

In this example, a diamond is a kind of jewelry. A pizza is a kind of food. Therefore, the correct answer is D.

Question 1

bright $\rightarrow$ dark : easy $\rightarrow$

(A) simple (B) difficult (C) safe (D) cheap (E) calm

Question 2

banana $\rightarrow$ yellow : strawberry $\rightarrow$

(A) blue (B) purple (C) red (D) green (E) orange

Question 3

cake $\rightarrow$ bakery : steak $\rightarrow$

(A) restaurant (B) school (C) hospital (D) museum (E) library

Question 4

season $\rightarrow$ spring : week $\rightarrow$

(A) calendar (B) month (C) Sunday (D) year (E) time

Question 5

soccer $\rightarrow$ referee : baseball $\rightarrow$

(A) player (B) coach (C) umpire (D) passenger (E) messenger

Question 6

good → reward : bad →

(A) profit (B) bonus (C) award (D) cost (E) penalty

Question 7

hands → gloves : feet →

(A) clothes (B) pants (C) jacket (D) socks (E) jump

Question 8

car → driver : airplane →

(A) astronaut (B) pilot (C) captain (D) passenger (E) attendant

Question 9

legs → run : arms →

(A) throw (B) jump (C) jog (D) walk (E) hop

Question 10

California → state : English →

(A) name (B) country (C) city (D) weather (E) language

Question 11

hospital → nurse : school →

(A) doctor (B) waitress (C) teacher (D) mechanic (E) reporter

Question 12

give → receive : save →

(A) send (B) spend (C) enjoy (D) travel (E) play

Question 13

water → boat : snow →

(A) golf (B) kite (C) eagle (D) moon (E) skis

Question 14

glue → sticky : icy road →

(A) dry (B) calm (C) warm (D) peaceful (E) slippery

Question 15

movies → film director : poems →

(A) singer (B) athlete (C) painter (D) poet (E) actress

Question 16

below → above : before →

(A) near (B) beneath (C) out (D) after (E) in

Question 17

chef → cook : waiter →

(A) repair (B) eat (C) fix (D) draw (E) serve

Question 18

cotton candy → sugar : cheese →

(A) water (B) milk (C) salt (D) jam (E) bread

Question 19

party → celebrate : race →

(A) relax (B) forget (C) compete (D) help (E) pay

Question 20

square → four : pentagon →

(A) two (B) three (C) five (D) six (E) eight

Question 21

pen → write : brush →

(A) paint (B) clean (C) hear (D) touch (E) see

Question 22

United States → The president : Florida →

(A) governor (B) artist (C) accountant (D) librarian (E) doctor

Sentence Completion

Directions: In each question, a sentence with a missing word is given to you. Find the word that best completes the sentence.

Below is an example of a sentence completion question:

Example

A rope is hard to cut because it is so _________.

(A) thin (B) long (C) thick (D) tall (E) weak

A thick rope is hard to cut. Therefore, the correct answer is C.

Question 1

The food tastes ________ even though it was prepared by a chef.

(A) fantastic (B) good (C) terrible (D) fresh (E) awesome

Question 2

My uncle is proud ________ being a firefighter.

(A) in (B) by (C) of (D) at (E) with

Question 3

When my baby had a fever, I took him to a ________.

(A) doctor (B) lawyer (C) nutritionist (D) dentist (E) technician

Question 4

Jason ________ brings a calculator to school. He uses it every day.

(A) sometimes (B) never (C) always (D) occasionally (E) rarely

Question 5

Some snakes have venom so they are very ________.

(A) lethal (B) friendly (C) brave (D) intelligent (E) unpleasant

Question 6

When a comedian tells about a story of his friend, people can't stop ________.

(A) crying (B) laughing (C) eating (D) yawning (E) sneezing

Question 7

Rainy weather and gloomy skies can ________ your mood.

(A) stay (B) stop (C) bore (D) leave (E) affect

Question 8

I ________ lemon trees in my yard.

(A) planted (B) harvested (C) produced (D) made (E) caught

Question 9

The soldiers were ordered to ________ at their posts.

(A) volunteer (B) remain (C) rescue (D) climb (E) discover

Question 10

His ________ mom is always worrying that something terrible will happen to him.

(A) relaxed (B) nervous (C) calm (D) jealous (E) cheerful

Question 11

Daniel is the second ________ boy in his school.

(A) shorter (B) taller (C) tallest (D) heavy (E) strong

Question 12

We prayed she would ________ from her illness.

(A) return (B) lose (C) solve (D) find (E) recover

Question 13

Dinosaurs became ________. You won't see them today.

(A) appeared (B) alive (C) extinct (D) small (E) fragile

Question 14

While I was working, the cat meowed and the dog ________.

(A) quacked (B) chirped (C) barked (D) hissed (E) growled

Question 15

I ________ my dog off with fresh water whenever he swims in the ocean.

(A) flush (B) stain (C) pull (D) rinse (E) hold

Question 16

I always walk my dog on a ________.

(A) rope (B) wheel (C) lead (D) leash (E) shadow

Question 17

Matthew lives in a ________. He is always on the road to travel new places.

(A) house (B) cave (C) hut (D) trailer (E) shelter

Question 18

Pelicans continually ________ near the water and dive for fish.

(A) play (B) sleep (C) hover (D) settle (E) hurry

Question 19

My mom wants to ________ me sweaters.

(A) need (B) neat (C) wash (D) dry (E) knit

Question 20

My brother graduated from a high school. He worked painting houses to earn money for ________.

(A) college (B) work (C) hospital (D) fun (E) teaching

Verbal Classification

Directions: The three words in each question are somehow related. Determine how they are similar and find the word that is most similar to the three words.

Below is an example of a verbal Classification question:

Example

earthquake **hurricane** **tornado**

(A) fire (B) disaster (C) wind (D) rain (E) ambulance

A natural disaster is a major adverse event resulting from natural processes of the Earth including earthquakes, hurricanes, and tornadoes. Therefore, the correct answer is B.

Question 1

lion cheetah cat

(A) tiger (B) bear (C) dog (D) shark (E) owl

Question 2

apartment hut shelter

(A) water (B) storage (C) cabin (D) farm (E) road

Question 3

Venus Mars Jupiter

(A) Moon (B) Sun (C) Star (D) Sky (E) Earth

Question 4

tall beautiful soft

(A) color (B) rainbow (C) loud (D) fruit (E) fish

Question 5

boat paddle steamer ship

(A) yacht (B) aircraft (C) bus (D) parachute (E) balloon

Question 6

Swiss Mozzarella Cheddar

(A) Boston (B) America (C) Europe (D) Feta (E) Croissant

Question 7

coal wood gas

(A) Star (B) compass (C) diesel (D) station (E) market

Question 8

bark trunk branch

(A) soil (B) forest (C) roots (D) metal (E) trip

Question 9

puddings cakes ice cremes

(A) fries (B) flour (C) hot dog (D) pies (E) pizza

Question 10

fear joy disgust

(A) height (B) handsome (C) surprise (D) appearance (E) weight

Question 11

CD NO ST

(A) AD (B) ET (C) MA (D) XY (E) WI

Question 12

square circle triangle

(A) rectangle (B) drawing (C) notebook (D) sign (E) flag

Question 13

lilac lily daffodil

(A) plant (B) city (C) flower (D) size (E) flavor

Question 14

tumble topple collapse

(A) love (B) fall (C) run (D) exercise (E) walk

Question 15

ketchup mustard mayonnaise

(A) condiment (B) hot dog (C) hamburger (D) salad (E) bottle

Question 16

brass aluminum copper

(A) road (B) stone (C) metal (D) ingredient (E) wood

Question 17

maple palm oak

(A) bread (B) cut (C) saw (D) tropical (E) tree

Question 18

bat cat rat

(A) hat (B) mat (C) project (D) helmet (E) goat

Question 19

history math literature

(A) training (B) library (C) magazine (D) strength (E) science

Question 20

bench chair couch

(A) desk (B) ladder (C) fireplace (D) sofa (E) computer

QUANTITATIVE BATTERY

1. NUMBER ANALOGIES

2. NUMBER PUZZLES

3. NUMBER SERIES

Number Analogies

Directions: In each question, three pairs of numbers are given to you. Determine the relationship between the first two pairs of numbers. Find the number that has the same relationship when paired with the number in the third pair.

Below is an example of a number analogies question:

Example

$[\mathbf{5} \rightarrow \mathbf{2}]$ $[\mathbf{8} \rightarrow \mathbf{5}]$ $[\mathbf{12} \rightarrow ?]$

(A) 7 (B) 8 (C) 9 (D) 10 (E) 11

In this example, the second number of each pair is three less than the first number; that is, $5 - 3 = 2$ and $8 - 3 = 5$, and $12 - 3 = 9$. Therefore, the correct answer is C.

Question 1

$[\mathbf{5} \rightarrow \mathbf{10}]$ $[\mathbf{3} \rightarrow \mathbf{8}]$ $[\mathbf{7} \rightarrow ?]$

(A) 8 (B) 9 (C) 10 (D) 11 (E) 12

Question 2

$[\mathbf{2} \rightarrow \mathbf{4}]$ $[\mathbf{4} \rightarrow \mathbf{8}]$ $[\mathbf{8} \rightarrow ?]$

(A) 10 (B) 12 (C) 14 (D) 16 (E) 18

Question 3

$[\mathbf{9} \rightarrow \mathbf{6}]$ $[\mathbf{7} \rightarrow \mathbf{4}]$ $[\mathbf{11} \rightarrow ?]$

(A) 4 (B) 5 (C) 6 (D) 7 (E) 8

Question 4

$[\mathbf{3} \rightarrow \mathbf{14}]$ $[\mathbf{7} \rightarrow \mathbf{18}]$ $[\mathbf{11} \rightarrow ?]$

(A) 18 (B) 19 (C) 20 (D) 21 (E) 22

Question 5

$[\mathbf{26} \rightarrow \mathbf{13}]$ $[\mathbf{24} \rightarrow \mathbf{12}]$ $[\mathbf{22} \rightarrow ?]$

(A) 9 (B) 10 (C) 11 (D) 12 (E) 13

Question 6

[**2** $\to$ **4**] [**3** $\to$ **9**] [**4** $\to$?]

(A) 6 (B) 8 (C) 10 (D) 12 (E) 16

Question 7

[**12** $\to$ **2**] [**56** $\to$ **6**] [**79** $\to$?]

(A) 6 (B) 7 (C) 8 (D) 9 (E) 10

Question 8

[**1 : 15** $\to$ **1 : 30**] [**3 : 25** $\to$ **3 : 40**] [**5 : 40** $\to$?]

(A) 5:55 (B) 6:00 (C) 6:10 (D) 6:15 (E) 6:25

Question 9

[**13** $\to$ **4**] [**17** $\to$ **8**] [**24** $\to$?]

(A) 15 (B) 14 (C) 13 (D) 12 (E) 11

Question 10

[**25** $\to$ **50**] [**40** $\to$ **65**] [**53** $\to$?]

(A) 58 (B) 68 (C) 78 (D) 88 (E) 98

Question 11

$[\mathbf{2} \rightarrow \mathbf{6}]$ $[\mathbf{4} \rightarrow \mathbf{12}]$ $[\mathbf{5} \rightarrow ?]$

(A) 15 (B) 14 (C) 13 (D) 12 (E) 11

Question 12

$[\mathbf{234} \rightarrow \mathbf{3}]$ $[\mathbf{156} \rightarrow \mathbf{5}]$ $[\mathbf{471} \rightarrow ?]$

(A) 7 (B) 5 (C) 4 (D) 2 (E) 1

Question 13

$[\mathbf{2} \rightarrow \mathbf{5}]$ $[\mathbf{3} \rightarrow \mathbf{7}]$ $[\mathbf{6} \rightarrow ?]$

(A) 10 (B) 11 (C) 12 (D) 13 (E) 14

Question 14

$[\mathbf{9} \rightarrow \mathbf{3}]$ $[\mathbf{12} \rightarrow \mathbf{4}]$ $[\mathbf{18} \rightarrow ?]$

(A) 2 (B) 3 (C) 4 (D) 5 (E) 6

Question 15

$[\mathbf{1:25} \rightarrow \mathbf{1:05}]$ $[\mathbf{3:40} \rightarrow \mathbf{3:20}]$ $[\mathbf{8:00} \rightarrow ?]$

(A) 7:45 (B) 7:40 (C) 7:35 (D) 7:30 (E) 7:25

Question 16

[**8** → **3**] [**12** → **5**] [**20** → ?]

(A) 7 (B) 8 (C) 9 (D) 10 (E) 11

Question 17

[**3** → **333**] [**5** → **555**] [**8** → ?]

(A) 800 (B) 808 (C) 880 (D) 888 (E) 899

Question 18

[**Mar 9** → **Mar 10**] [**Oct 15** → **Oct 16**] [**May 31** → ?]

(A) May 32 (B) June 1 (C) April 1 (D) March 1 (E) July 1

Number Puzzles

Directions: In each question, a mathematical equation with a question mark is given to you. Find the number that will replace the question mark so that the equation or inequality is true.

Below is an example number puzzles question:

Example

$\mathbf{11} \quad + \quad \boxed{?} \quad = \quad \mathbf{40}$

(A) 29 (B) 39 (C) 49 (D) 59 (E) 69

In this example, $11 + \boxed{29} = 40$. Therefore, the correct answer is A.

Question 1

$$\boxed{?} + 8 + 9 = 25$$

(A) 6 (B) 7 (C) 8 (D) 9 (E) 10

Question 2

$$17 = \boxed{?} - 2 + 5$$

(A) 17 (B) 16 (C) 15 (D) 14 (E) 13

Question 3

$$2 \times \boxed{?} = 2 + 3 + 5$$

(A) 3 (B) 4 (C) 5 (D) 6 (E) 7

Question 4

$$14 + 15 = 17 - 6 + \boxed{?}$$

(A) 14 (B) 15 (C) 16 (D) 17 (E) 18

Question 5

$$9 + \boxed{?} - 6 = 20 - 10$$

(A) 7 (B) 8 (C) 9 (D) 10 (E) 11

Question 6

$\boxed{?} - 6 - 15 = 4 + 8$

(A) 23 (B) 27 (C) 33 (D) 37 (E) 43

Question 7

$1 + 2 + 3 + 4 = 2 \times \boxed{?}$

(A) 4 (B) 5 (C) 6 (D) 7 (E) 8

Question 8

$13 + 9 - 8 = 21 - \boxed{?} + 6$

(A) 10 (B) 11 (C) 12 (D) 13 (E) 14

Question 9

$2 \times 2 \times 2 = \boxed{?} + 6$

(A) 1 (B) 2 (C) 3 (D) 4 (E) 5

Question 10

$\boxed{?} > 2 + 3 + 4$

(A) 6 (B) 7 (C) 8 (D) 9 (E) 10

Question 11

$$\mathbf{17} + \boxed{?} = \mathbf{12} + \mathbf{9} + \mathbf{15}$$

(A) 19 (B) 18 (C) 17 (D) 16 (E) 15

Question 12

$$\mathbf{31} + \mathbf{26} = \boxed{?} + \mathbf{13} + \mathbf{22}$$

(A) 21 (B) 22 (C) 23 (D) 24 (E) 25

Question 13

$$\mathbf{33} + \boxed{?} + \mathbf{44} = \mathbf{44} + \mathbf{55} + \mathbf{33}$$

(A) 53 (B) 54 (C) 55 (D) 56 (E) 57

Question 14

$$\boxed{?} + \mathbf{2} < \mathbf{3} + \mathbf{5} + \mathbf{7}$$

(A) 12 (B) 13 (C) 14 (D) 15 (E) 16

Question 15

$$\mathbf{14} + \mathbf{23} - \mathbf{31} = \boxed{?} - \mathbf{11} - \mathbf{15}$$

(A) 30 (B) 31 (C) 32 (D) 33 (E) 34

Question 16

$\boxed{?} \times \mathbf{4} = \mathbf{2} \times \mathbf{3} \times \mathbf{4}$

(A) 2 (B) 3 (C) 4 (D) 5 (E) 6

Number Series

Directions: In each question, a list of numbers including a box with a question mark follows some type of pattern. Find the number that replaces the question mark so that a list of numbers follow the same type of pattern.

Below is an example of a number series question:

Example

2 4 6 8 10 12 ?

(A) 13 (B) 14 (C) 15 (D) 16 (E) 17

In this example, the numbers are increasing by 2. So the number that replaces the question mark is $12 + 2 = 14$. Therefore, the correct answer is B.

Question 1

19 16 13 ? 7 4 1

(A) 12 (B) 11 (C) 10 (D) 9 (E) 8

Question 2

1 2 4 8 16 ? 64

(A) 28 (B) 30 (C) 32 (D) 34 (E) 36

Question 3

? 14 24 34 44 54 64

(A) 4 (B) 6 (C) 8 (D) 10 (E) 12

Question 4

1 2 4 7 11 16 ?

(A) 21 (B) 22 (C) 23 (D) 24 (E) 25

Question 5

74 69 64 59 54 ? 44

(A) 51 (B) 50 (C) 49 (D) 48 (E) 47

Question 6

23 41 55 23 [?] 55 23

(A) 23 (B) 41 (C) 49 (D) 51 (E) 55

Question 7

12 12 19 [?] 26 26 33

(A) 16 (B) 17 (C) 18 (D) 19 (E) 20

Question 8

[?] 160 80 40 20 10 5

(A) 240 (B) 260 (C) 280 (D) 300 (E) 320

Question 9

8 5 9 4 10 3 [?]

(A) 13 (B) 12 (C) 11 (D) 10 (E) 9

Question 10

1 3 9 27 81 [?] 729

(A) 162 (B) 181 (C) 200 (D) 225 (E) 243

Question 11

30 45 60 75 90 105 ?

(A) 140 (B) 135 (C) 130 (D) 120 (E) 120

Question 12

10 9 12 11 14 13 ?

(A) 14 (B) 15 (C) 16 (D) 17 (E) 18

Question 13

100 89 78 67 56 45 ?

(A) 38 (B) 37 (C) 36 (D) 35 (E) 34

Question 14

50 5 40 10 30 15 ?

(A) 20 (B) 25 (C) 30 (D) 35 (E) 40

Question 15

8 24 12 36 18 54 ?

(A) 25 (B) 26 (C) 27 (D) 28 (E) 29

Question 16

1 2 2 3 3 3 ?

(A) 7 (B) 6 (C) 5 (D) 4 (E) 4

Question 17

2 5 11 23 47 95 ?

(A) 171 (B) 181 (C) 191 (D) 201 (E) 211

Question 18

1 4 9 16 25 36 ?

(A) 47 (B) 48 (C) 49 (D) 50 (E) 51

NONVERBAL BATTERY

1. FIGURE MATRICES
2. PAPER FOLDING
3. FIGURE CLASSIFICATION

Figure Matrices

Directions: In each question, look at the figures on the top row and determine how the two figures are related. Choose the figure from the answer choices that goes with the bottom left figure in a similar way as shown on the top row.

Below is an example of a figure matrices question:

Example

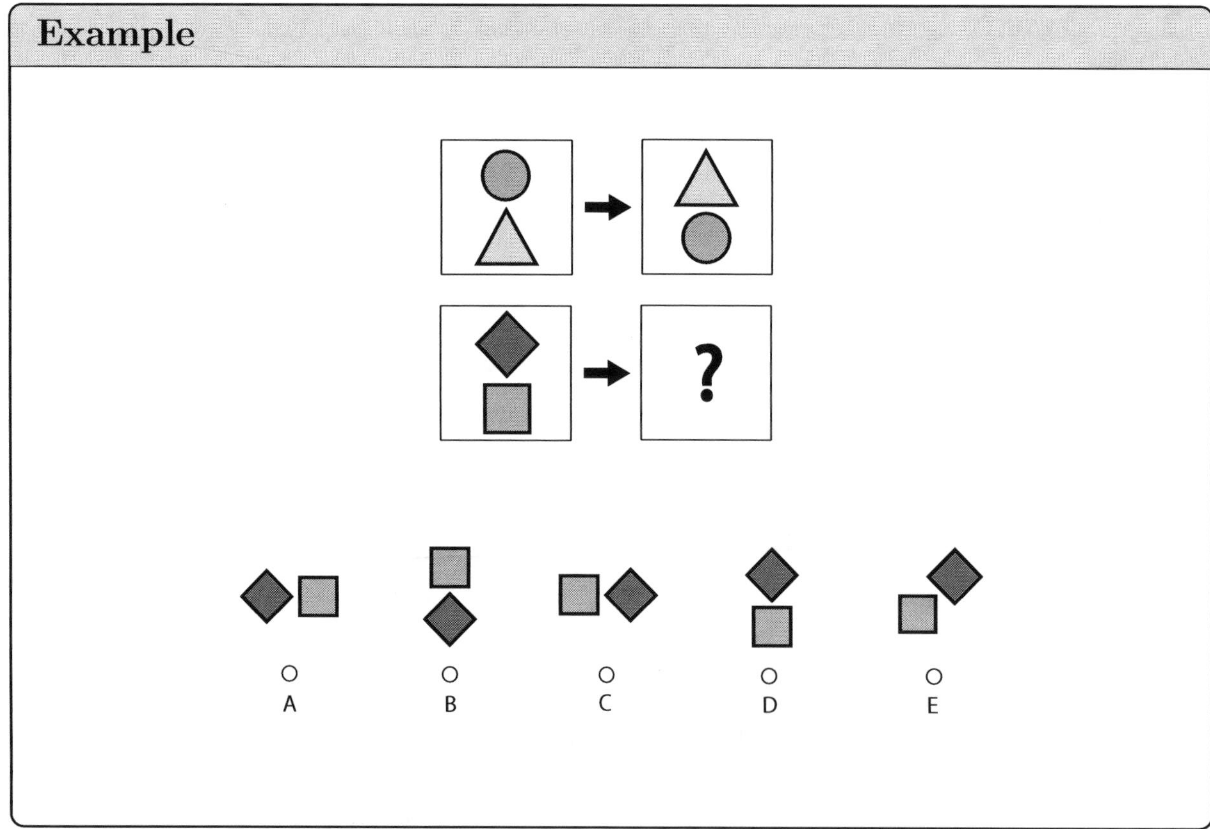

In the first figure, there are two shapes: a circle is at the top and a triangle is at the bottom. However, the arrangements are reversed in the second figure. A triangle is at the top and a circle is at the bottom. If you reverse the arrangements of shapes in the third figure, you get the figure in (B). Therefore, the correct answer is B.

Question 1

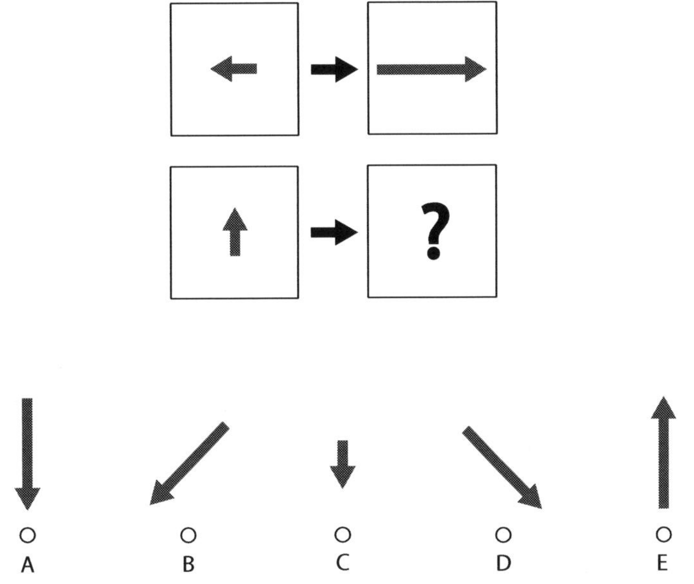

Question 2

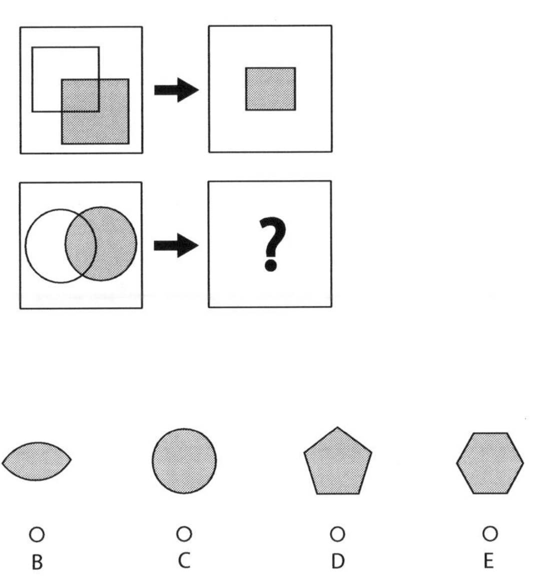

Question 3

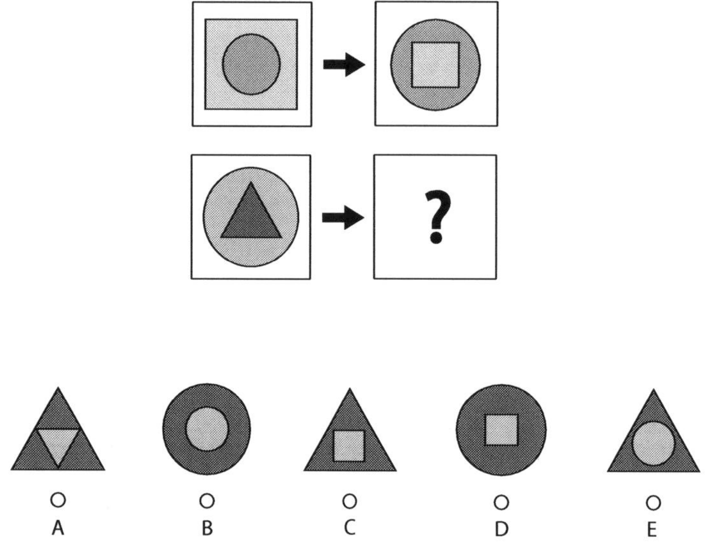

Question 4

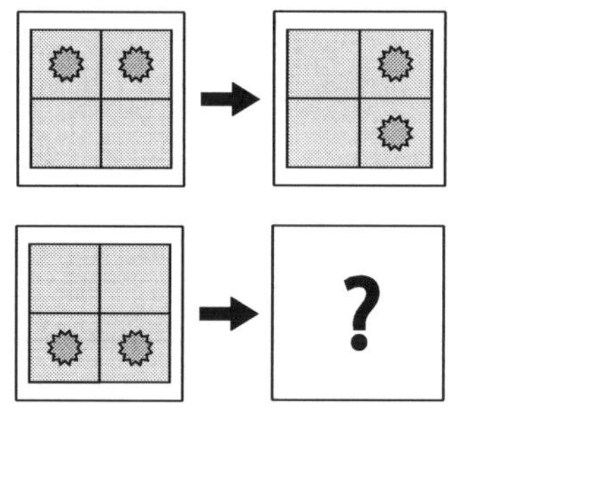

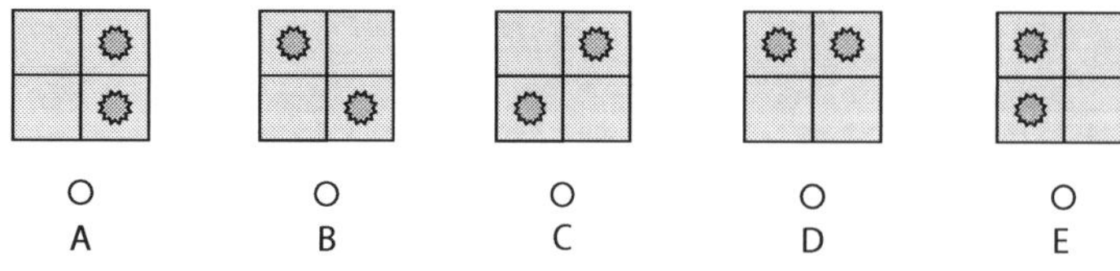

Question 5

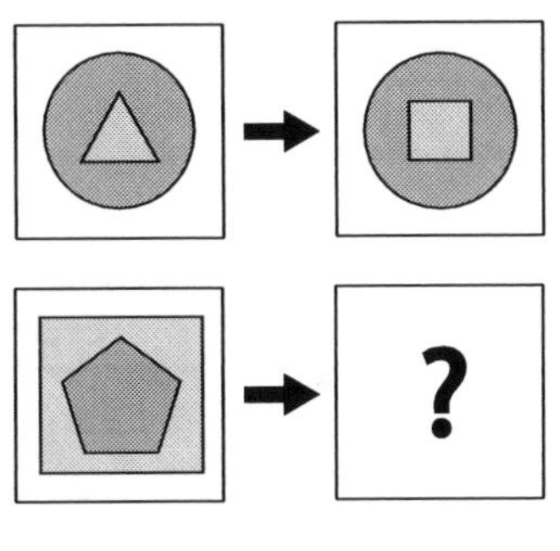

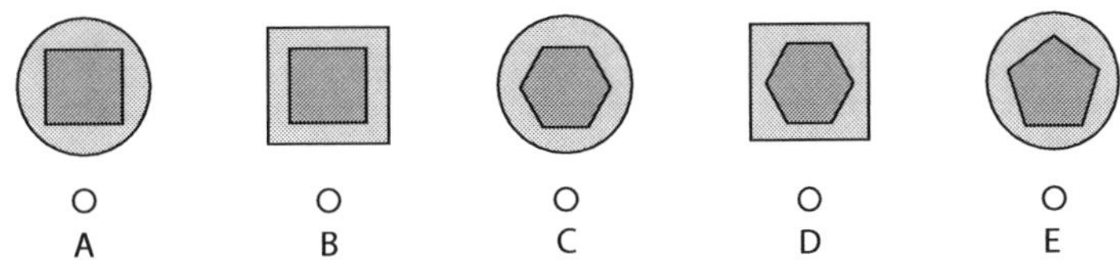

Question 6

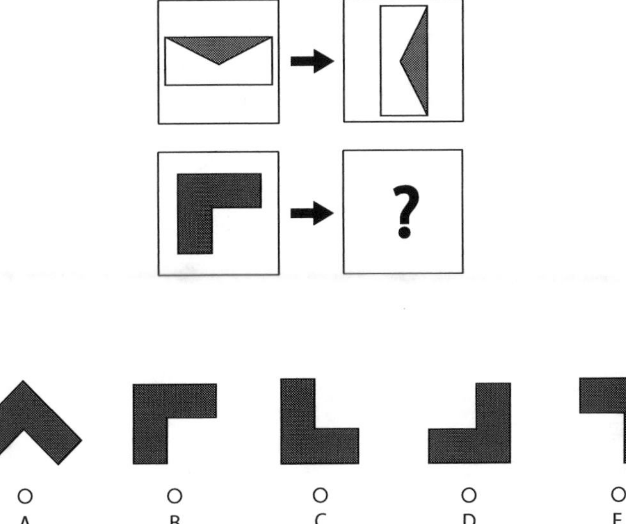

Question 7

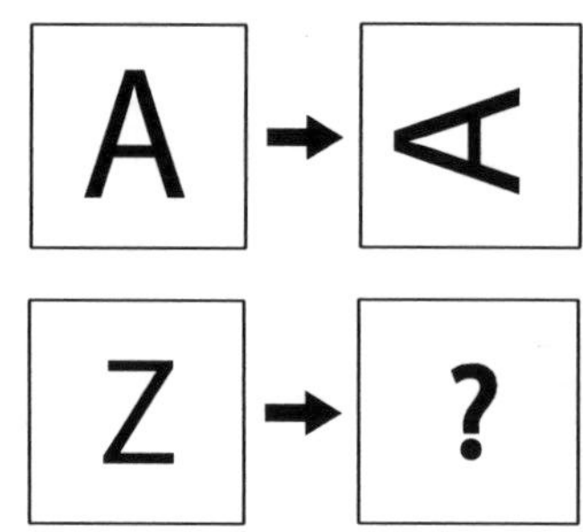

A B C D E

Question 8

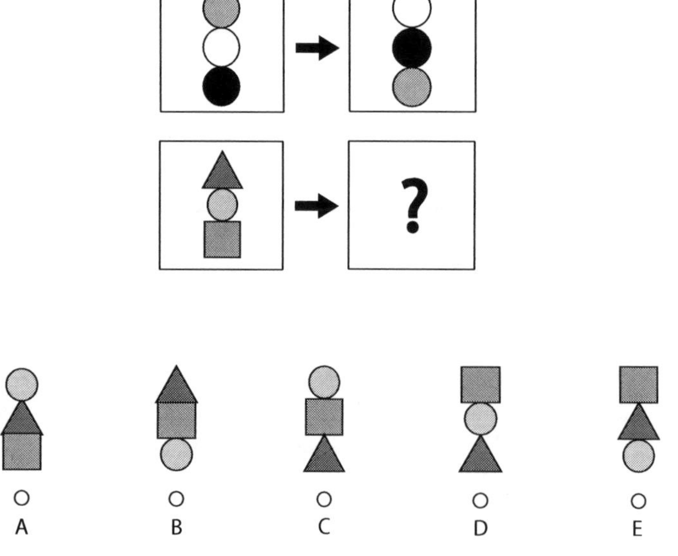

Question 9

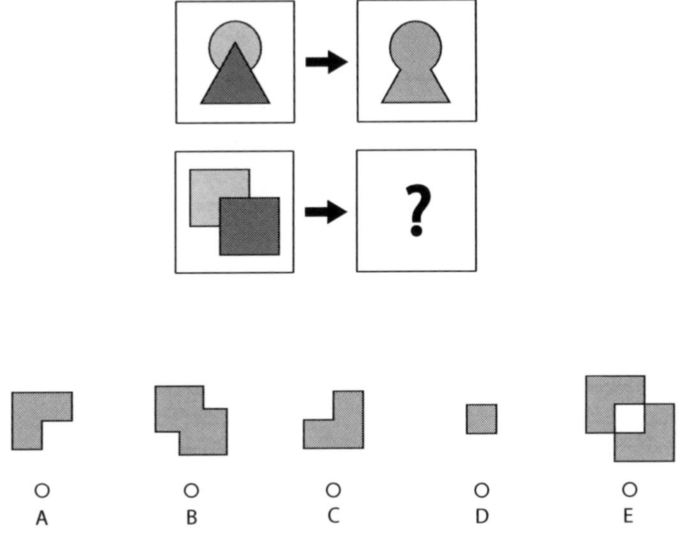

Question 10

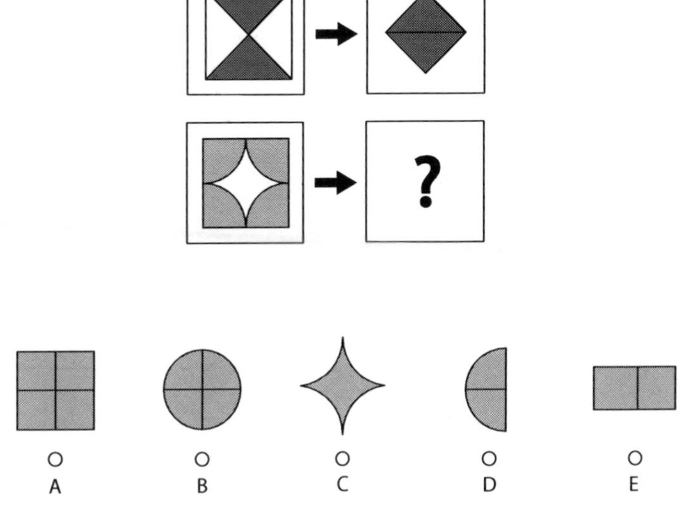

Question 11

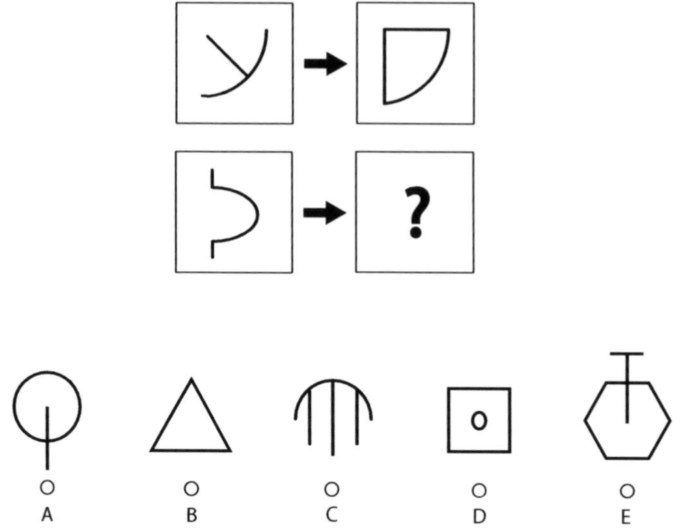

Question 12

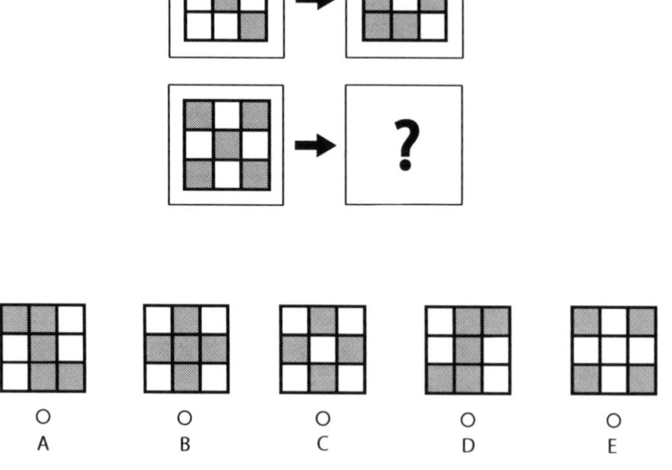

Question 13

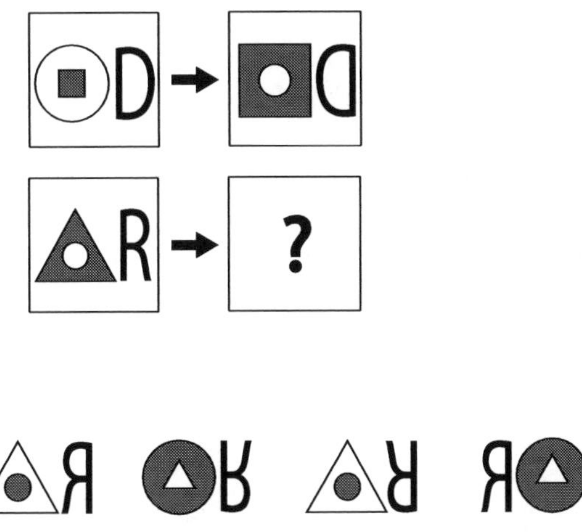

A B C D E

Question 14

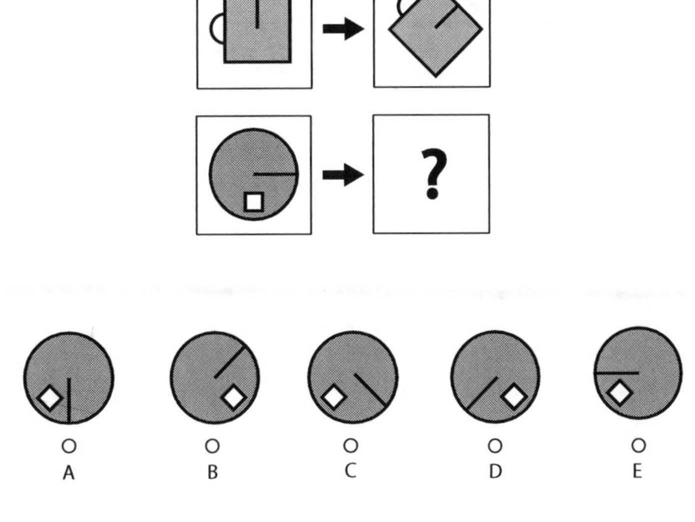

A B C D E

Question 15

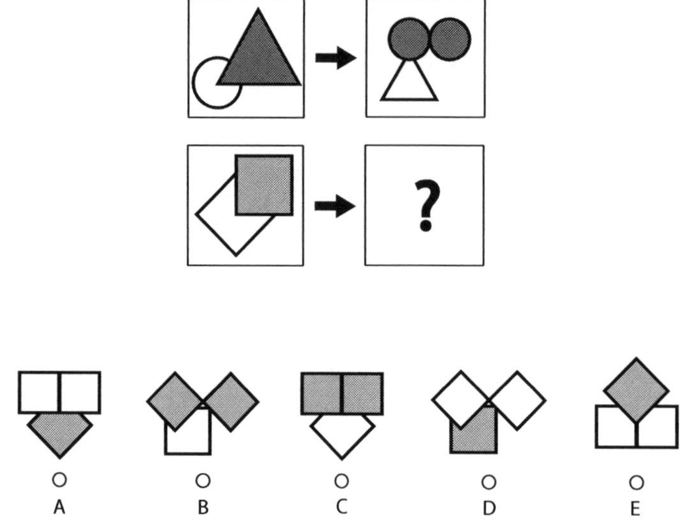

Question 16

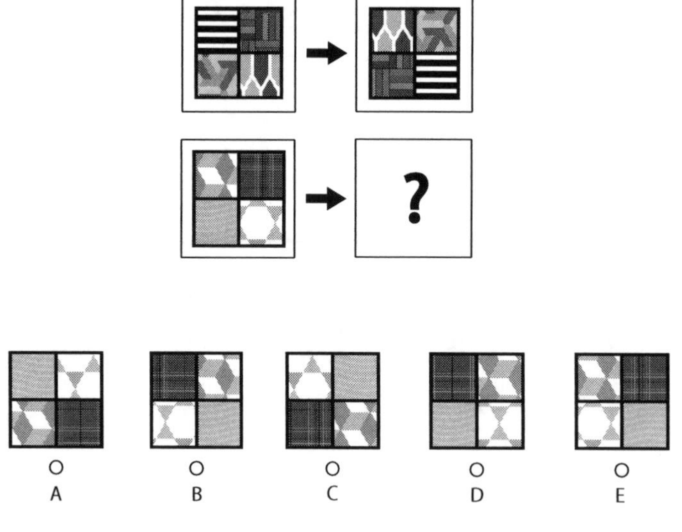

Question 17

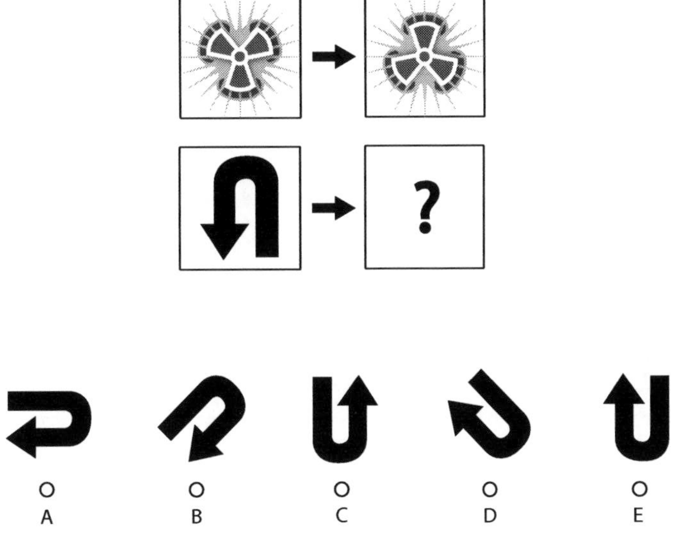

Question 18

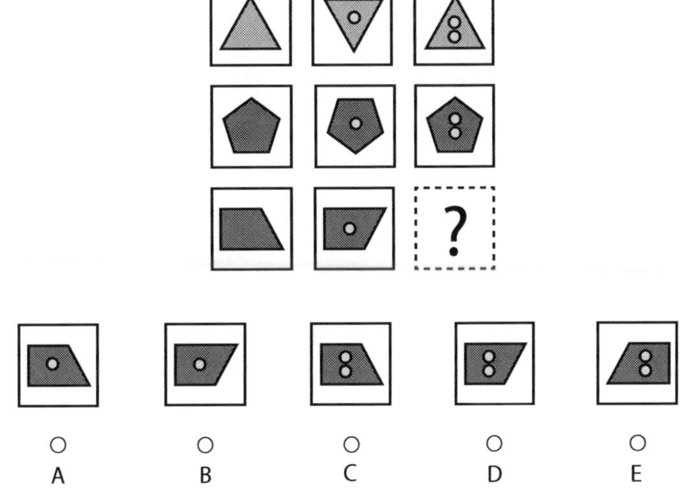

Question 19

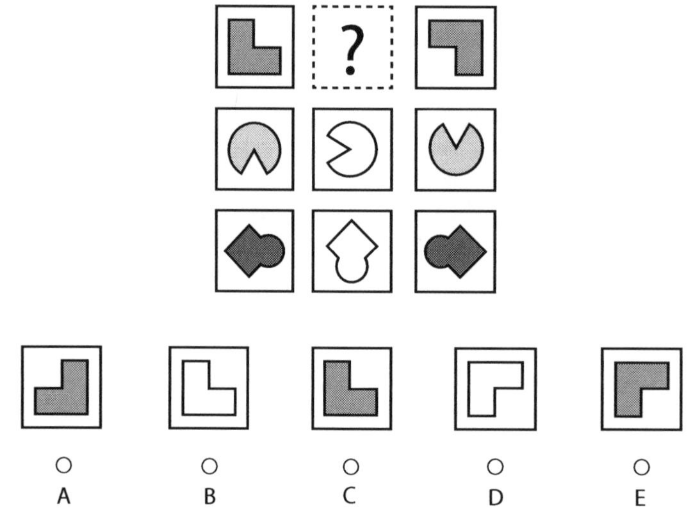

Question 20

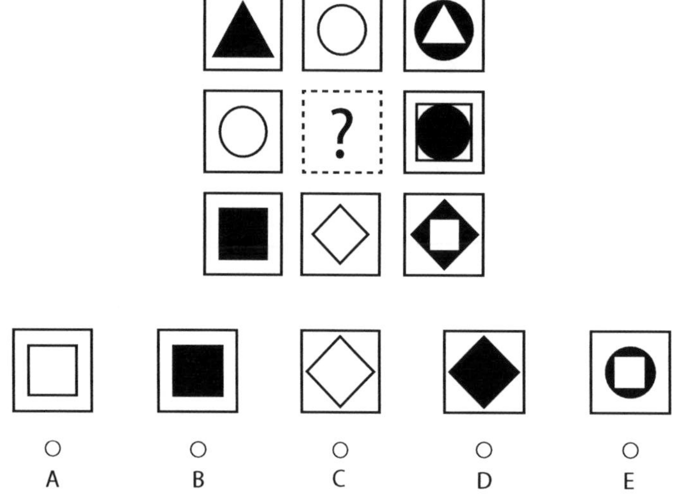

Paper Folding

Directions: In each question, a square paper is folded completely and then either holes or other shapes are punched into the paper. Choose the picture from the answer choices that shows you how the paper will look like when it is unfolded completely.

Below is an example of a paper folding question:

Example

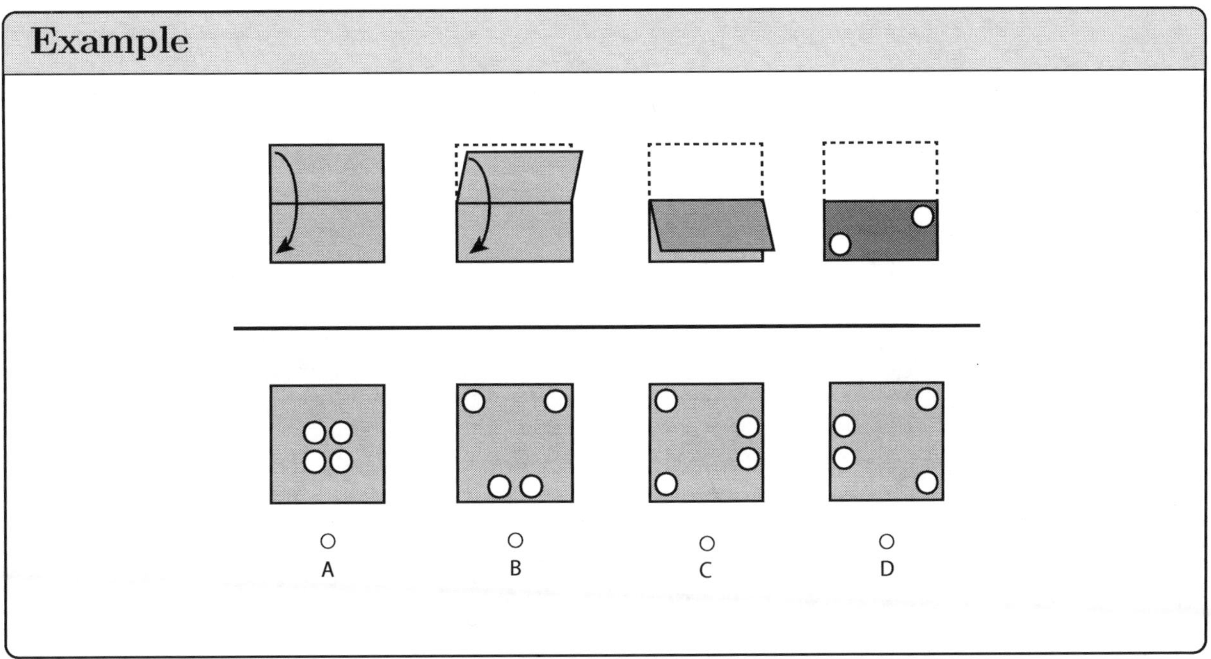

The paper is folded horizontally once. So there will be 4 holes if it is unfolded completely as shown below.

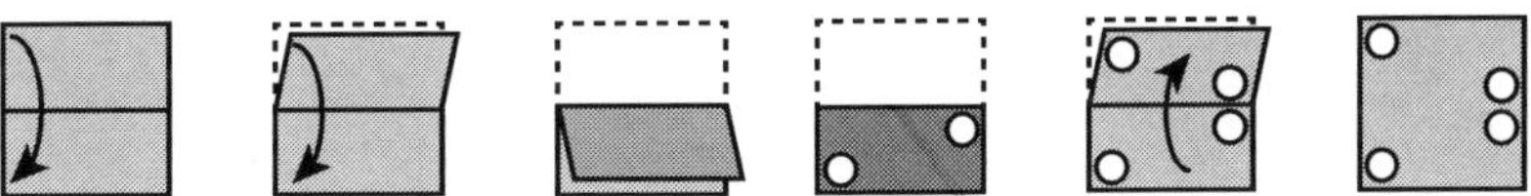

Therefore, the correct answer is C.

Question 1

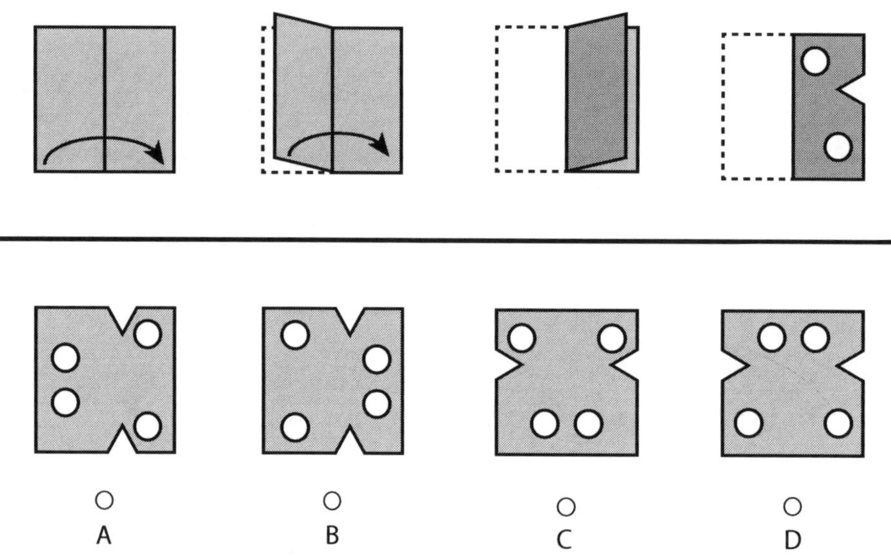

Question 2

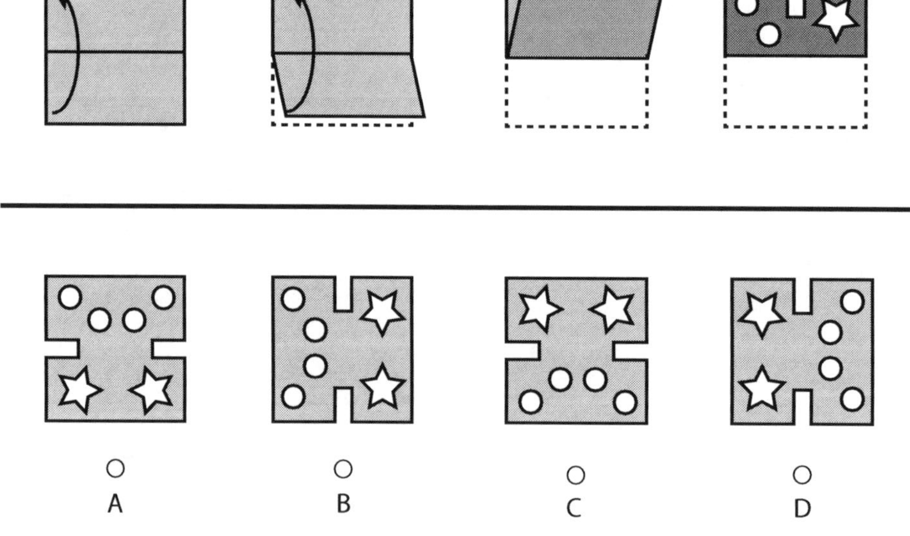

Question 3

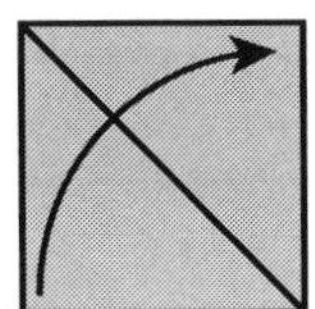 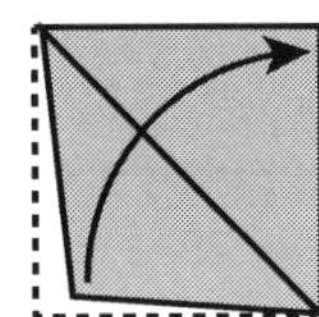 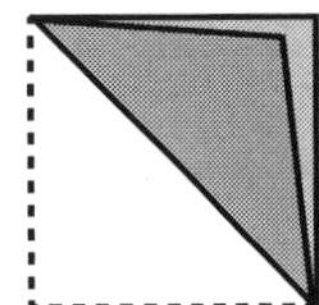 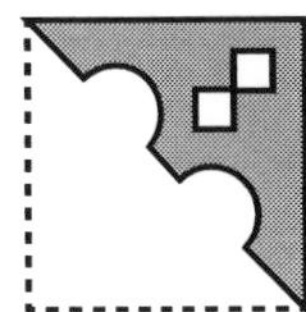

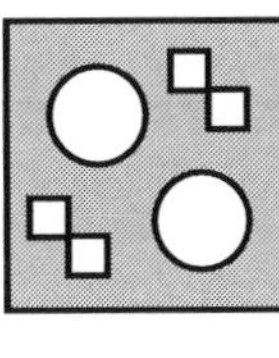
○ A

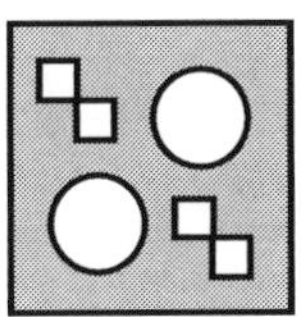
○ B

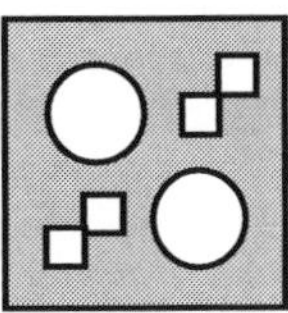
○ C

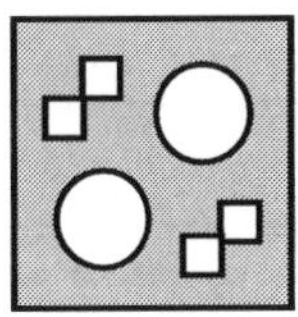
○ D

Question 4

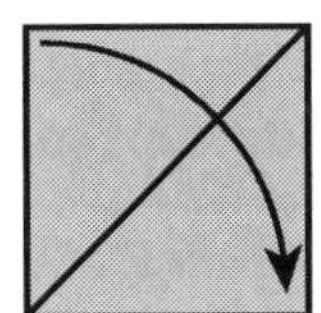 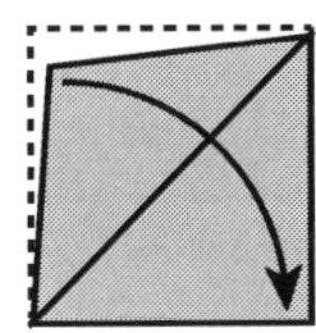 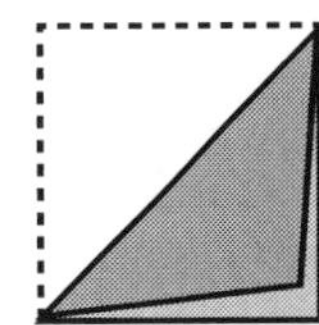 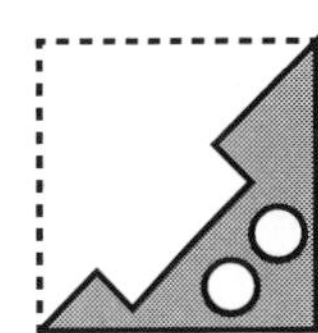

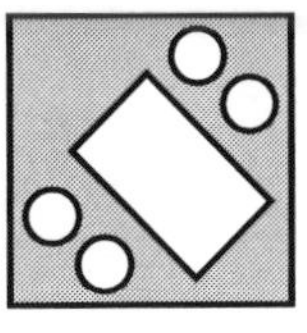
○ A

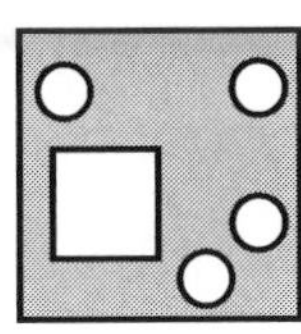
○ B

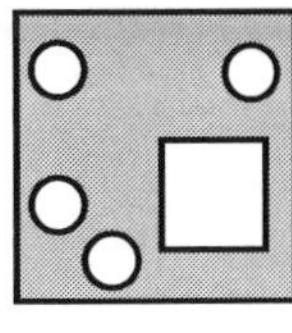
○ C

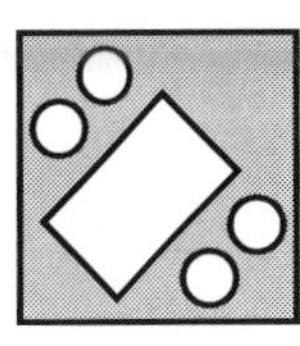
○ D

Question 5

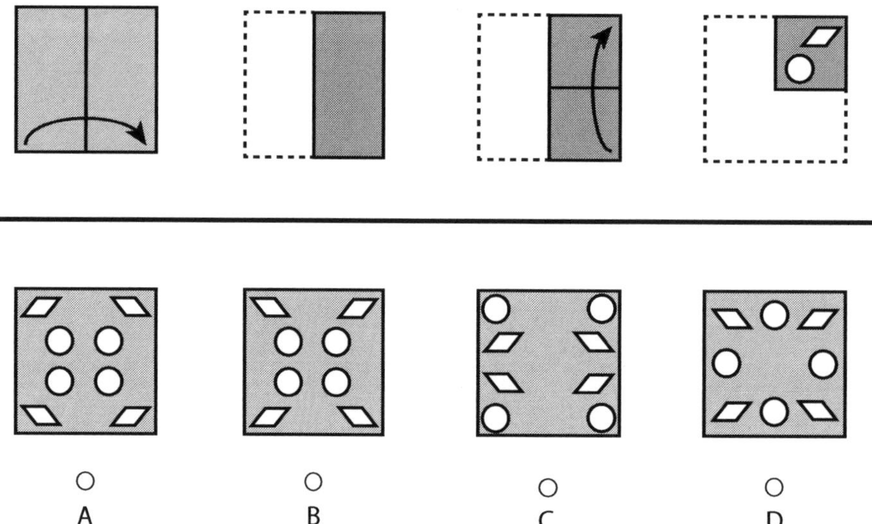

Question 6

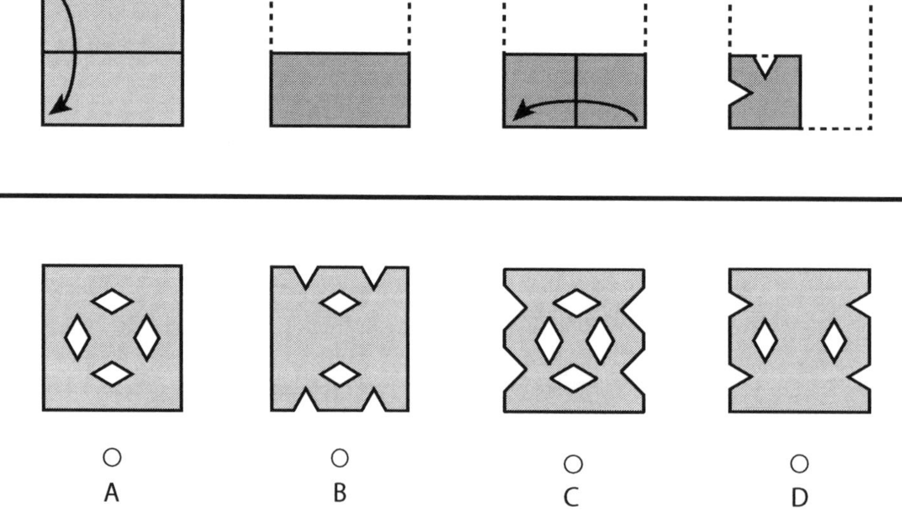

Question 7

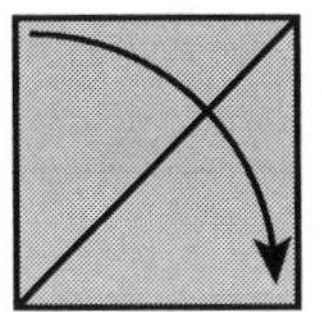 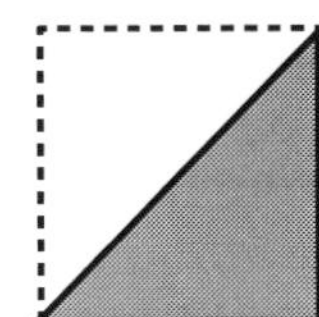 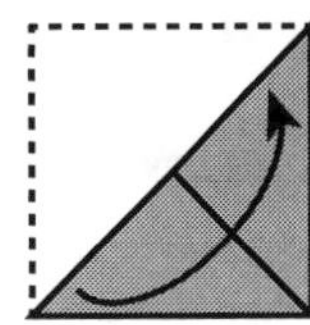 

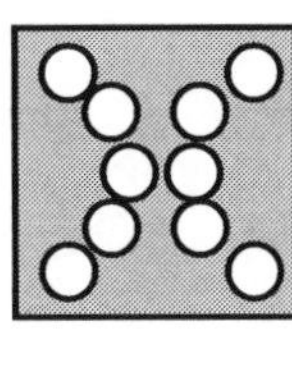 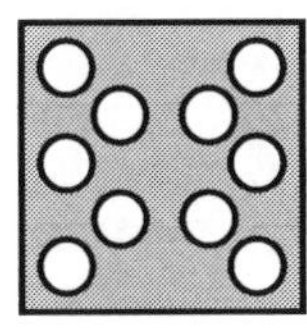 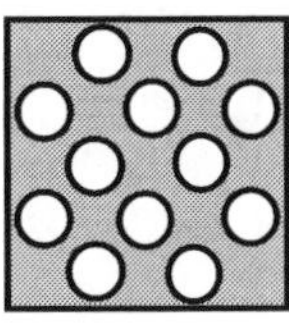 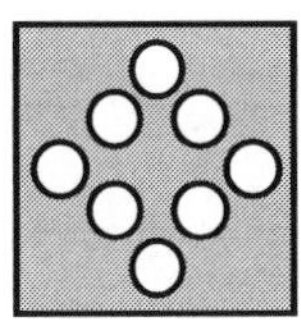

○ A ○ B ○ C ○ D

Question 8

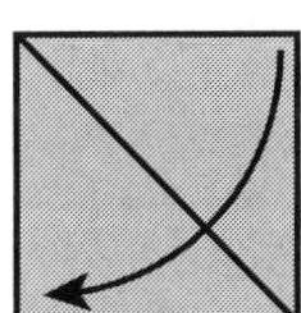 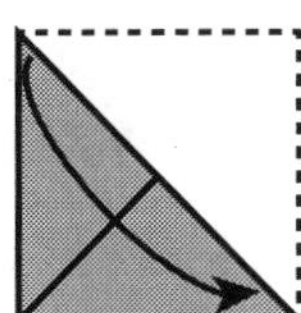 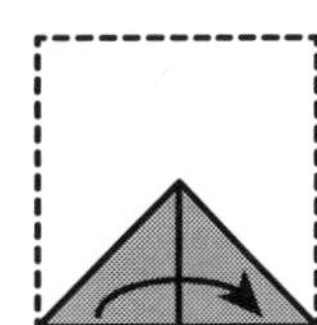 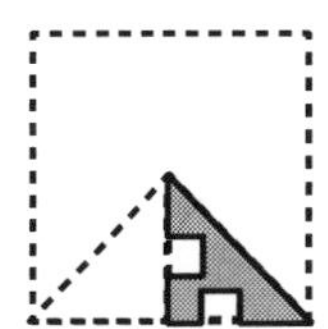

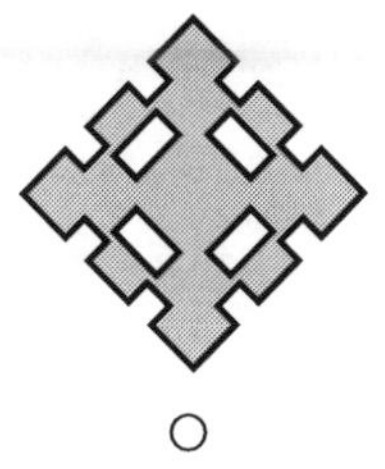  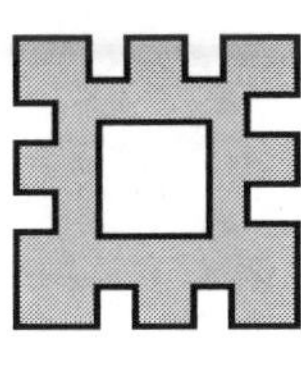 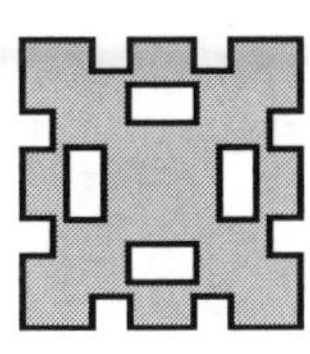 

○ A ○ B ○ C ○ D

Question 9

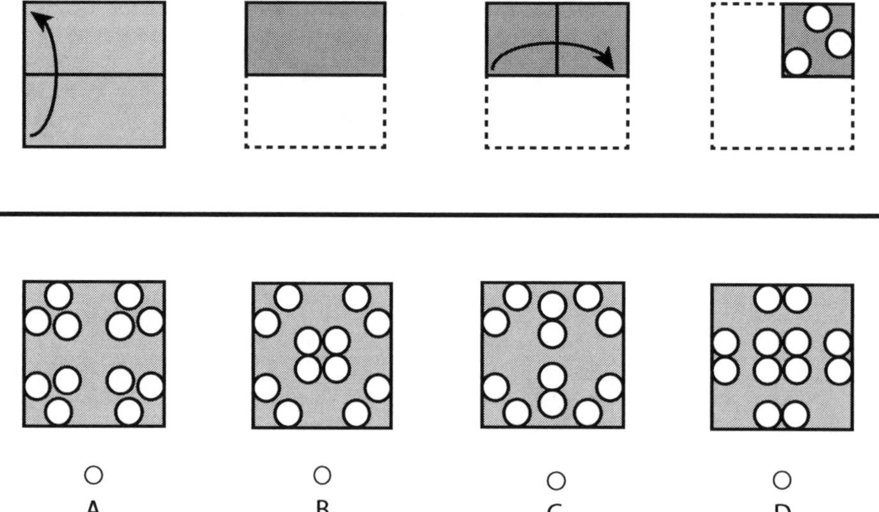

Question 10

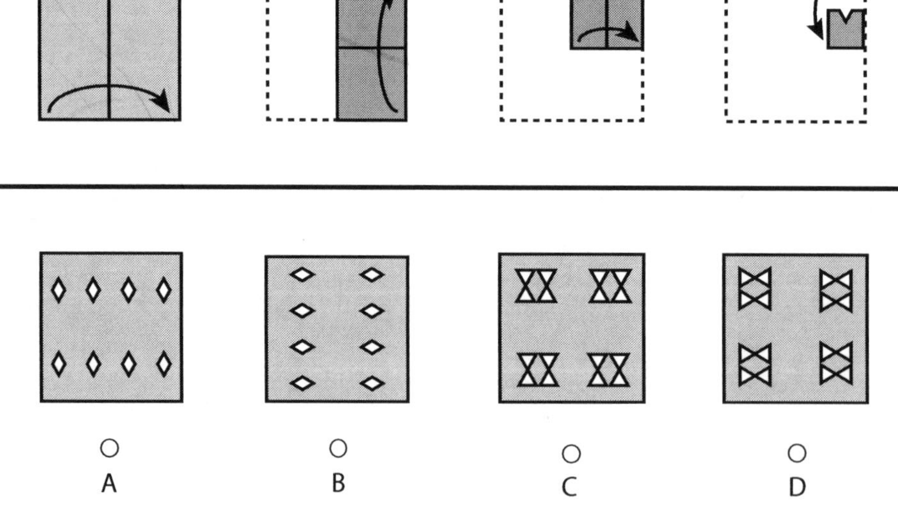

Question 11

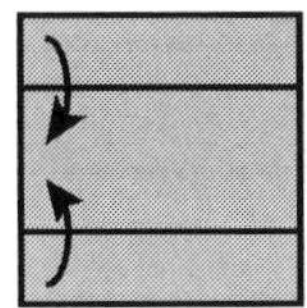 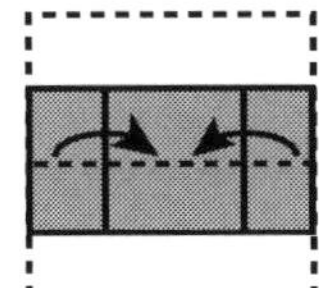 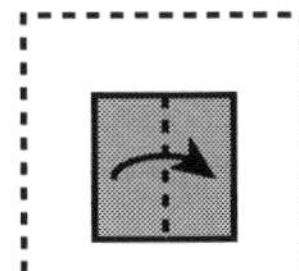 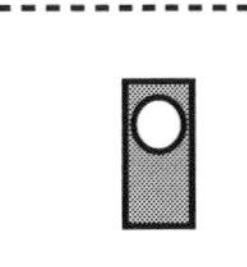

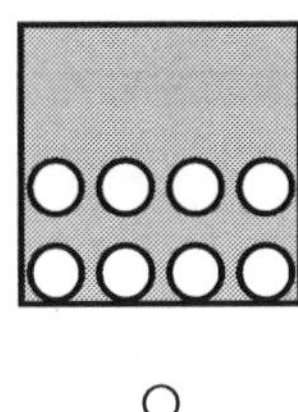
○ A

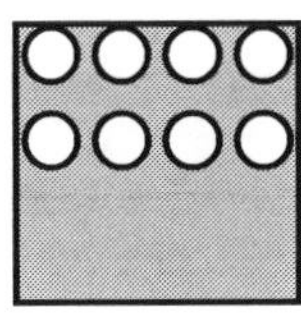
○ B

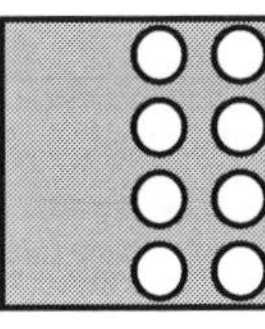
○ C

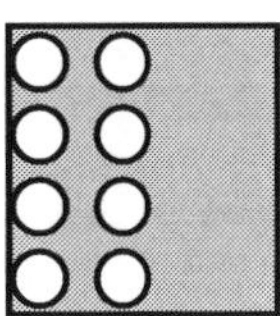
○ D

Question 12

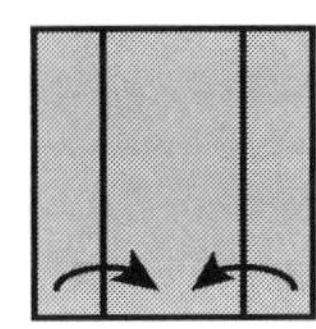 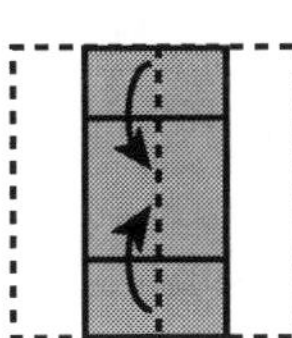  

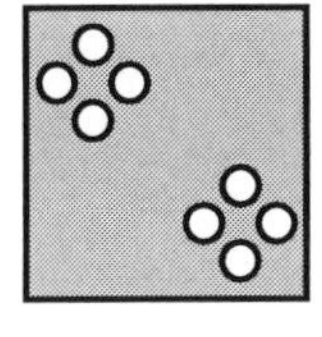
○ A

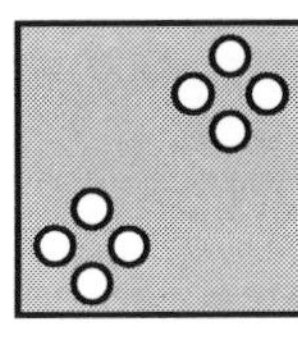
○ B

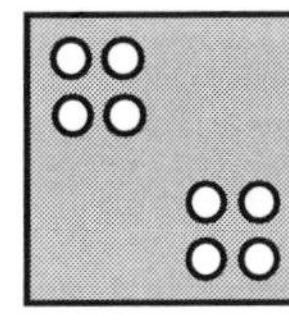
○ C

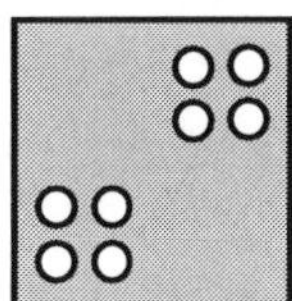
○ D

Question 13

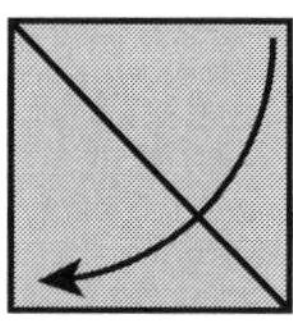
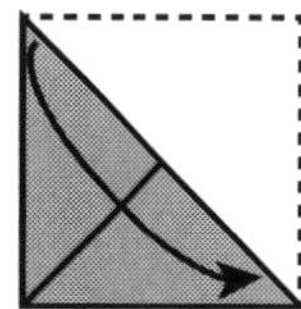
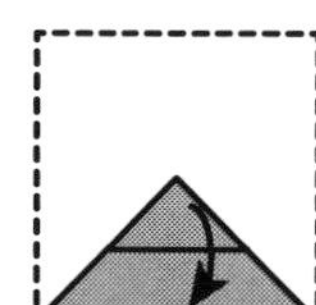

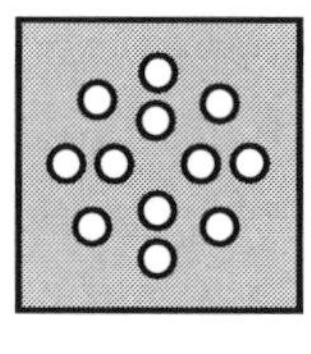

○ A

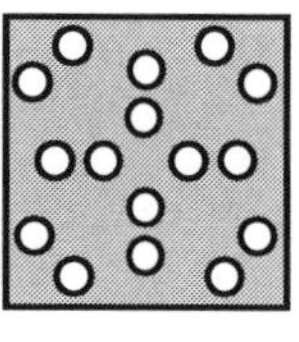

○ B

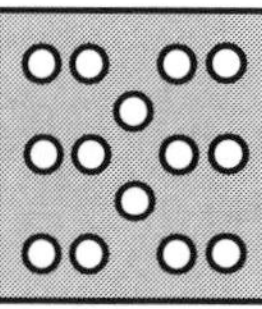

○ C

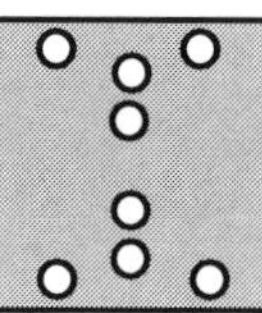

○ D

Question 14

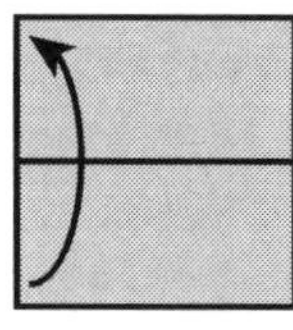
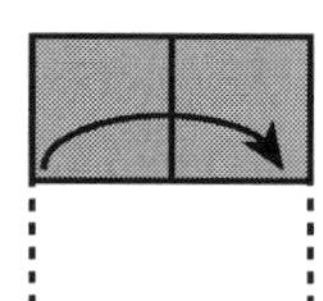
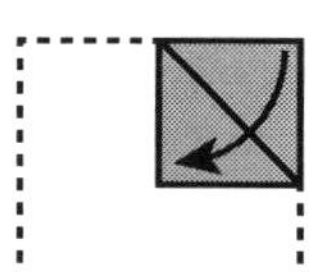
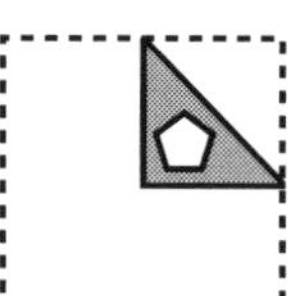

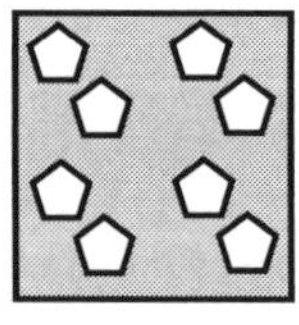

○ A

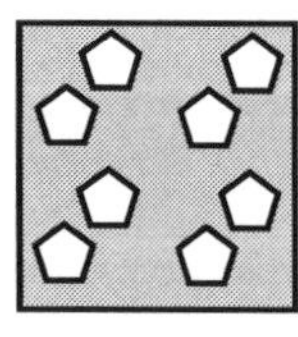

○ B

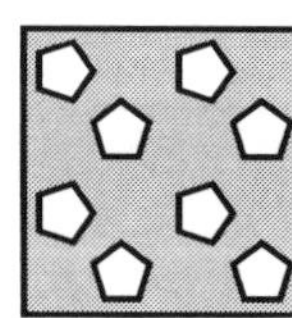

○ C

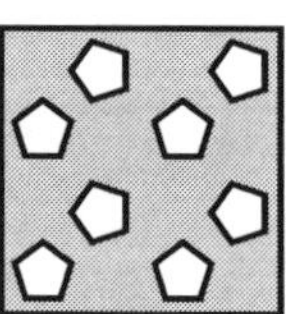

○ D

Question 15

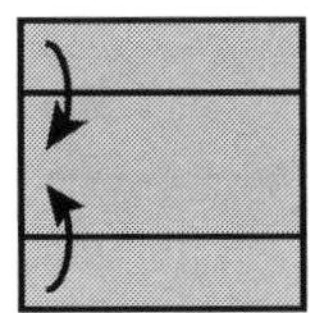 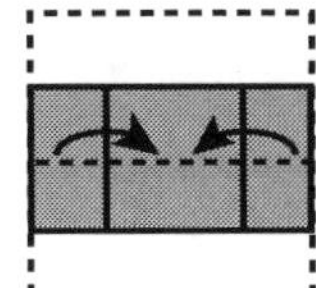  

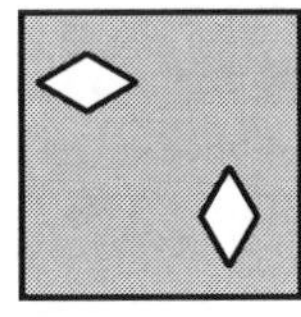 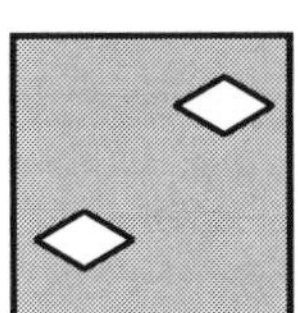 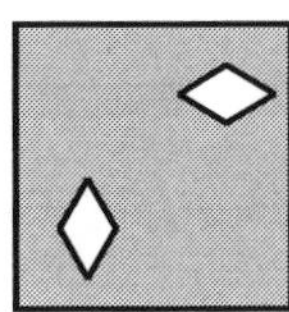 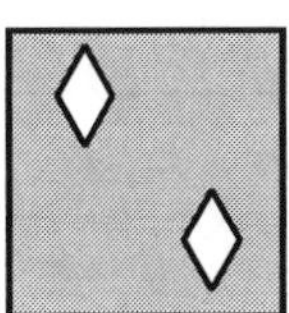

○ A ○ B ○ C ○ D

Question 16

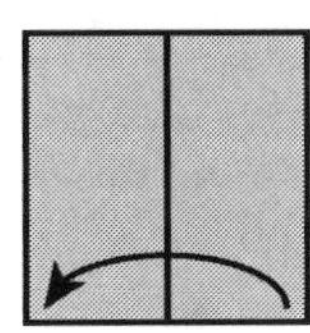 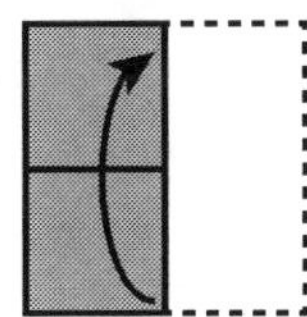 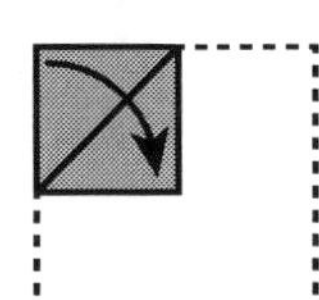 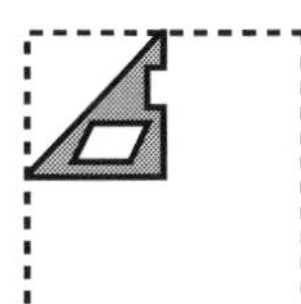

○ A ○ B ○ C ○ D

Figure Classification

Directions: In each question, look at the three figures in the top row and determine how they are related. The four figures in the second row are answer choices. Choose the figure from the answer choices that is most similar to the figures on the top row.

Below is an example of a figure classification question:

Example

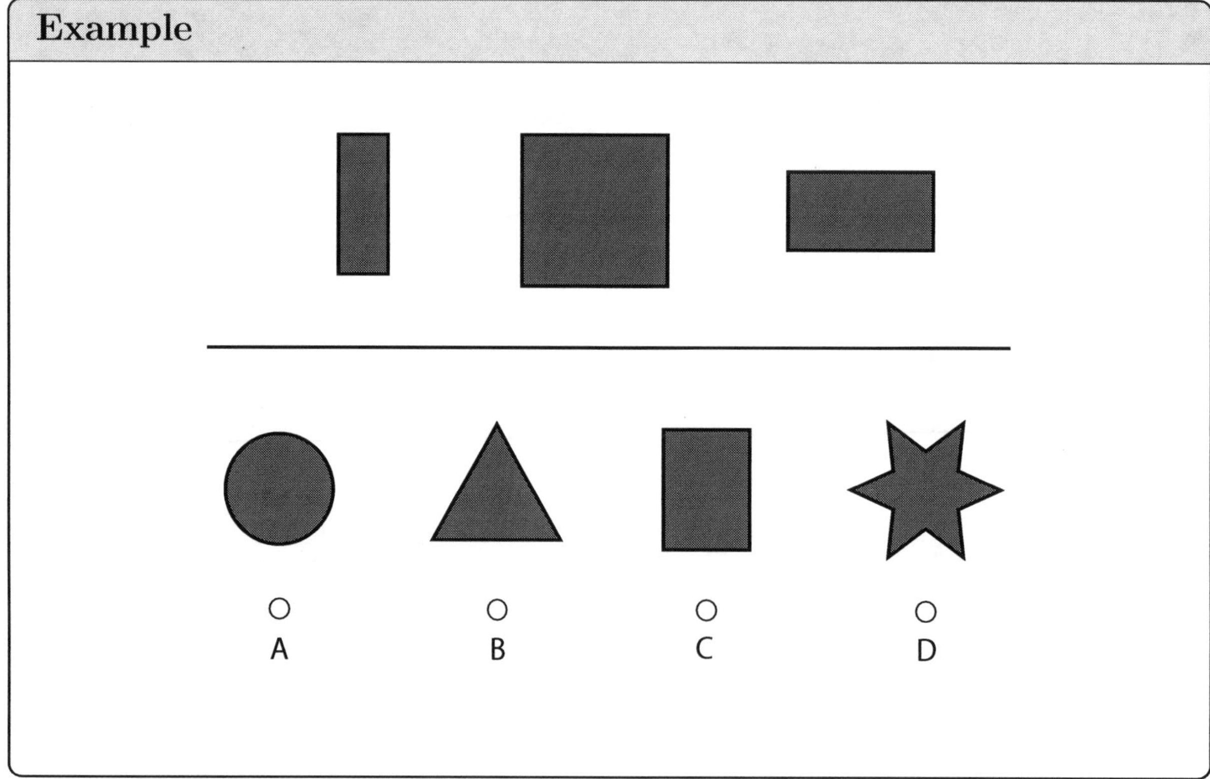

In this example, the three figures in the top row are rectangles. Therefore, the correct answer is C.

Question 1

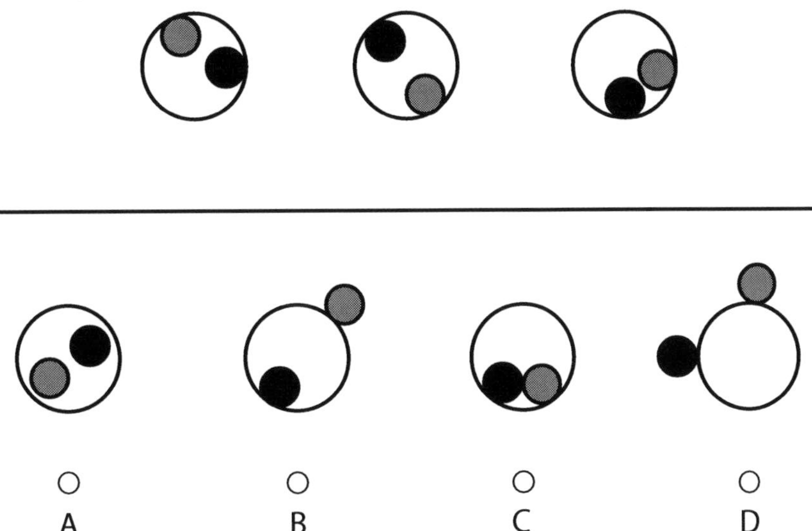

Question 2

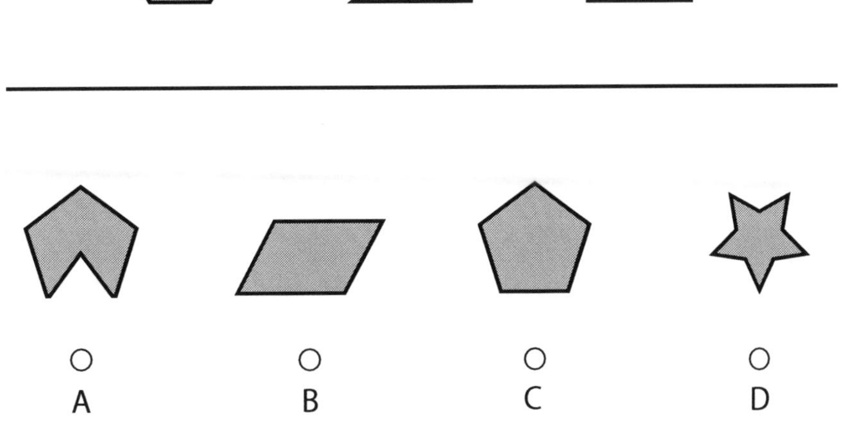

Question 3

○ A ○ B ○ C ○ D

Question 4

  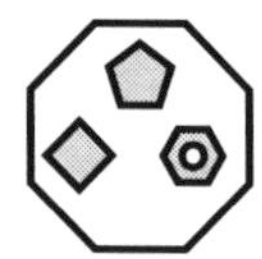 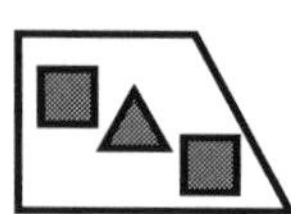

○ A ○ B ○ C ○ D

Question 5

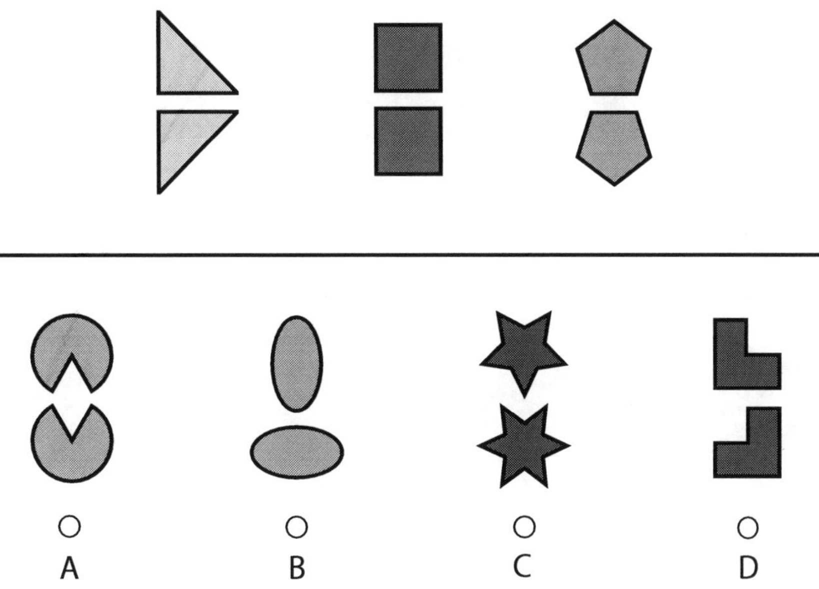

Question 6

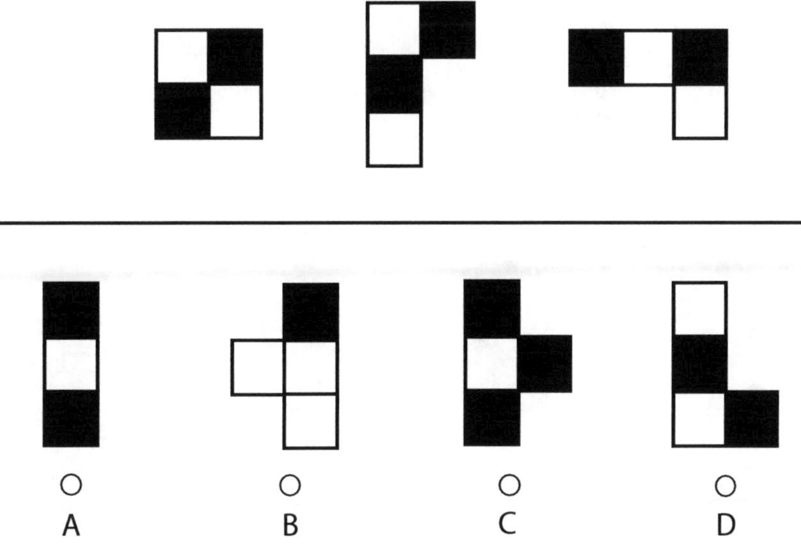

Question 7

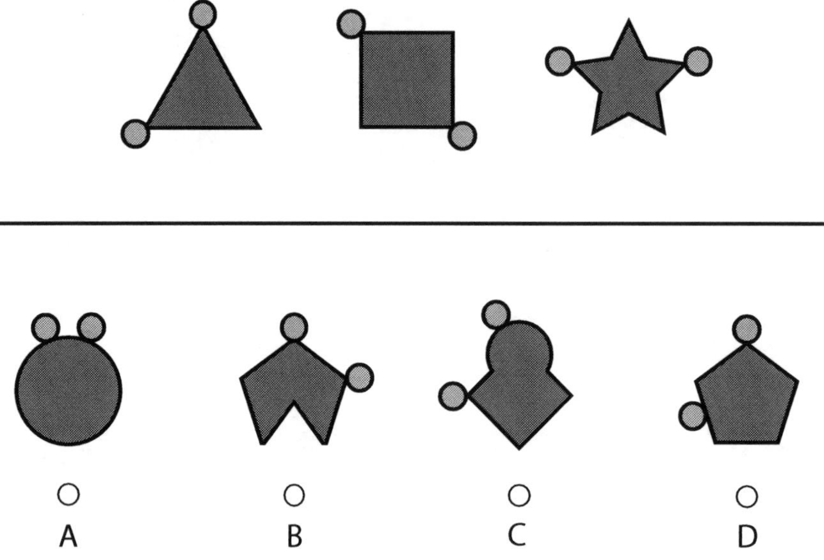

Question 8

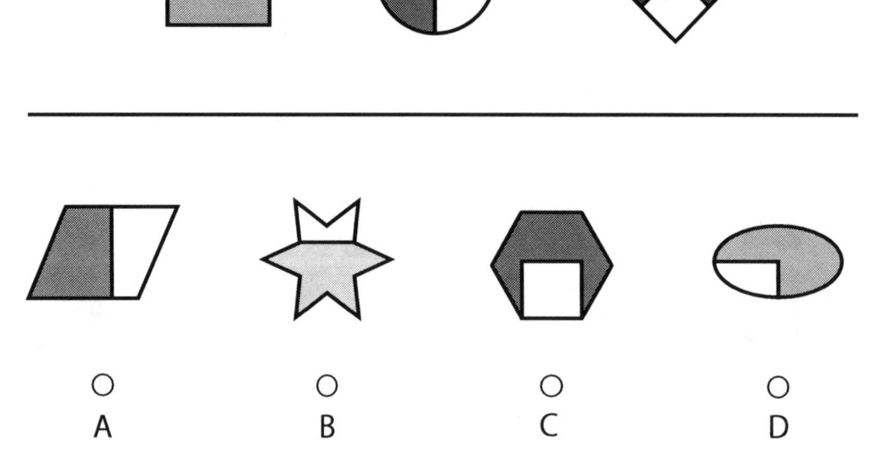

Question 9

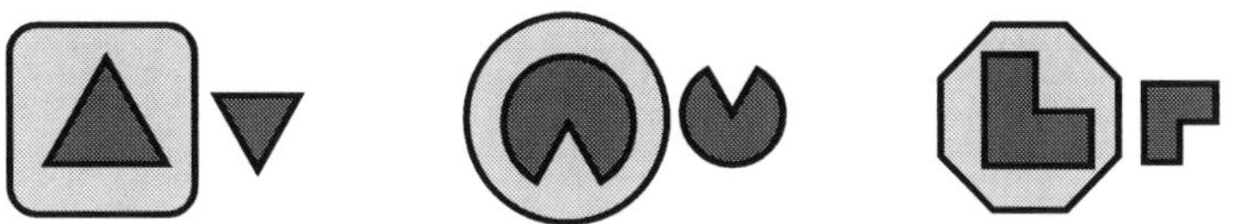

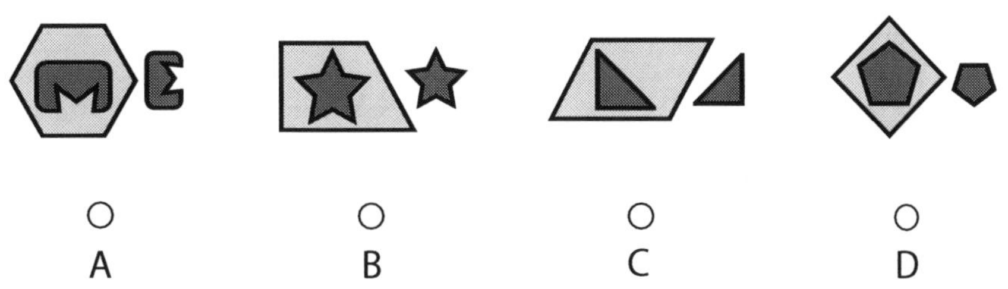

A B C D

Question 10

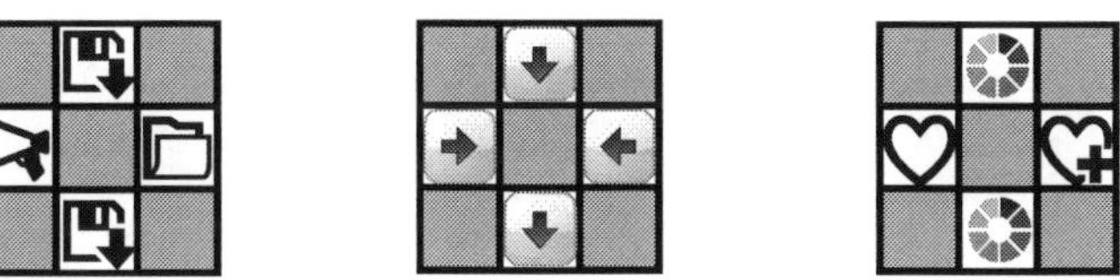

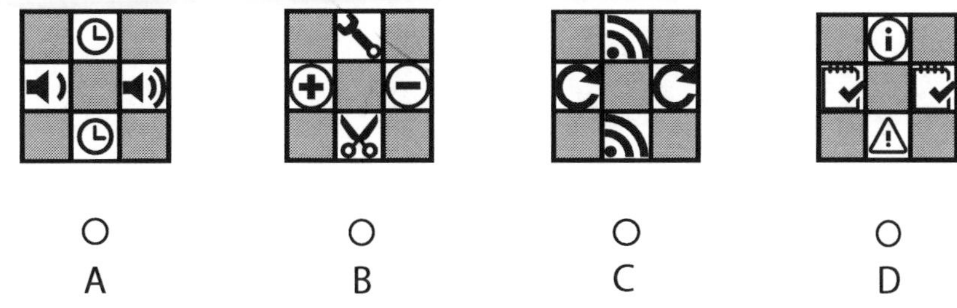

A B C D

Question 11

 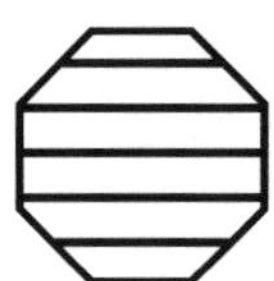 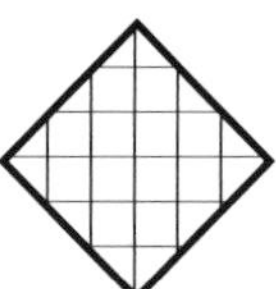

 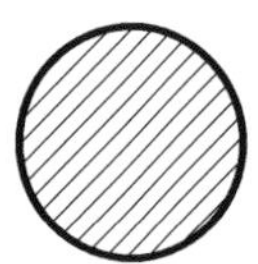  

○ A ○ B ○ C ○ D

Question 12

 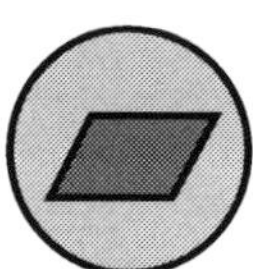 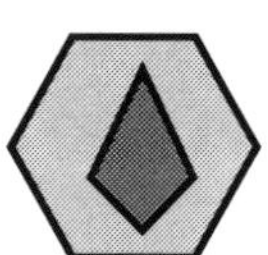

  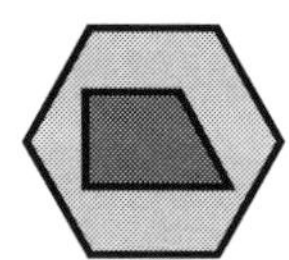 

○ A ○ B ○ C ○ D

Question 13

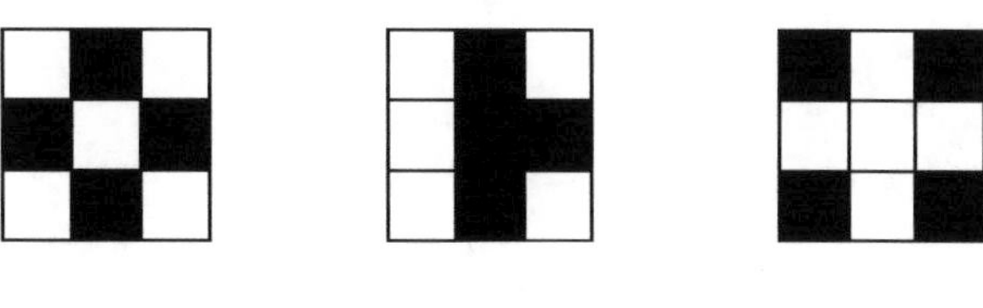

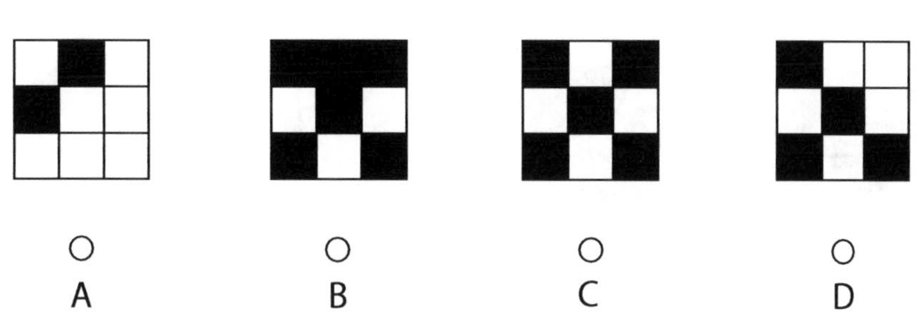

Question 14

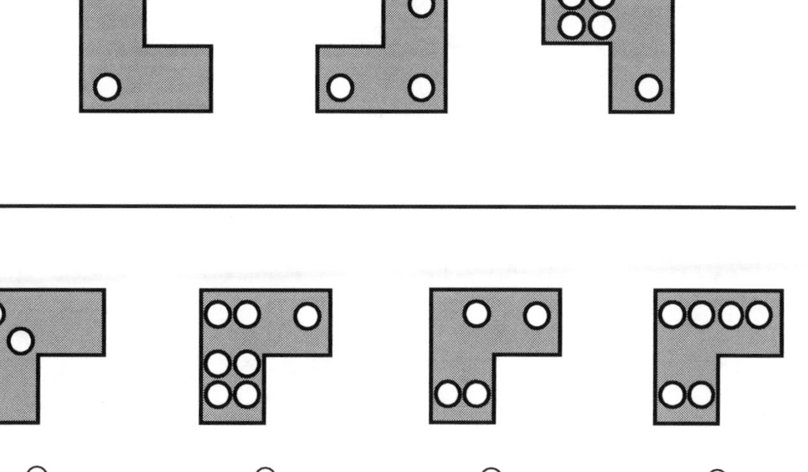

A B C D

Question 15

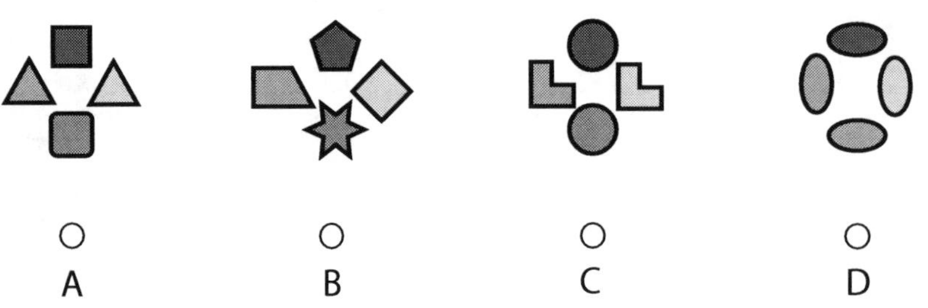

Question 16

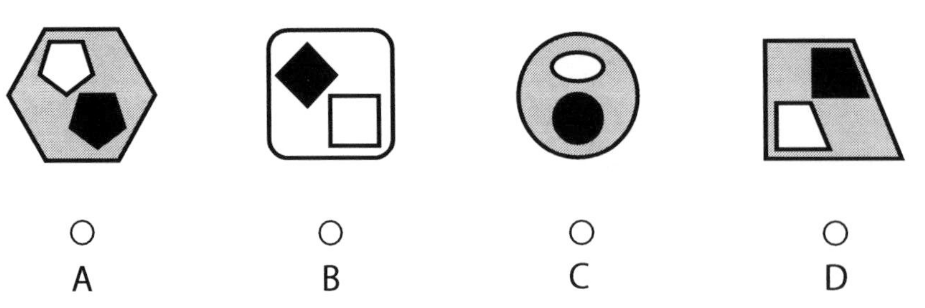

Question 17

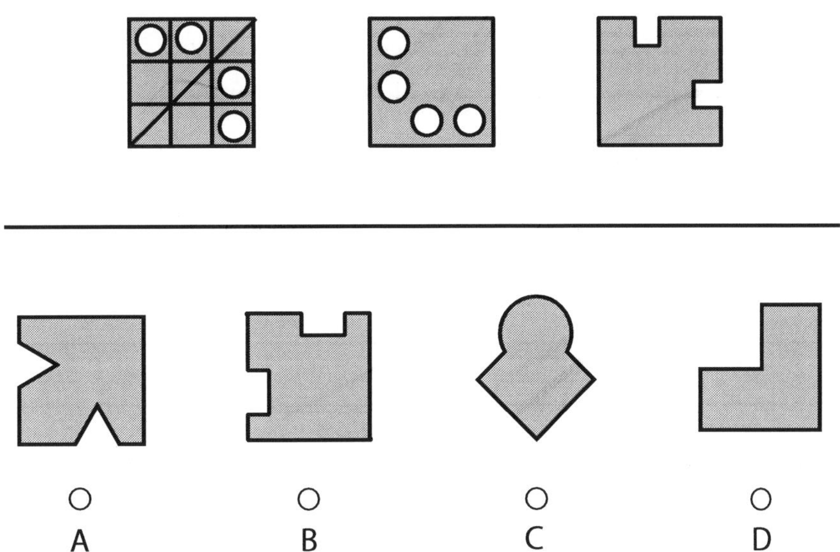

Question 18

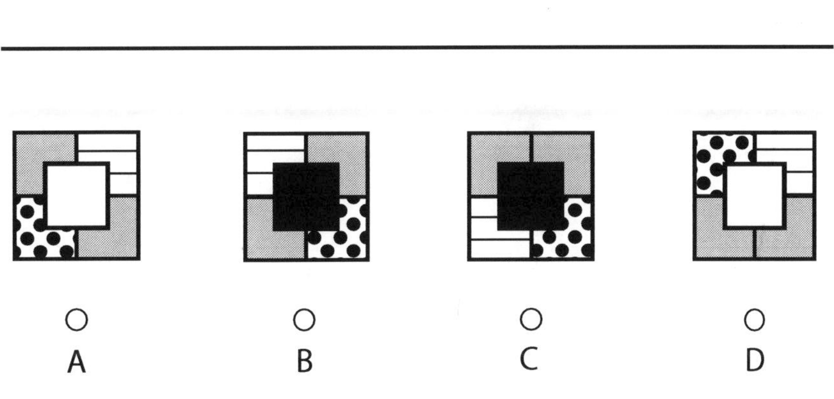

Question 19

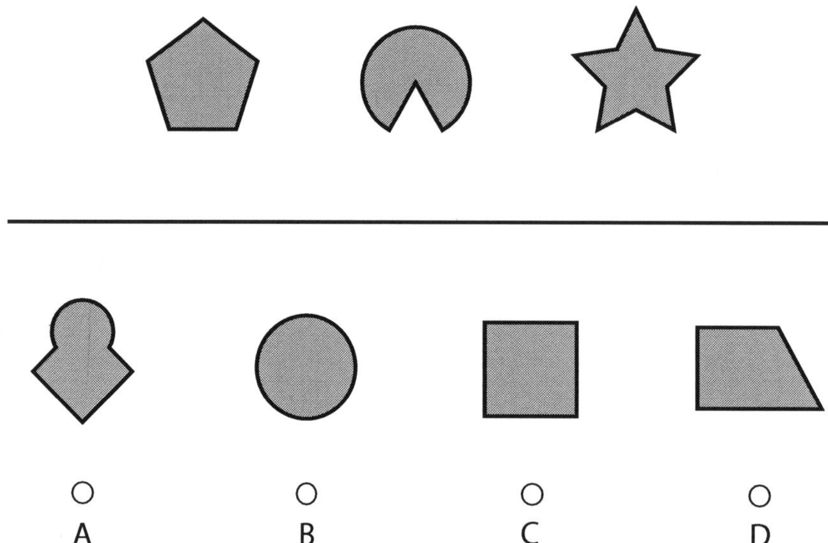

Question 20

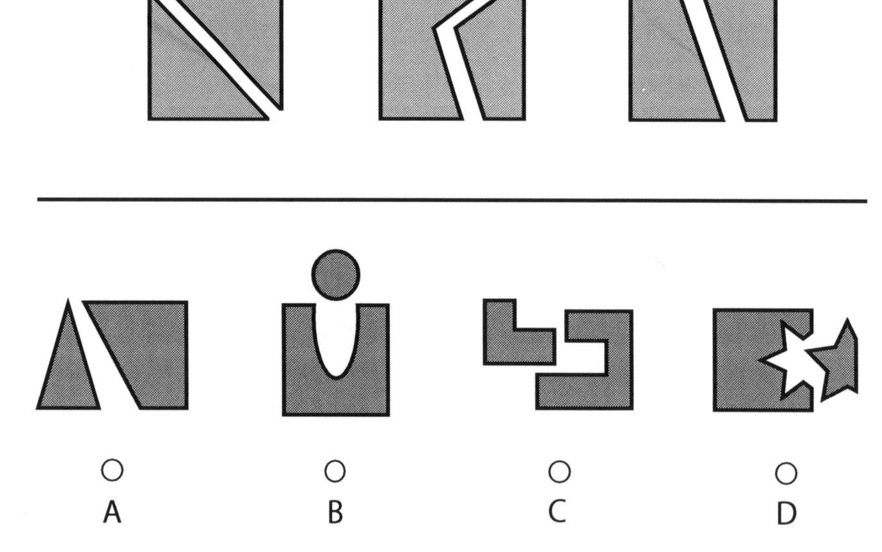

PRACTICE TEST 2

VERBAL BATTERY

1. VERBAL ANALOGIES

2. SENTENCE COMPLETION

3. VERBAL CLASSIFICATION

Verbal Analogies

Directions: In each question, three words are given to you. The first two words are somehow related. Find the word that relates to the third word in the same way that the first two words are related.

Below is an example of a verbal analogies question:

Example

diamond → jewelry : pizza →

(A) hamburger (B) soda (C) ketchup (D) food (E) exercise

In this example, a diamond is a kind of jewelry. A pizza is a kind of food. Therefore, the correct answer is D.

Question 1

cat → kitten : bear →

(A) calf (B) chick (C) baby (D) pub (E) cub

Question 2

scale → measure : saw →

(A) see (B) taste (C) hit (D) pull (E) cut

Question 3

letter → alphabet : steering wheel →

(A) car (B) control (C) direction (D) circle (E) rotation

Question 4

fire → hot : candy →

(A) bitter (B) sweet (C) chocolate (D) color (E) melt

Question 5

ignition key → car : match →

(A) peer (B) fire (C) touch (D) competition (E) game

Question 6

difficult → complicated : funny →

(A) sad (B) hilarious (C) emotional (D) serious (E) tragic

Question 7

farmer → produce : teacher →

(A) learn (B) educate (C) play (D) forgive (E) ignore

Question 8

talk → listen : laugh →

(A) giggle (B) chuckle (C) smile (D) cry (E) fortune

Question 9

cup → drink : chair →

(A) seat (B) stand (C) run (D) comfortable (E) tense

Question 10

finger → hand : leaf →

(A) wood (B) paper (C) tile (D) tree (E) plastic

Question 11

jaguar $\rightarrow$ mountain : whale $\rightarrow$

(A) desert (B) forrest (C) ocean (D) jungle (E) city

Question 12

bitter $\rightarrow$ sweet : weak $\rightarrow$

(A) cheerful (B) fragile (C) pleasant (D) lame (E) strong

Question 13

big $\rightarrow$ huge : little $\rightarrow$

(A) gigantic (B) tall (C) tiny (D) size (E) amount

Question 14

instrument $\rightarrow$ piano : gender $\rightarrow$

(A) personality (B) name (C) female (D) income (E) age

Question 15

traffic lights $\rightarrow$ control : password $\rightarrow$

(A) protect (B) public (C) secret (D) hide (E) reveal

Question 16

silent → noisy : safe →

(A) dangerous (B) easy (C) secure (D) loud (E) rapid

Question 17

wrench → tool : apple →

(A) eat (B) delicious (C) green (D) vegetable (E) fruit

Question 18

run → ran : sing →

(A) song (B) singed (C) sung (D) sanged (E) sang

Question 19

lens → camera : pedals →

(A) ship (B) truck (C) car (D) bus (E) bicycle

Question 20

school → student : court →

(A) designer (B) artist (C) librarian (D) jury (E) actress

Question 21

neck → necklace : wrist →

(A) hat (B) bracelet (C) glasses (D) ring (E) diamond

Question 22

bean → pod : nut →

(A) cover (B) bin (C) exterior (D) shell (E) crack

Sentence Completion

Directions: In each question, a sentence with a missing word is given to you. Find the word that best completes the sentence.

Below is an example of a sentence completion question:

Example

A rope is hard to cut because it is so ________.

(A) thin (B) long (C) thick (D) tall (E) weak

A thick rope is hard to cut. Therefore, the correct answer is C.

Question 1

Each time I travel, I learn about what to bring to be ________.

(A) discovered (B) prepared (C) frightened (D) afraid (E) surprised

Question 2

After I ________ ketchup and mustard on meat, I eat my sandwich.

(A) touch (B) spread (C) hold (D) grab (E) snatch

Question 3

I ________ containers with potting soil to plant flowers.

(A) feel (B) draw (C) fill (D) empty (E) complete

Question 4

My vacation was fun. Hopefully we can go ________ to the same place next year.

(A) back (B) forward (C) after (D) over (E) by

Question 5

Jenny wakes up late every morning. She often leaves her bed ________.

(A) open (B) unmade (C) organized (D) unhealthy (E) balanced

Question 6

It is very important to wear a ________ to stay safe in a boat.

(A) shoes (B) hat (C) life jacket (D) sun glasses (E) swimwear

Question 7

The blue crab is found ________ in the Atlantic ocean.

(A) below (B) alive (C) deep (D) active (E) apart

Question 8

Ben is excited about moving ________ Texas to New York.

(A) in (B) at (C) by (D) over (E) from

Question 9

As dumpsters are almost full, our environment is getting ________.

(A) dirty (B) free (C) dry (D) rich (E) smooth

Question 10

We had to go home early. There was a sudden ________.

(A) rainstorm (B) traffic (C) sleep (D) moment (E) search

Question 11

My family went ________ vacation last month.

(A) to (B) in (C) by (D) on (E) up

Question 12

My cat made a mess on the floor. I had to ________ it up.

(A) organize (B) learn (C) clear (D) clean (E) look

Question 13

A full-grown salmon is ready to ________ eggs.

(A) lie (B) laid (C) lay (D) set (E) put

Question 14

Beavers ________ dams with sticks and mud.

(A) build (B) destroy (C) prepare (D) use (E) pick

Question 15

As soon as we arrive at the campsite, we will ________ up the tent.

(A) move (B) make (C) cover (D) construct (E) set

Question 16

I heard the rain make loud ________ noises on the roof.

(A) static (B) electronic (C) rolling (D) crunchy (E) plunking

Question 17

Joshua saw a dog walking down the street. He wanted to ________ the dog.

(A) meet (B) squeeze (C) water (D) hug (E) pat

Question 18

The English class ended. So students ________ up their bags.

(A) filled (B) packed (C) closed (D) rubbed (E) stretched

Question 19

"Please move out of my way! Let me ________!".

(A) away (B) in (C) through (D) to (E) by

Question 20

Squirrels love ________ from tree to tree.

(A) leaning (B) hopping (C) playing (D) standing (E) parking

Verbal Classification

Directions: The three words in each question are somehow related. Determine how they are similar and find the word that is most similar to the three words.

Below is an example of a verbal Classification question:

Example

earthquake **hurricane** **tornado**

(A) fire (B) disaster (C) wind (D) rain (E) ambulance

A natural disaster is a major adverse event resulting from natural processes of the Earth including earthquakes, hurricanes, and tornadoes. Therefore, the correct answer is B.

Question 1

Thanksgiving Independence day Labor day

(A) Sunday (B) holiday (C) Winter (D) turkey (E) trip

Question 2

blue yellow red

(A) color (B) hat (C) pencil (D) flag (E) shape

Question 3

rain snow hail

(A) water (B) river (C) temperature (D) sleet (E) winter

Question 4

group assembly crowd

(A) regiment (B) grade (C) school (D) strength (E) flower

Question 5

trust belief confidence

(A) doubt (B) lying (C) denial (D) suspicion (E) faith

Question 6

Sweden France Canada

(A) New York (B) Chicago (C) Beijing (D) London (E) South Korea

Question 7

pork lamb chicken

(A) wool (B) zoo (C) cage (D) potato (E) beef

Question 8

heavy-eyed tired sleepy

(A) awake (B) drowsy (C) alert (D) busy (E) active

Question 9

parsley sage dill

(A) carrot (B) cucumber (C) eggplant (D) onion (E) basil

Question 10

inch yard mile

(A) ounce (B) foot (C) hour (D) pound (E) day

Question 11

sourdough biscuit baguette

(A) bread (B) jam (C) butter (D) flavor (E) breakfast

Question 12

stock pot skillet roasting pan

(A) kitchen (B) laundry (C) cleaning (D) bath (E) recipe

Question 13

talent capability skill

(A) expertise (B) stress (C) play (D) study (E) argue

Question 14

hip hop rap rock

(A) history (B) science (C) education (D) subject (E) music

Question 15

copy imitation reproduction

(A) impression (B) genuine (C) real (D) idea (E) magazine

Question 16

novel poetry nonfiction

(A) sports (B) literature (C) artist (D) product (E) material

Question 17

lodging accommodation housing

(A) goal (B) residence (C) health (D) style (E) information

Question 18

shape structure form

(A) nature (B) round (C) appearance (D) imagination (E) description

Question 19

ear apple ice

(A) busy (B) cake (C) umbrella (D) time (E) dictionary

Question 20

applaud admire honor

(A) punishment (B) name (C) congratulate (D) criticize (E) oath

QUANTITATIVE BATTERY

1. NUMBER ANALOGIES
2. NUMBER PUZZLES
3. NUMBER SERIES

Number Analogies

Directions: In each question, three pairs of numbers are given to you. Determine the relationship between the first two pairs of numbers. Find the number that has the same relationship when paired with the number in the third pair.

Below is an example of a number analogies question:

Example

[**5** → **2**] [**8** → **5**] [**12** → ?]

(A) 7 (B) 8 (C) 9 (D) 10 (E) 11

In this example, the second number of each pair is three less than the first number; that is, $5 - 3 = 2$ and $8 - 3 = 5$, and $12 - 3 = 9$. Therefore, the correct answer is C.

Question 1

[**8** $\rightarrow$ **6**] [**11** $\rightarrow$ **9**] [**24** $\rightarrow$?]

(A) 23 (B) 22 (C) 21 (D) 20 (E) 19

Question 2

[**5** $\rightarrow$ **55**] [**50** $\rightarrow$ **100**] [**36** $\rightarrow$?]

(A) 86 (B) 88 (C) 90 (D) 96 (E) 99

Question 3

[**40** $\rightarrow$ **20**] [**60** $\rightarrow$ **30**] [**90** $\rightarrow$?]

(A) 50 (B) 45 (C) 42 (D) 40 (E) 35

Question 4

[**30** $\rightarrow$ **15**] [**25** $\rightarrow$ **10**] [**56** $\rightarrow$?]

(A) 45 (B) 44 (C) 43 (D) 42 (E) 41

Question 5

[**10** $\rightarrow$ **30**] [**20** $\rightarrow$ **60**] [**30** $\rightarrow$?]

(A) 65 (B) 75 (C) 80 (D) 90 (E) 100

Question 6

$[\mathbf{134} \rightarrow \mathbf{34}]$ $[\mathbf{362} \rightarrow \mathbf{62}]$ $[\mathbf{783} \rightarrow ?]$

(A) 73 (B) 78 (C) 83 (D) 87 (E) 92

Question 7

$[\mathbf{10} \rightarrow \mathbf{100}]$ $[\mathbf{50} \rightarrow \mathbf{500}]$ $[\mathbf{100} \rightarrow ?]$

(A) 2000 (B) 1000 (C) 500 (D) 300 (E) 200

Question 8

$[\mathbf{618} \rightarrow \mathbf{6}]$ $[\mathbf{539} \rightarrow \mathbf{5}]$ $[\mathbf{895} \rightarrow ?]$

(A) 5 (B) 6 (C) 7 (D) 8 (E) 9

Question 9

$[\mathbf{3:25} \rightarrow \mathbf{3:15}]$ $[\mathbf{9:40} \rightarrow \mathbf{9:30}]$ $[\mathbf{7:05} \rightarrow ?]$

(A) 6:55 (B) 6:75 (C) 6:95 (D) 7:00 (E) 7:04

Question 10

$[\mathbf{5} \rightarrow \mathbf{25}]$ $[\mathbf{6} \rightarrow \mathbf{36}]$ $[\mathbf{9} \rightarrow ?]$

(A) 99 (B) 81 (C) 54 (D) 45 (E) 42

Question 11

$[\mathbf{3} \rightarrow \mathbf{10}]$ $[\mathbf{4} \rightarrow \mathbf{13}]$ $[\mathbf{7} \rightarrow ?]$

(A) 21 (B) 22 (C) 23 (D) 24 (E) 25

Question 12

$[\mathbf{319} \rightarrow \mathbf{39}]$ $[\mathbf{193} \rightarrow \mathbf{13}]$ $[\mathbf{279} \rightarrow ?]$

(A) 97 (B) 79 (C) 72 (D) 53 (E) 29

Question 13

$[\mathbf{3:00} \rightarrow \mathbf{3:30}]$ $[\mathbf{6:15} \rightarrow \mathbf{6:45}]$ $[\mathbf{8:30} \rightarrow ?]$

(A) 8:45 (B) 8:60 (C) 9:00 (D) 9:15 (E) 9:30

Question 14

$[\mathbf{234} \rightarrow \mathbf{432}]$ $[\mathbf{637} \rightarrow \mathbf{736}]$ $[\mathbf{517} \rightarrow ?]$

(A) 571 (B) 624 (C) 671 (D) 715 (E) 751

Question 15

$[\mathbf{\$1.25} \rightarrow \mathbf{\$1.00}]$ $[\mathbf{\$2.50} \rightarrow \mathbf{\$2.25}]$ $[\mathbf{\$4.00} \rightarrow ?]$

(A) \$3.35 (B) \$3.45 (C) \$3.65 (D) \$3.75 (E) \$3.85

Question 16

$[\mathbf{33} \rightarrow \mathbf{16}]$ $[\mathbf{45} \rightarrow \mathbf{28}]$ $[\mathbf{56} \rightarrow ?]$

(A) 37 (B) 38 (C) 39 (D) 40 (E) 41

Question 17

$[\mathbf{5} \rightarrow \frac{\mathbf{5}}{\mathbf{2}}]$ $[\mathbf{7} \rightarrow \frac{\mathbf{7}}{\mathbf{2}}]$ $[\mathbf{9} \rightarrow ?]$

(A) 2 (B) 3 (C) 4 (D) $\frac{9}{2}$ (E) $\frac{11}{2}$

Question 18

$[\mathbf{10} \rightarrow \mathbf{29}]$ $[\mathbf{20} \rightarrow \mathbf{59}]$ $[\mathbf{30} \rightarrow ?]$

(A) 88 (B) 89 (C) 90 (D) 91 (E) 92

Number Puzzles

Directions: In each question, a mathematical equation with a question mark is given to you. Find the number that will replace the question mark so that the equation or inequality is true.

Below is an example of a number puzzles question:

Example

$\mathbf{11} \quad + \quad \boxed{?} \quad = \quad \mathbf{40}$

(A) 29 (B) 39 (C) 49 (D) 59 (E) 69

In this example, $11 + \boxed{29} = 40$. Therefore, the correct answer is A.

Question 1

$\boxed{?} = \mathbf{3} + \mathbf{8} + \mathbf{9}$

(A) 17 (B) 18 (C) 19 (D) 20 (E) 21

Question 2

$\mathbf{3} \times \boxed{?} = \mathbf{3} + \mathbf{3} + \mathbf{3} + \mathbf{3}$

(A) 3 (B) 4 (C) 5 (D) 6 (E) 7

Question 3

$\mathbf{8} + \mathbf{7} - \mathbf{3} < \boxed{?}$

(A) 9 (B) 10 (C) 11 (D) 12 (E) 13

Question 4

$\mathbf{7} - \boxed{?} = \mathbf{12} - \mathbf{10} + \mathbf{14} - \mathbf{12}$

(A) 6 (B) 5 (C) 4 (D) 3 (E) 2

Question 5

$\mathbf{5} + \mathbf{3} + \mathbf{4} = \mathbf{19} - \mathbf{2} - \boxed{?}$

(A) 1 (B) 2 (C) 3 (D) 4 (E) 5

Question 6

$$\mathbf{14} - \mathbf{10} + \mathbf{15} - \mathbf{9} = \boxed{?} + \mathbf{6}$$

(A) 2 (B) 3 (C) 4 (D) 5 (E) 6

Question 7

$$\mathbf{25} + \boxed{?} + \mathbf{37} = \mathbf{37} + \mathbf{14} + \mathbf{25}$$

(A) 10 (B) 12 (C) 14 (D) 16 (E) 18

Question 8

$$\boxed{?} - \mathbf{9} + \mathbf{8} = \mathbf{9} + \mathbf{8} + \mathbf{7}$$

(A) 21 (B) 23 (C) 25 (D) 27 (E) 29

Question 9

$$\mathbf{27} + \mathbf{13} = \boxed{?} \times \mathbf{4}$$

(A) 10 (B) 9 (C) 8 (D) 7 (E) 6

Question 10

$$\mathbf{19} + \mathbf{17} - \mathbf{22} = \mathbf{2} + \boxed{?} + \mathbf{8}$$

(A) 3 (B) 4 (C) 5 (D) 6 (E) 7

Question 11

$$6 \times 5 = 15 + 8 + \boxed{?} - 2$$

(A) 12 (B) 11 (C) 10 (D) 9 (E) 8

Question 12

$$16 + \boxed{?} > 8 + 9 + 10$$

(A) 8 (B) 9 (C) 10 (D) 11 (E) 12

Question 13

$$40 - 14 - 17 - 5 = \boxed{?}$$

(A) 2 (B) 3 (C) 4 (D) 5 (E) 6

Question 14

$$7 \times 4 = 7 + \boxed{?} + 7 + 7$$

(A) 7 (B) 6 (C) 5 (D) 4 (E) 3

Question 15

$$4 \times 7 \times 6 = \boxed{?} \times 4 \times 6$$

(A) 4 (B) 5 (C) 6 (D) 7 (E) 8

Question 16

$$\mathbf{6} + \mathbf{9} + \boxed{?} + \mathbf{5} = \mathbf{3} \times \mathbf{3} \times \mathbf{3}$$

(A) 10 (B) 9 (C) 8 (D) 7 (E) 6

Number Series

Directions: In each question, a list of numbers including a box with a question mark follows some type of pattern. Find the number that replaces the question mark so that a list of numbers follow the same type of pattern.

Below is an example of a number series question:

Example

2 4 6 8 10 12 [?]

(A) 13 (B) 14 (C) 15 (D) 16 (E) 17

In this example, the numbers are increasing by 2. So the number that replaces the question mark is $12 + 2 = 14$. Therefore, the correct answer is B.

Question 1

4 8 12 16 20 24 ?

(A) 26 (B) 28 (C) 30 (D) 32 (E) 34

Question 2

? 100 90 80 70 60 50

(A) 110 (B) 115 (C) 120 (D) 125 (E) 130

Question 3

2 15 28 41 ? 67 80

(A) 54 (B) 55 (C) 56 (D) 57 (E) 58

Question 4

256 128 ? 32 16 8 4

(A) 40 (B) 48 (C) 54 (D) 60 (E) 64

Question 5

76 68 60 ? 44 36 28

(A) 48 (B) 50 (C) 52 (D) 54 (E) 56

Question 6

17 [?] 17 33 17 33 17

(A) 17 (B) 25 (C) 33 (D) 38 (E) 43

Question 7

9 10 12 15 19 24 [?]

(A) 26 (B) 27 (C) 28 (D) 29 (E) 30

Question 8

25 3 22 4 19 5 [?]

(A) 14 (B) 15 (C) 16 (D) 17 (E) 18

Question 9

99 90 82 75 69 64 [?]

(A) 56 (B) 57 (C) 58 (D) 59 (E) 60

Question 10

6 23 40 57 [?] 91 108

(A) 72 (B) 74 (C) 76 (D) 78 (E) 80

Question 11

$\frac{2}{3}$ 2 6 18 54 ? 486

(A) 78 (B) 96 (C) 124 (D) 132 (E) 162

Question 12

21 1 29 1 37 1 ?

(A) 44 (B) 45 (C) 46 (D) 47 (E) 48

Question 13

34 44 38 48 42 52 ?

(A) 46 (B) 48 (C) 50 (D) 52 (E) 53

Question 14

232 210 188 166 144 ? 100

(A) 122 (B) 120 (C) 118 (D) 116 (E) 114

Question 15

1 2 5 14 41 122 ?

(A) 285 (B) 325 (C) (D) 365 (E) 405

Question 16

1 3 6 8 16 18 ?

(A) 40 (B) 36 (C) 32 (D) 28 (E) 20

Question 17

1 40 4 20 16 10 ?

(A) 5 (B) 22 (C) 36 (D) 64 (E) 88

Question 18

11 101 1001 ? 100001 1000001 10000001

(A) 10000 (B) 10001 (C) 10010 (D) 10100 (E) 11000

NONVERBAL BATTERY

1. FIGURE MATRICES
2. PAPER FOLDING
3. FIGURE CLASSIFICATION

Figure Matrices

Directions: In each question, look at the figures on the top row and determine how the two figures are related. Choose the figure from the answer choices that goes with the bottom left figure in a similar way as shown on the top row.

Below is an example of a figure matrices question:

Example

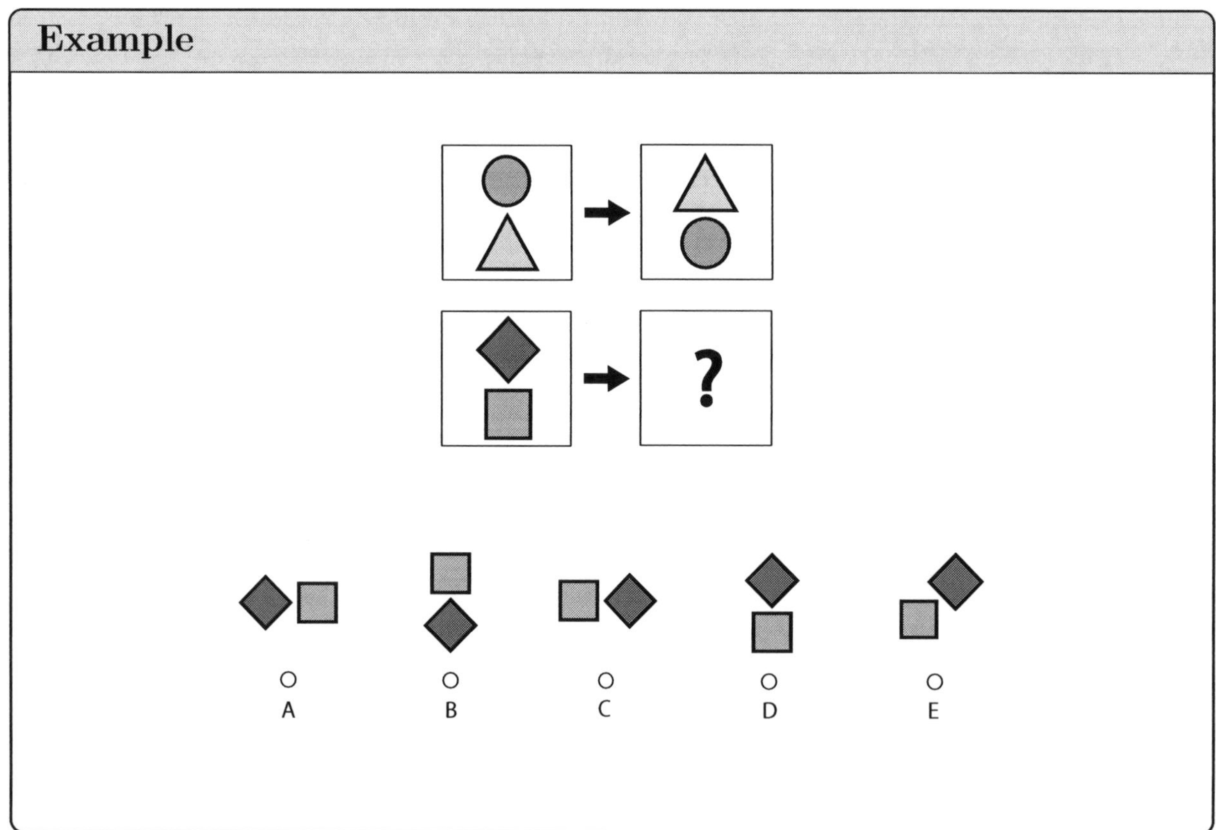

In the first figure, there are two shapes: a circle is at the top and a triangle is at the bottom. However, the arrangements are reversed in the second figure. A triangle is at the top and a circle is at the bottom. If you reverse the arrangements of shapes in the third figure, you get the figure in (B). Therefore, the correct answer is B.

Question 1

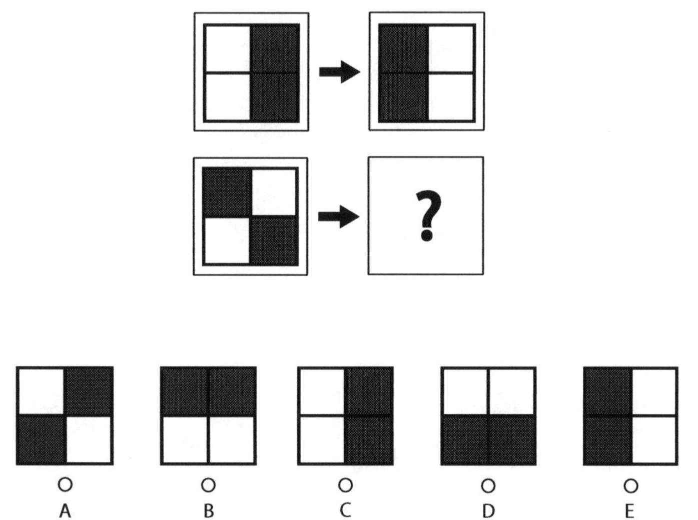

Question 2

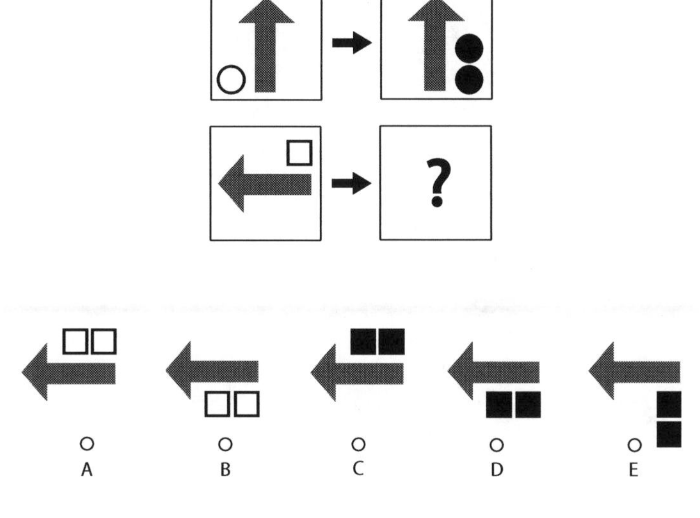

Question 3

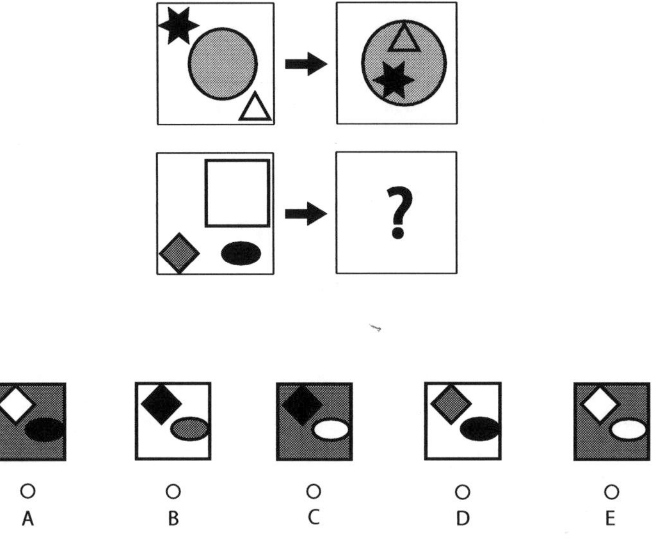

Question 4

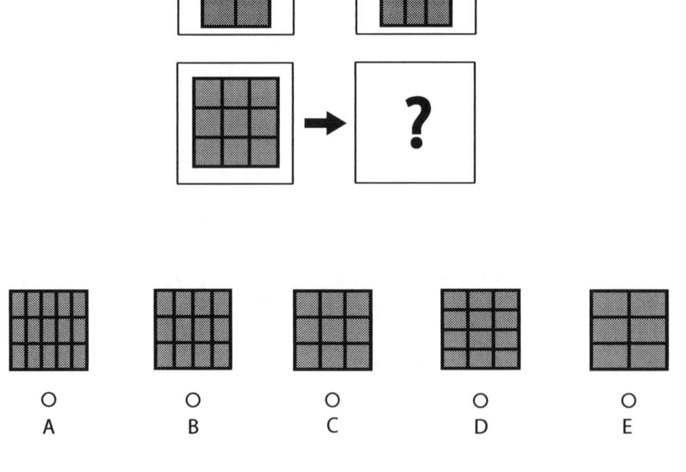

Question 5

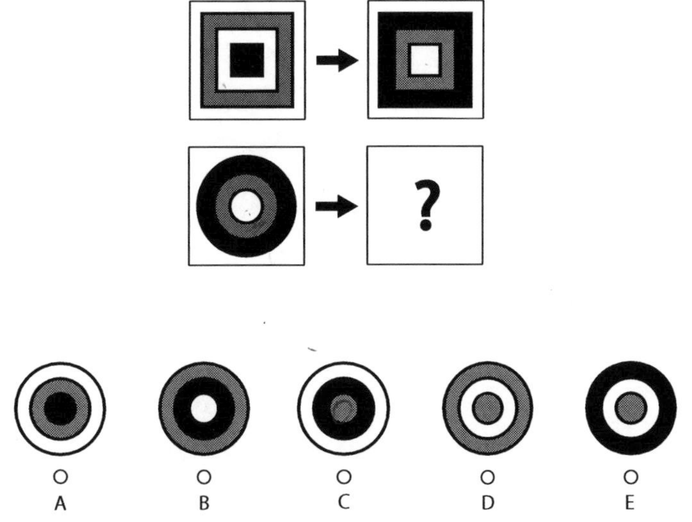

Question 6

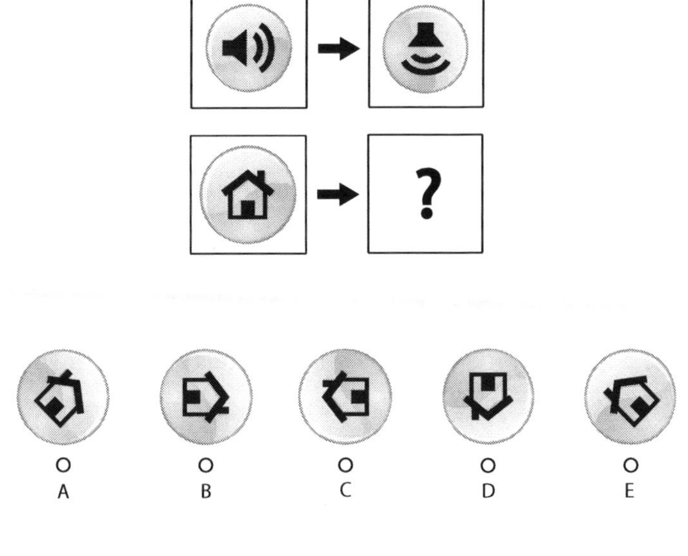

Question 7

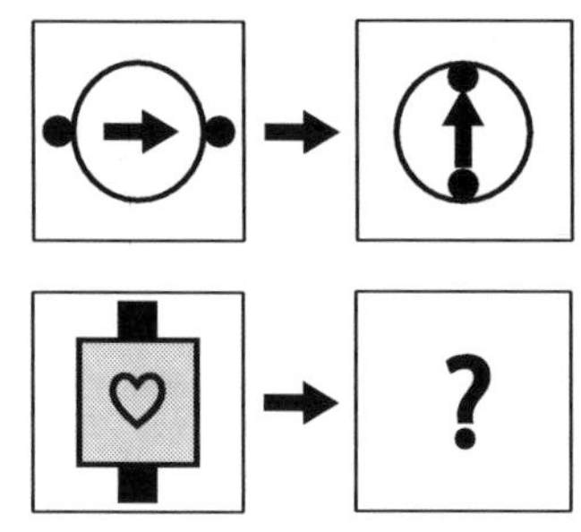

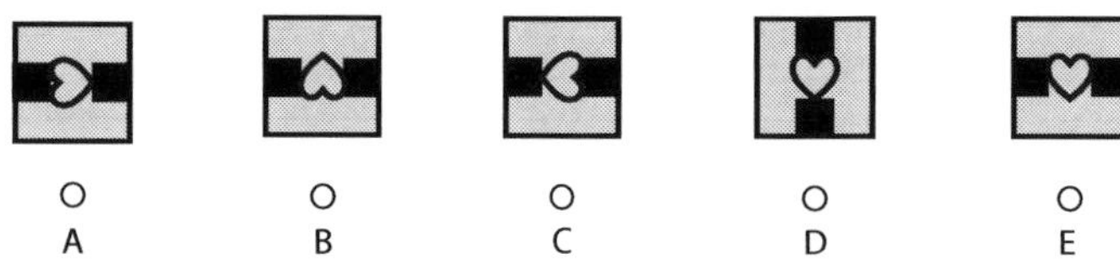

Question 8

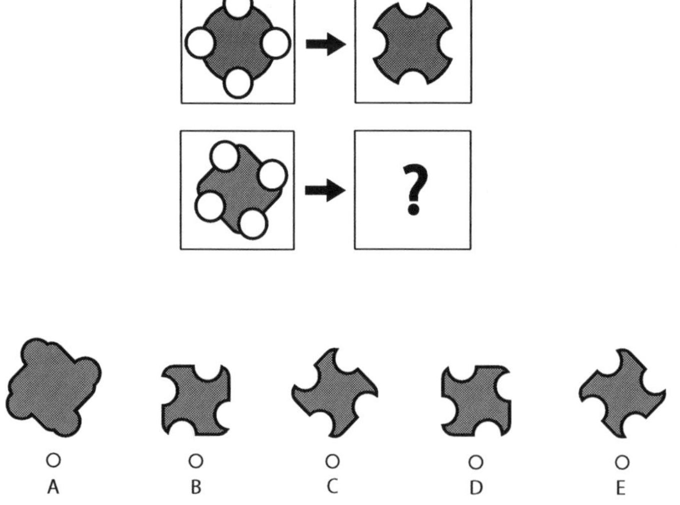

Question 9

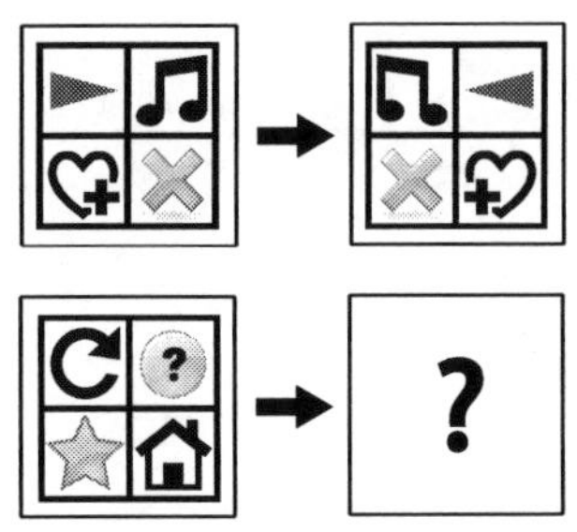

Question 10

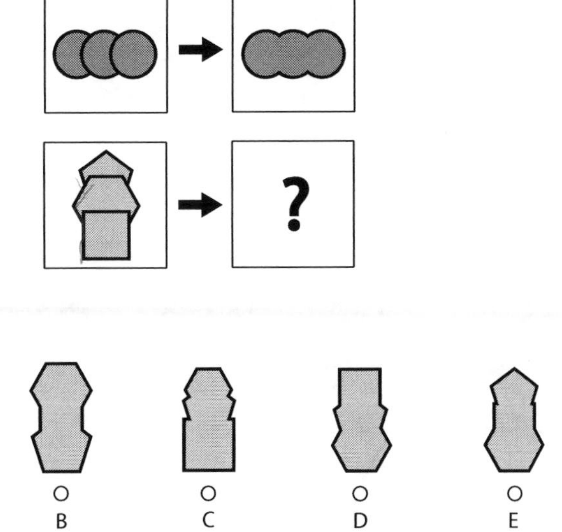

Question 11

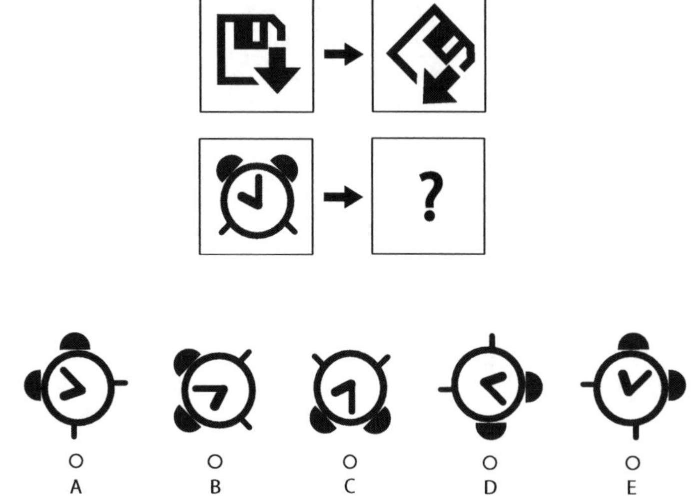

Question 12

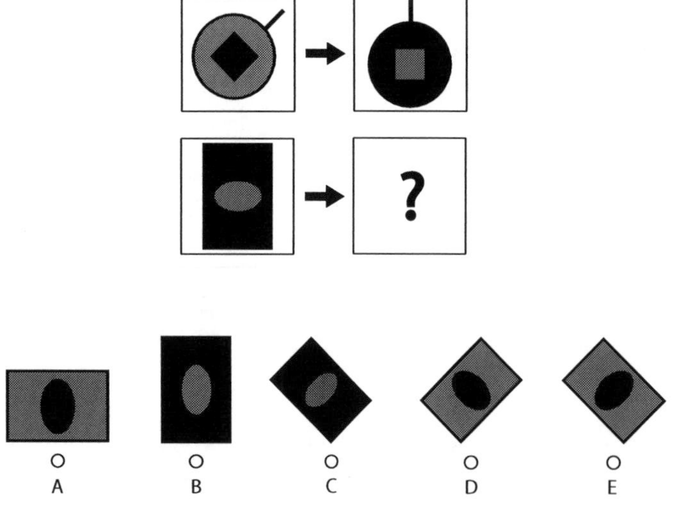

Question 13

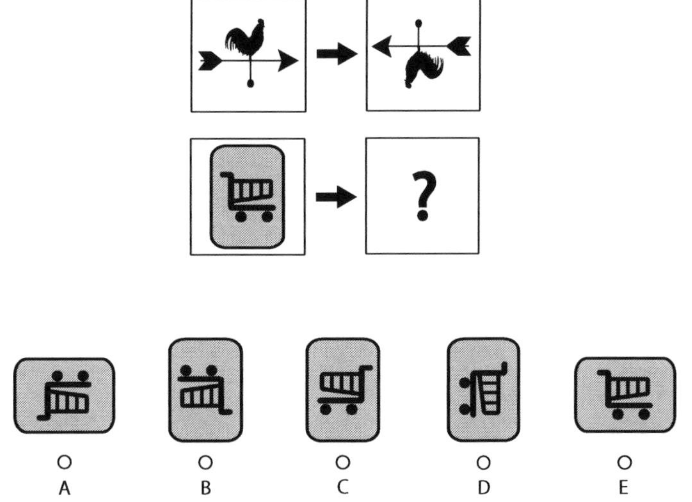

Question 14

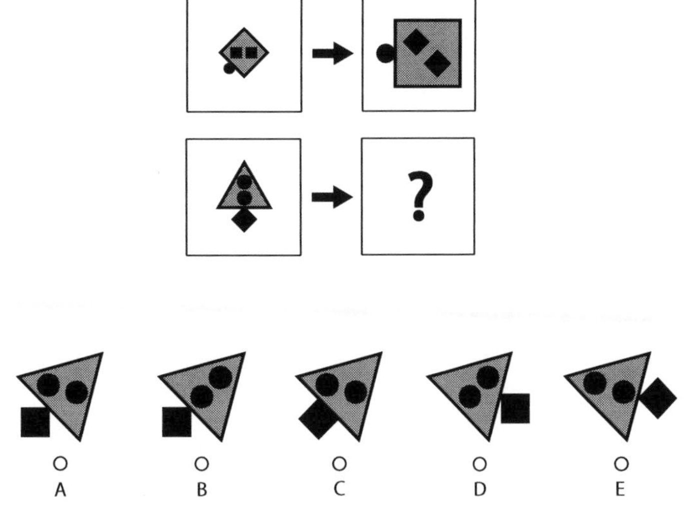

Question 15

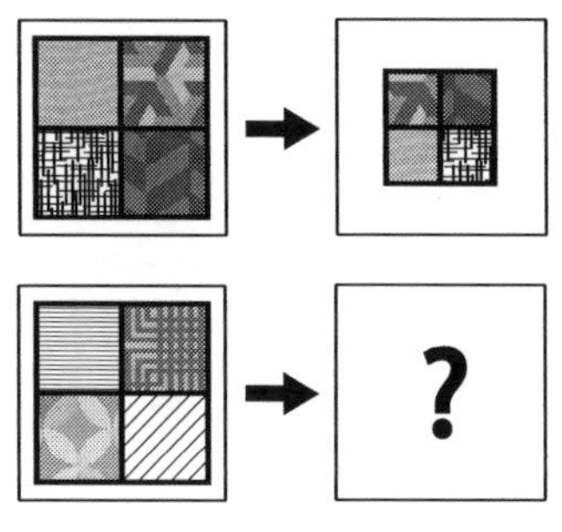

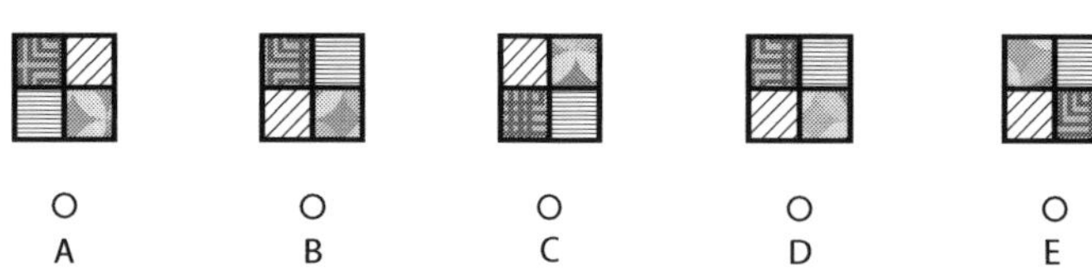

A B C D E

Question 16

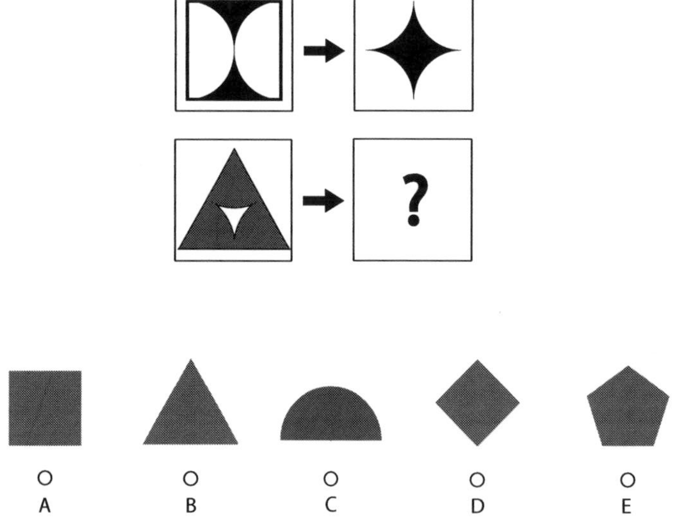

Question 17

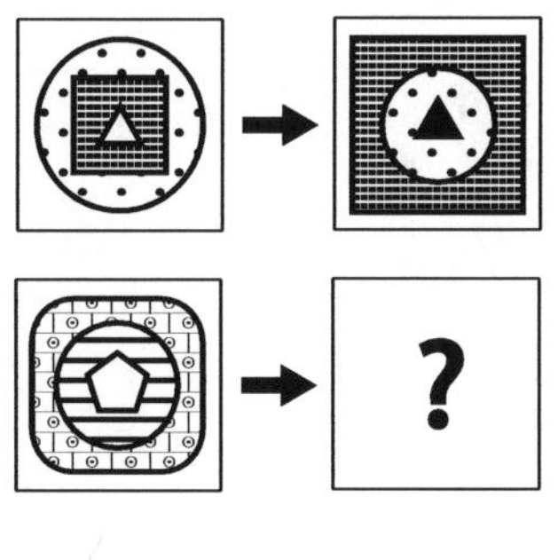

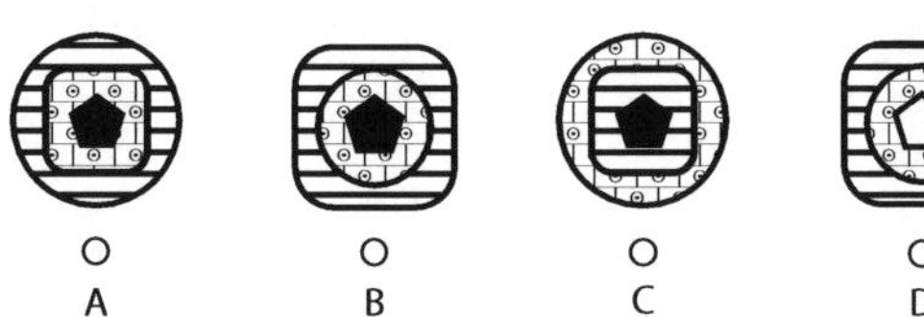

A B C D E

Question 18

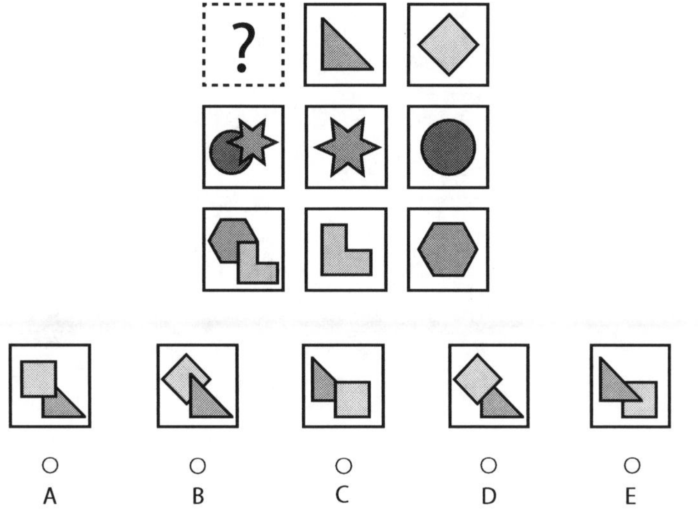

A B C D E

Question 19

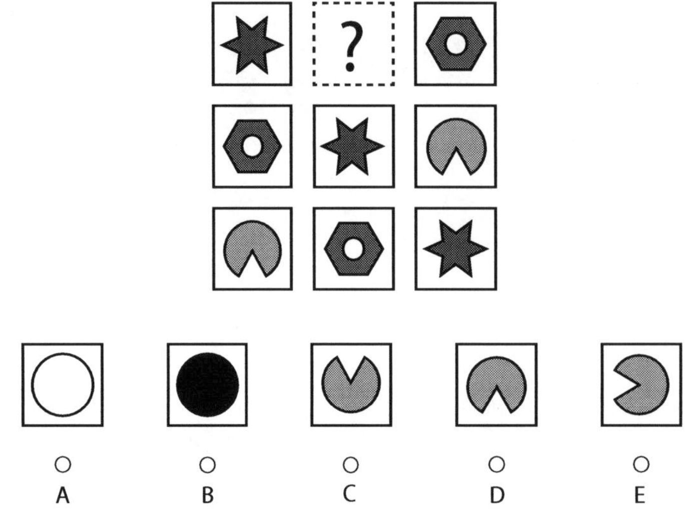

Question 20

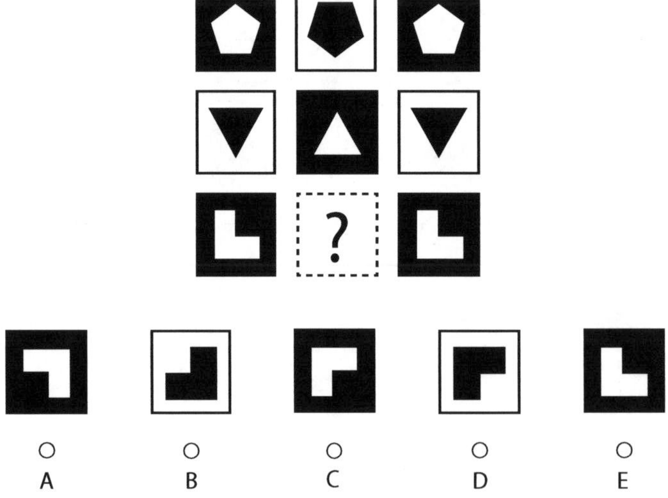

Paper Folding

Directions: In each question, a square paper is folded completely and then either holes or other shapes are punched into the paper. Choose the picture from the answer choices that shows you how the paper will look like when it is unfolded completely.

Below is an example of a paper folding question:

Example

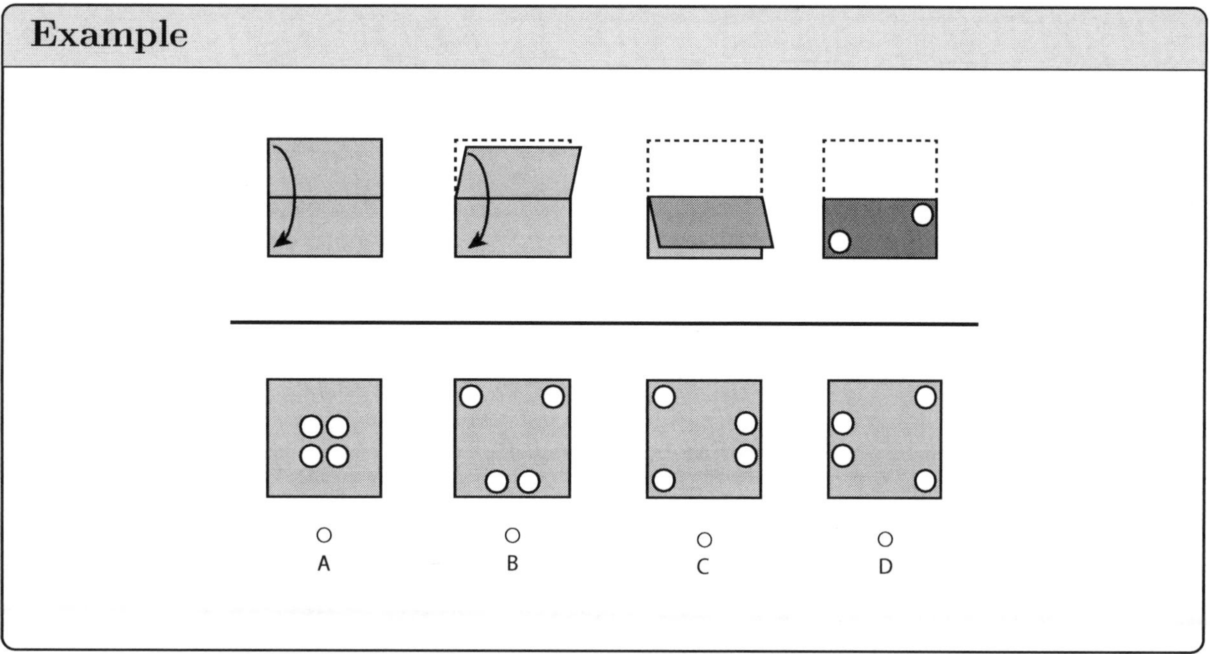

The paper is folded horizontally once. So there will be 4 holes if it is unfolded completely as shown below.

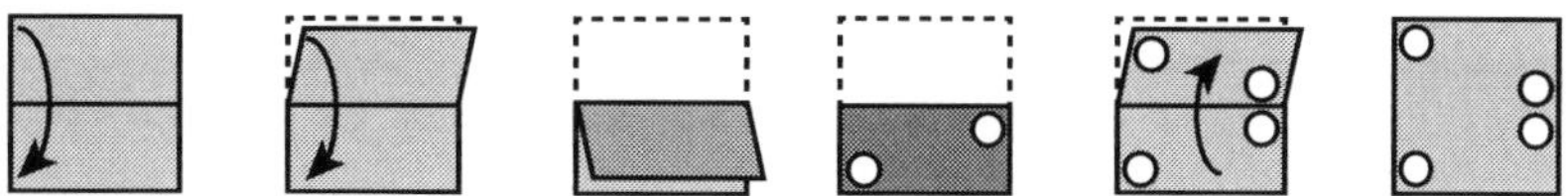

Therefore, the correct answer is C.

Question 1

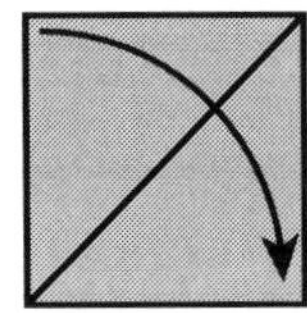
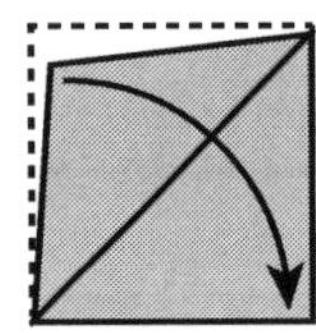
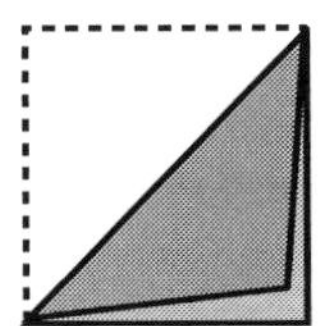
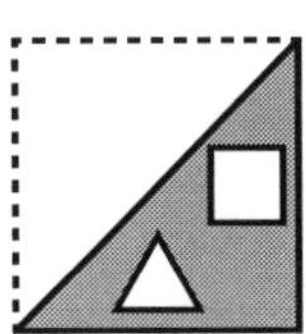

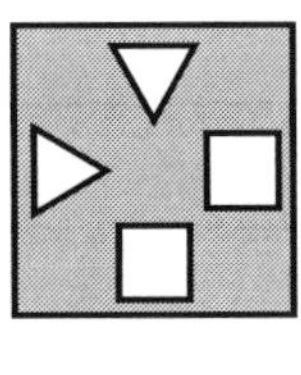
○ A

○ B

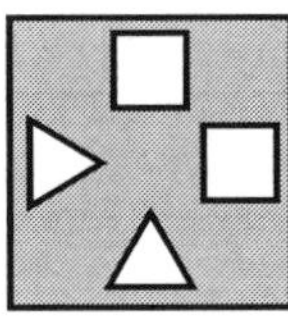
○ C

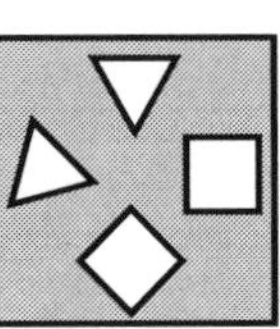
○ D

Question 2

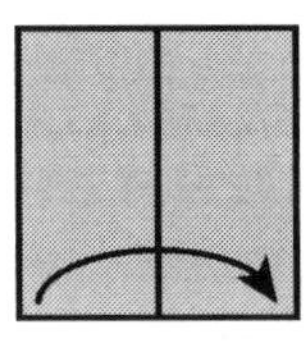
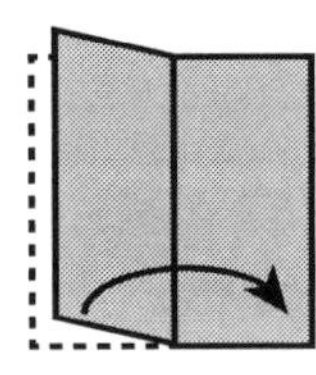
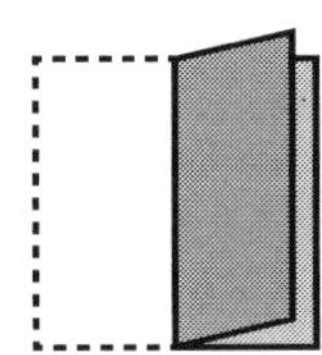
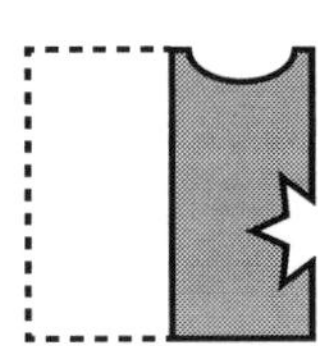

○ A

○ B

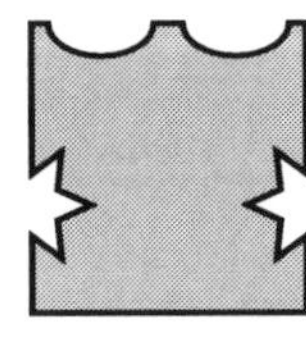
○ C

○ D

Question 3

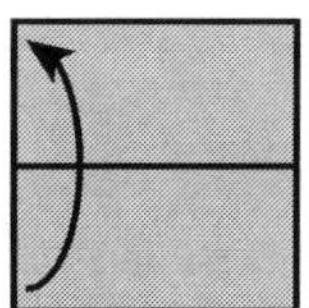 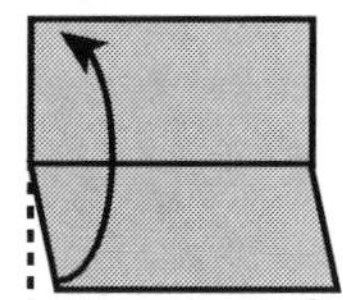 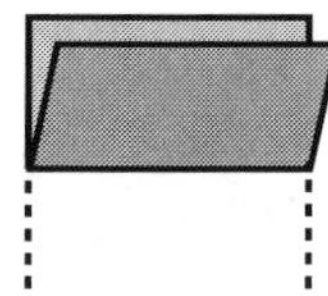 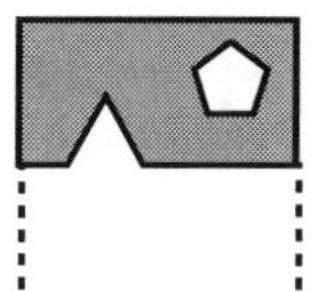

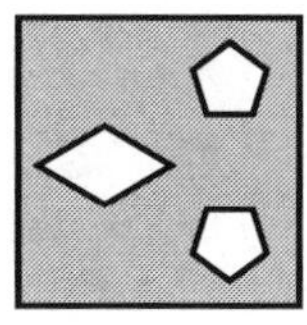 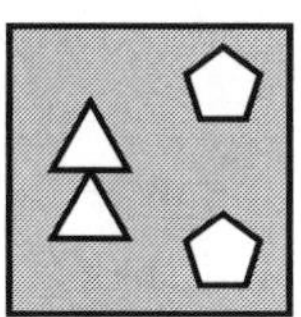 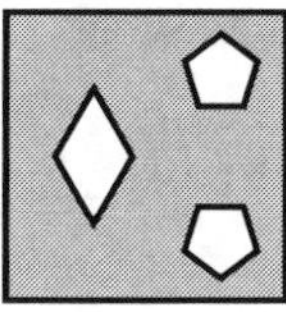 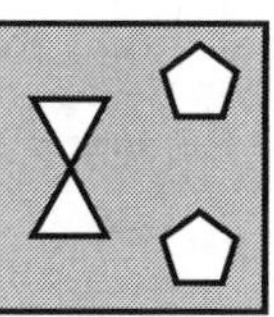

○ A ○ B ○ C ○ D

Question 4

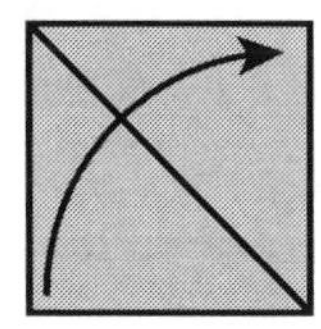 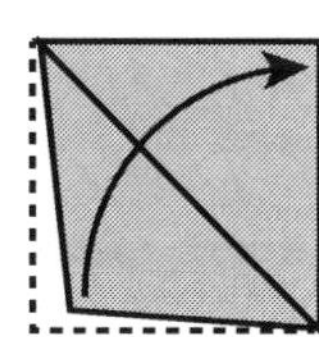 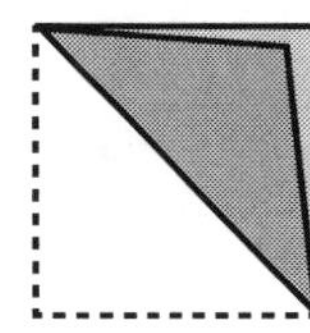 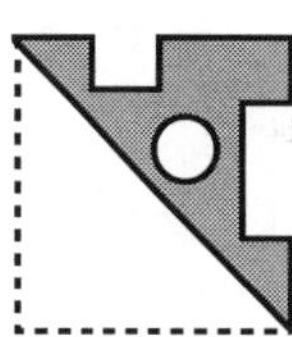

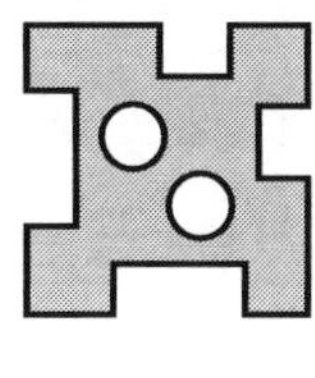 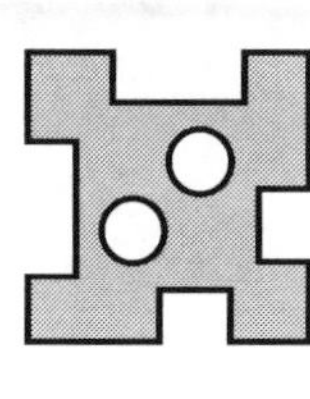  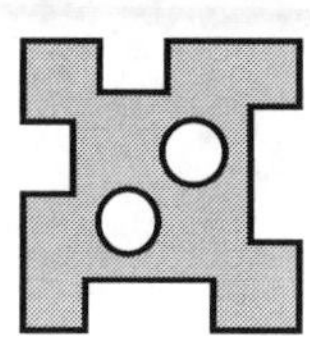

○ A ○ B ○ C ○ D

Question 5

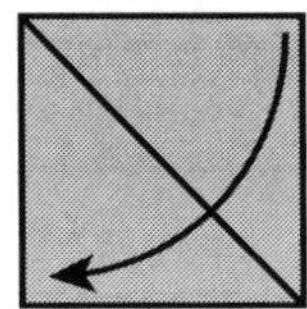
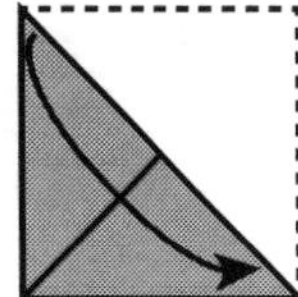
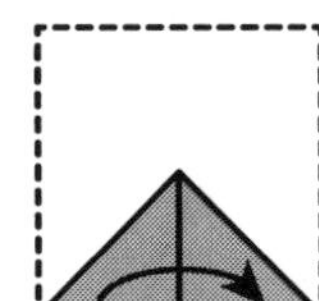
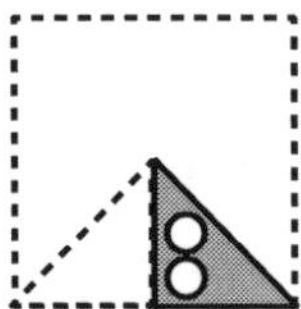

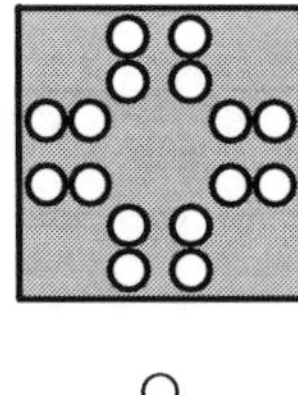
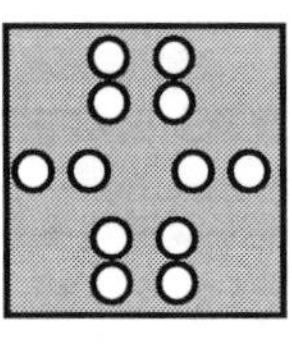
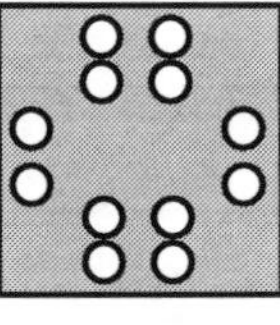
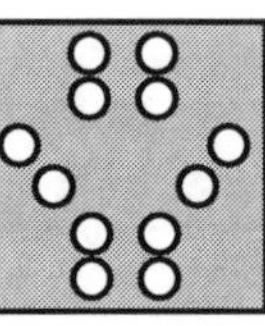

○ A ○ B ○ C ○ D

Question 6

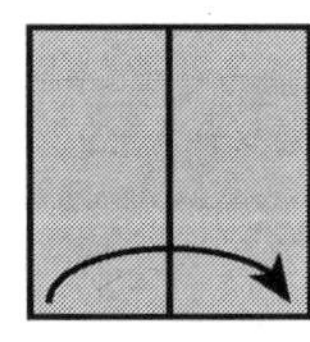
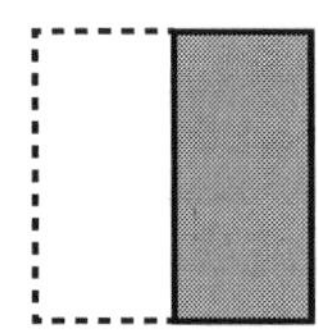
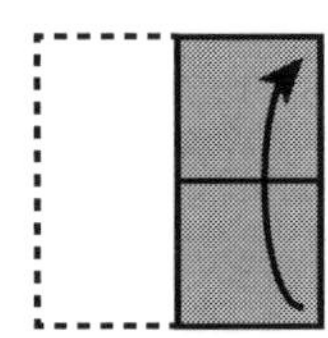
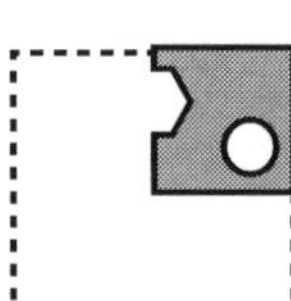

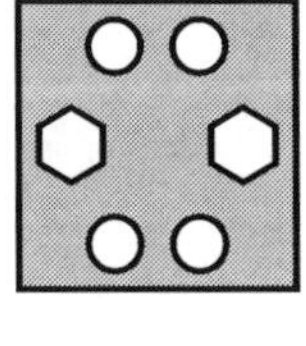
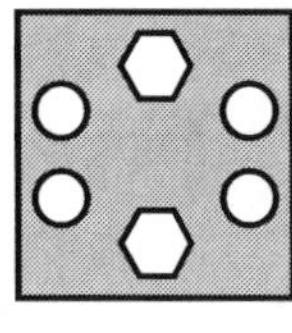
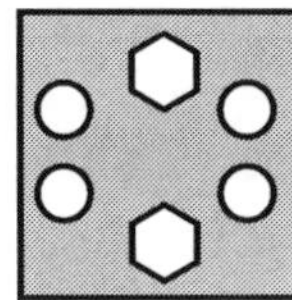
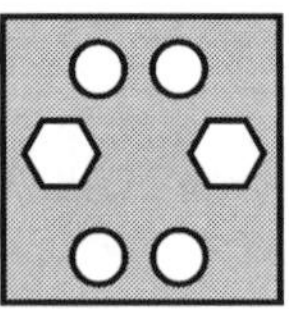

○ A ○ B ○ C ○ D

Question 7

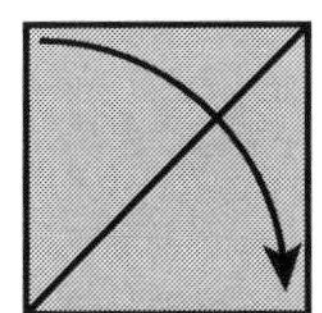
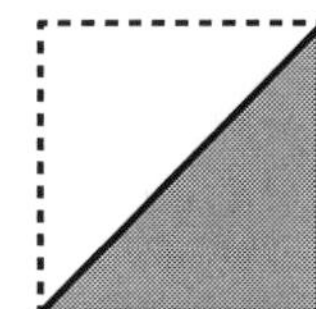
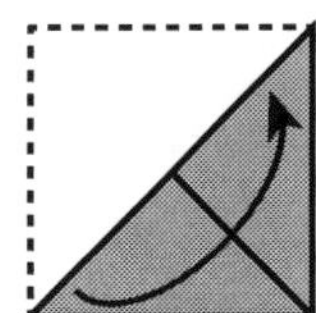

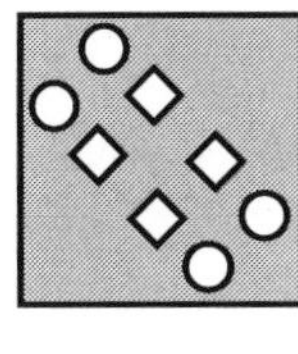
A

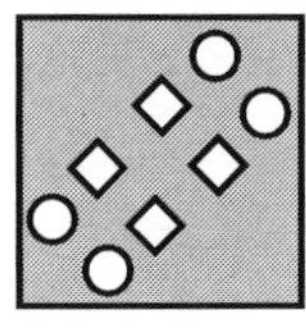
B

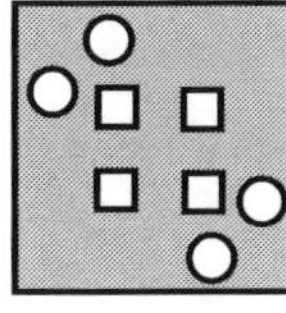
C

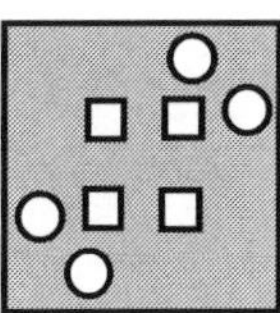
D

Question 8

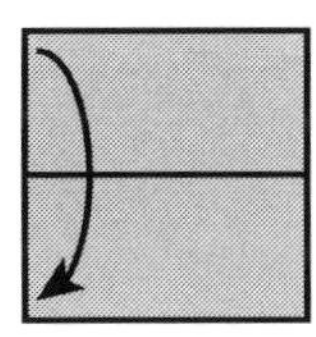
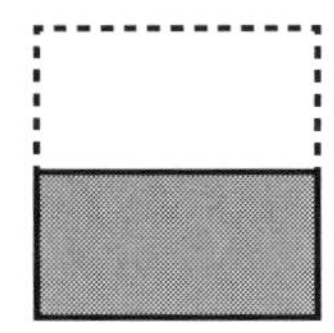
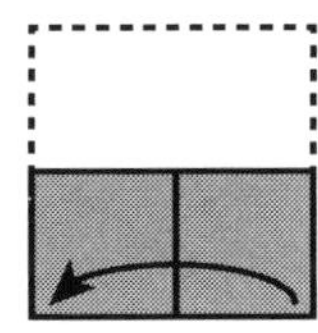
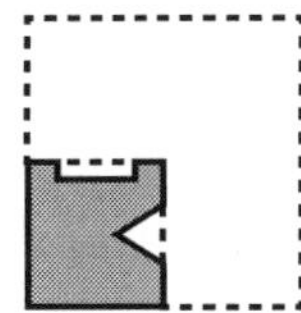

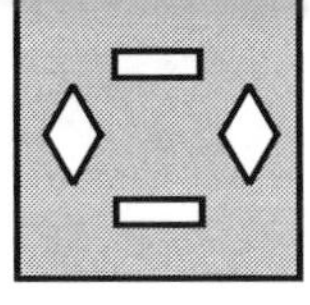
A

B

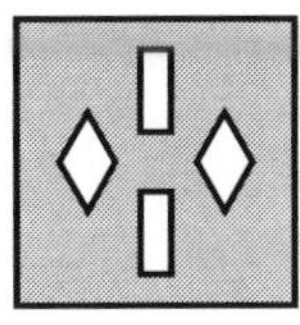
C

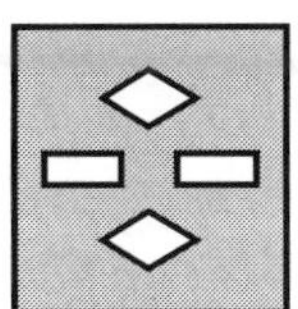
D

Question 9

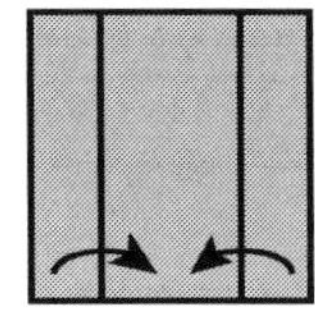
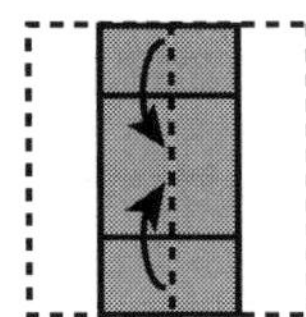

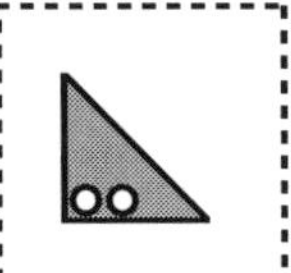

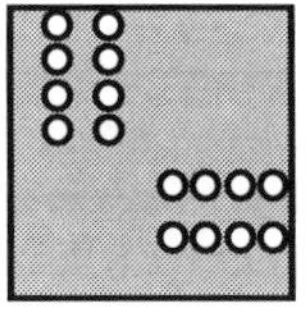
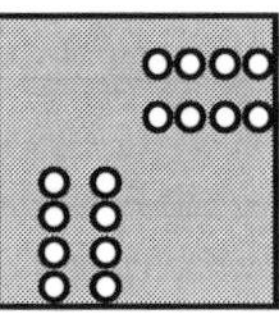
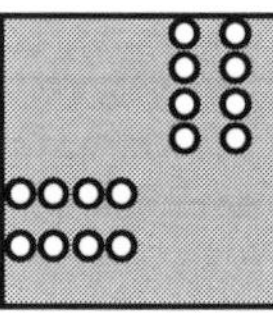
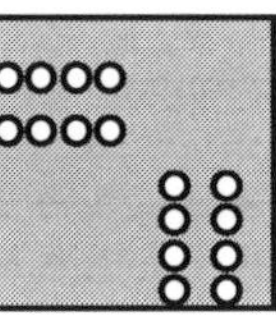

○ A ○ B ○ C ○ D

Question 10

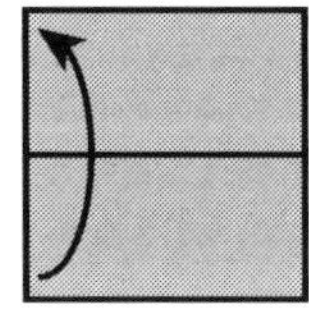
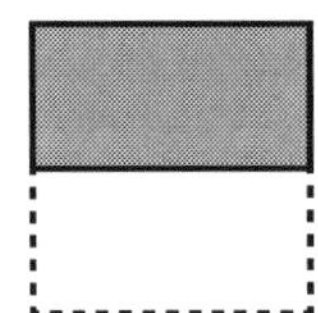
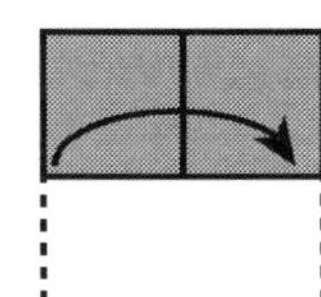
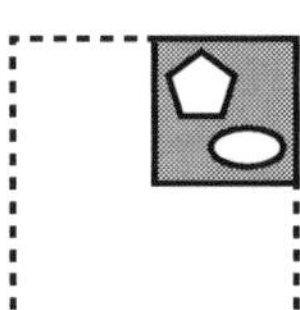

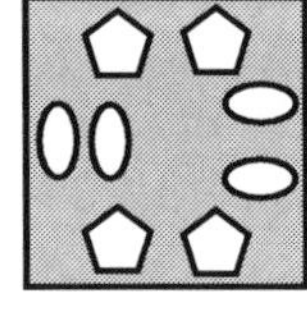
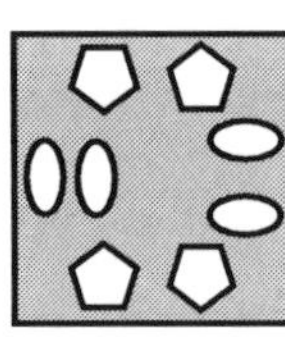
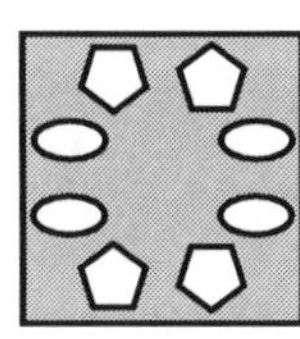
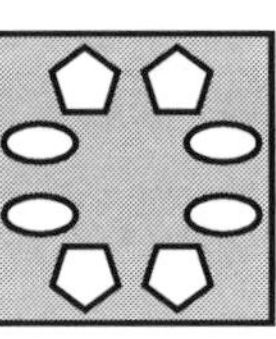

○ A ○ B ○ C ○ D

Question 11

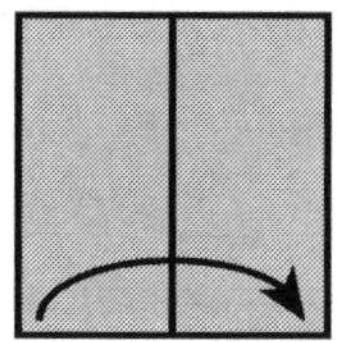
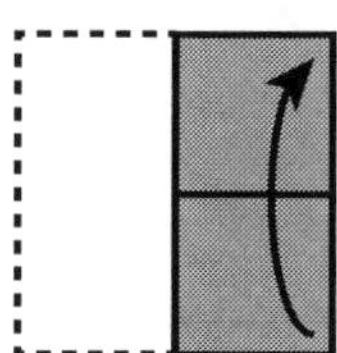
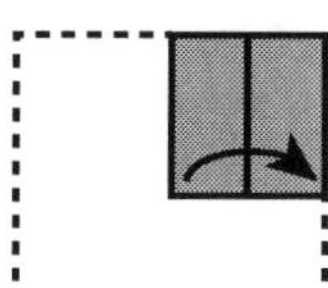
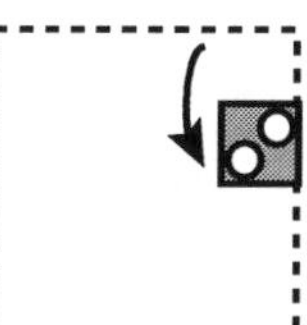

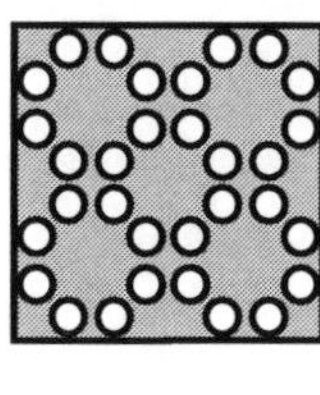

A

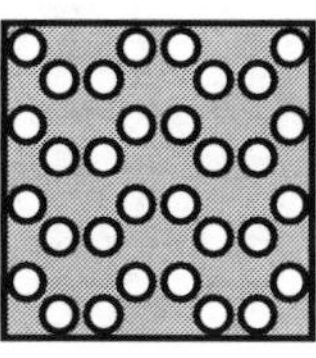
B

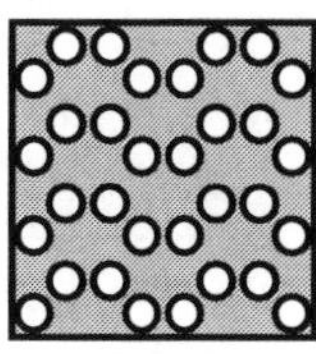
C

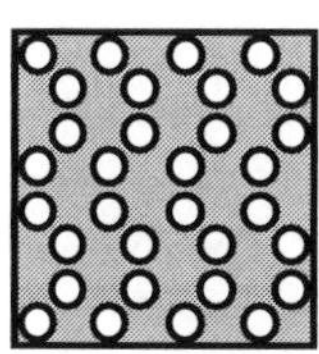
D

Question 12

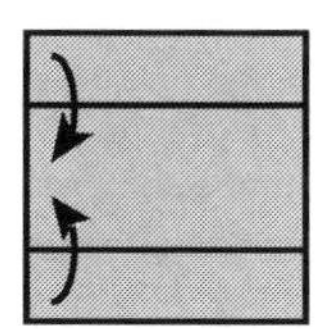
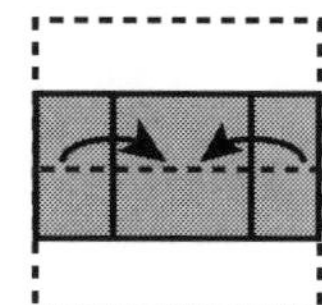
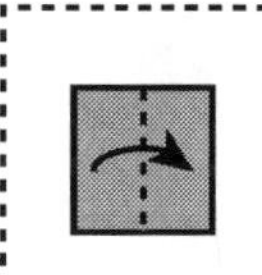
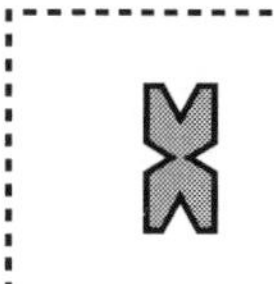

A

B

C

D

Question 13

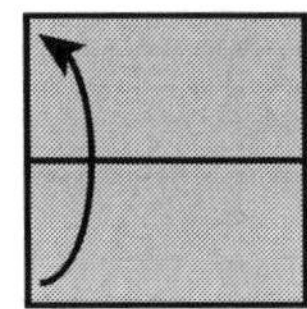 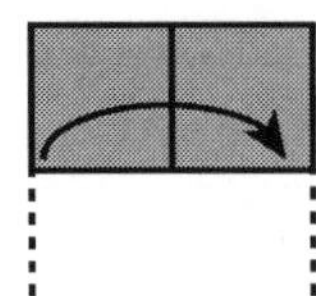 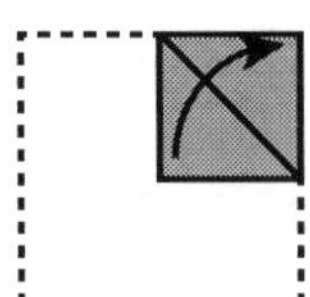 

○ A

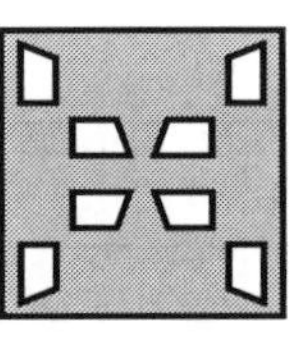
○ B

○ C

○ D

Question 14

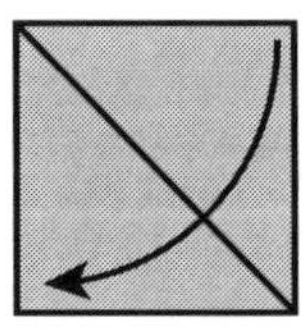 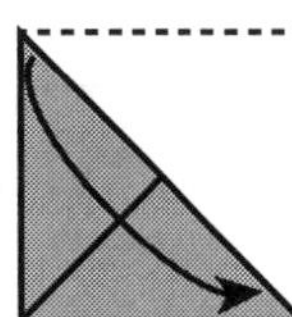 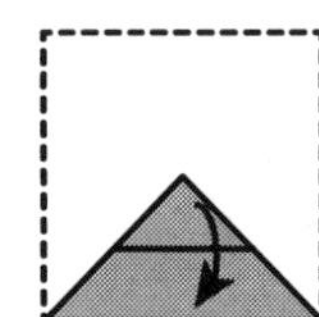 

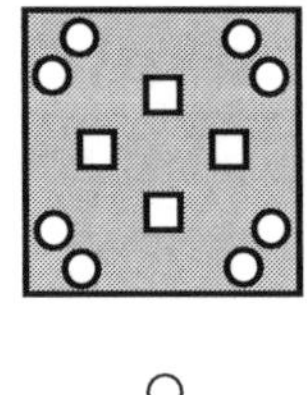

A

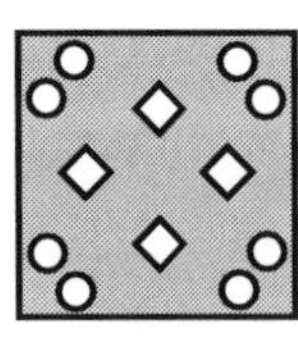
○ B

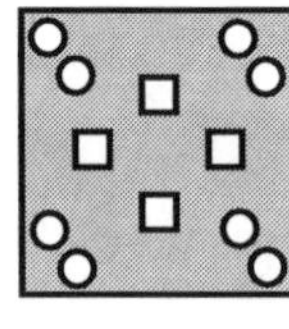
○ C

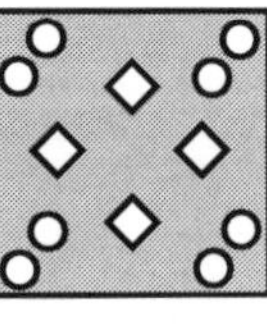
○ D

Question 15

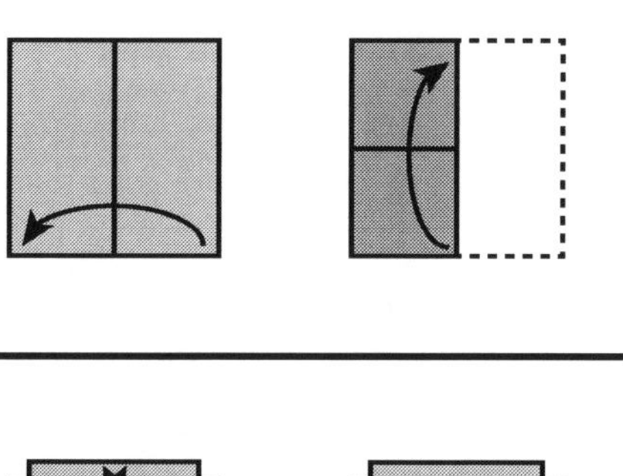

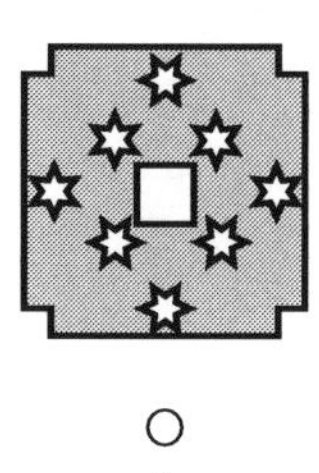
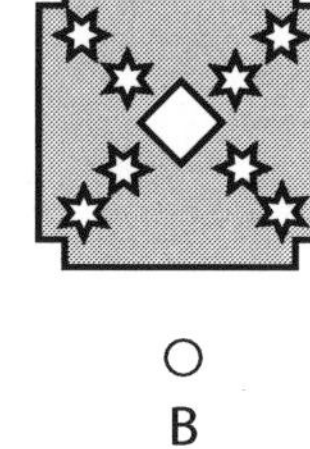
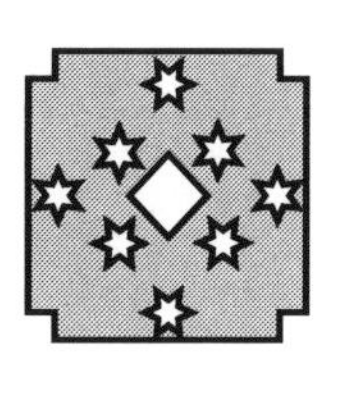
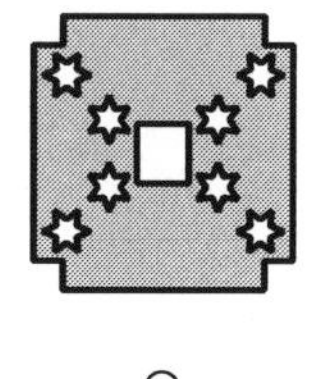

○ A ○ B ○ C ○ D

Question 16

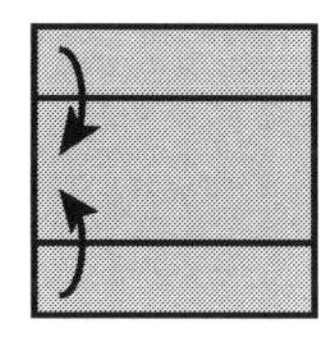
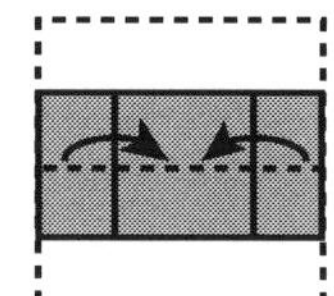
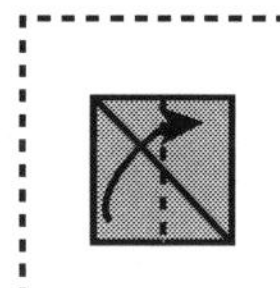

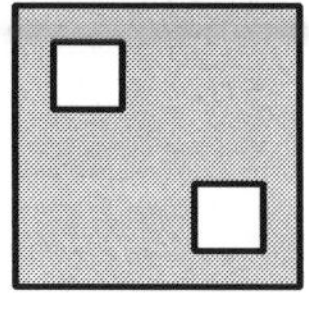
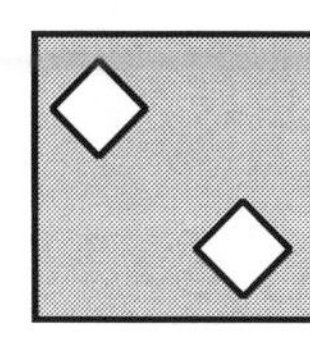
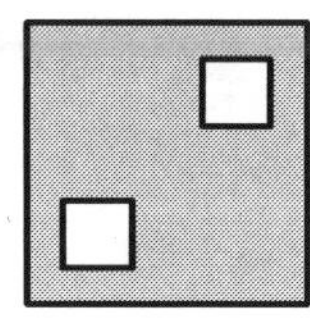
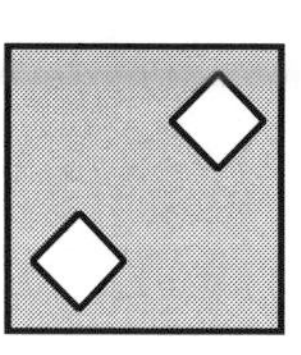

A ○ B ○ C ○ D

Figure Classification

Directions: In each question, look at the three figures in the top row and determine how they are related. The four figures in the second row are answer choices. Choose the figure from the answer choices that is most similar to the figures on the top row.

Below is an example of a figure classification question:

Example

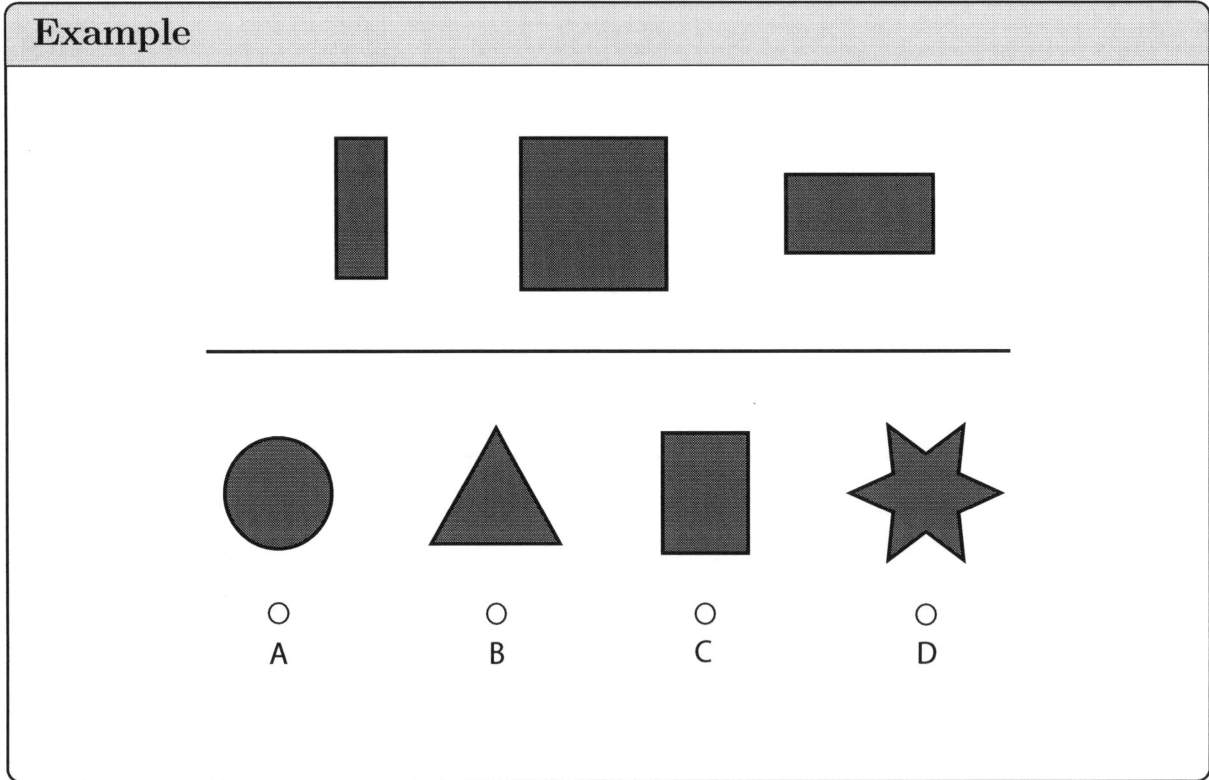

In this example, the three figures in the top row are rectangles. Therefore, the correct answer is C.

Question 1

○ A ○ B ○ C ○ D

Question 2

  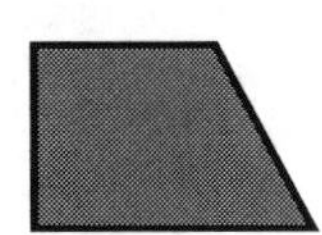 

○ A ○ B ○ C ○ D

Question 3

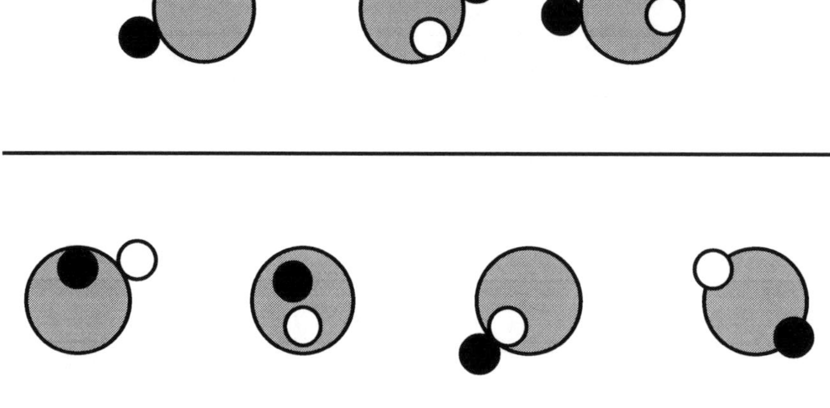

Question 4

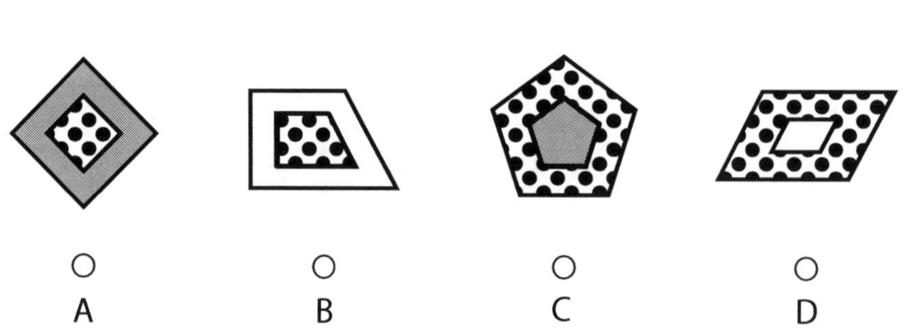

Question 5

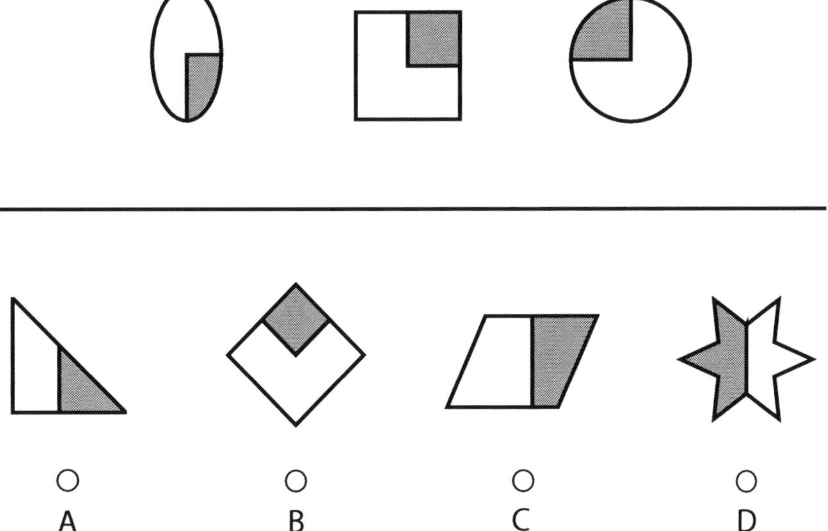

Question 6

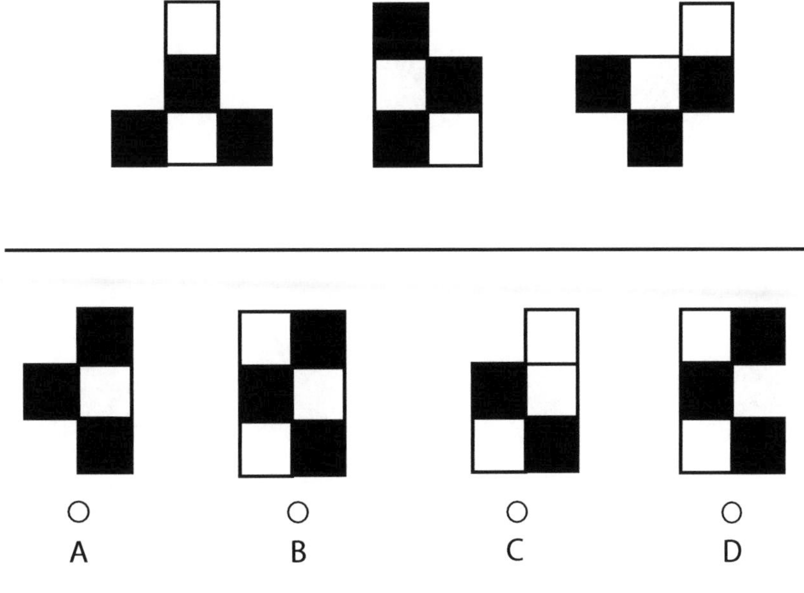

Question 7

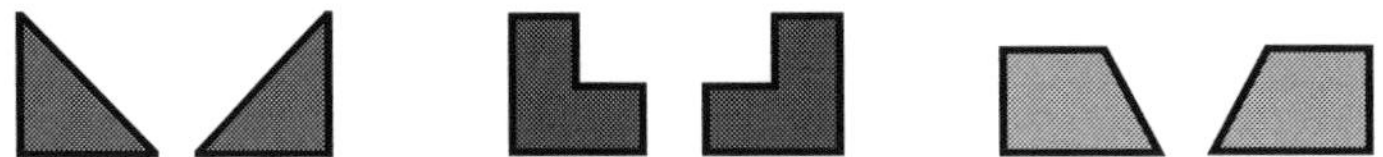

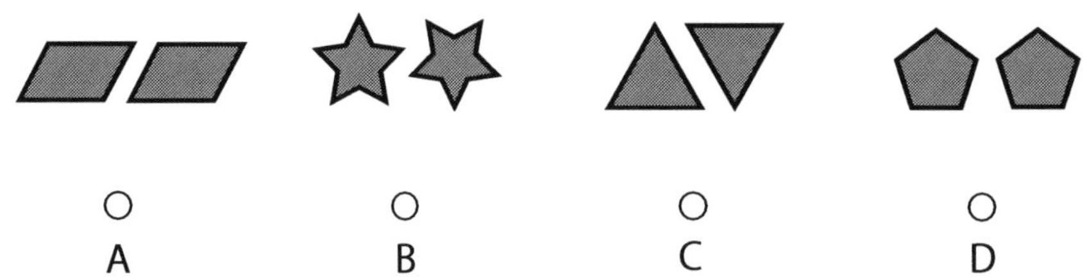

Question 8

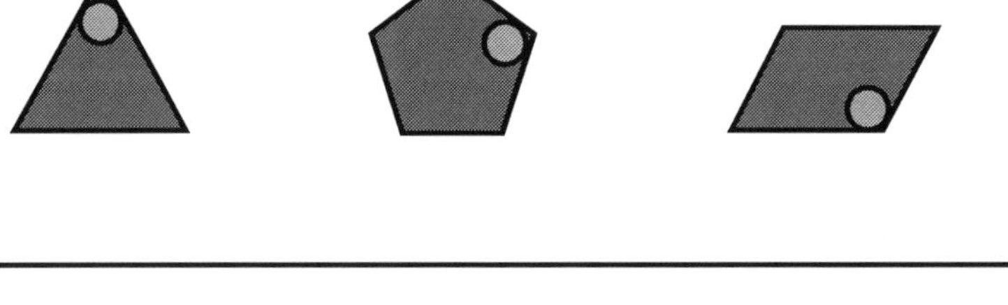

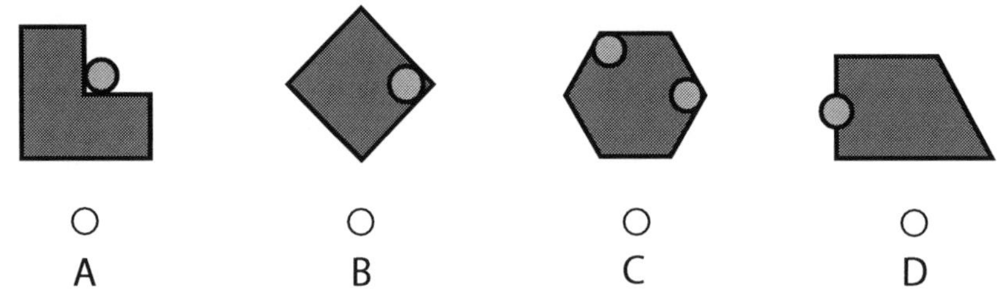

Question 9

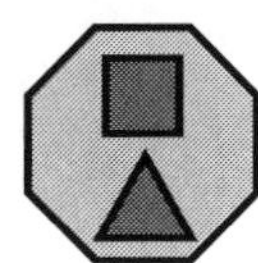  

 A ○ B ○ C ○ D

Question 10

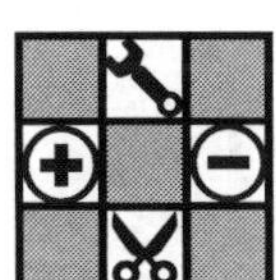  

 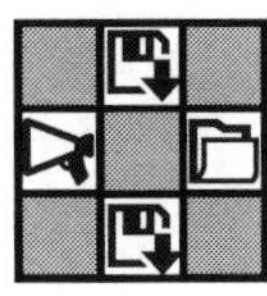 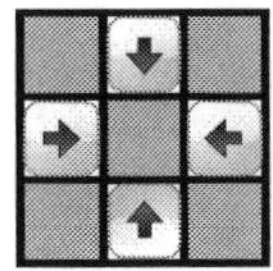 

 A ○ B ○ C ○ D

Question 11

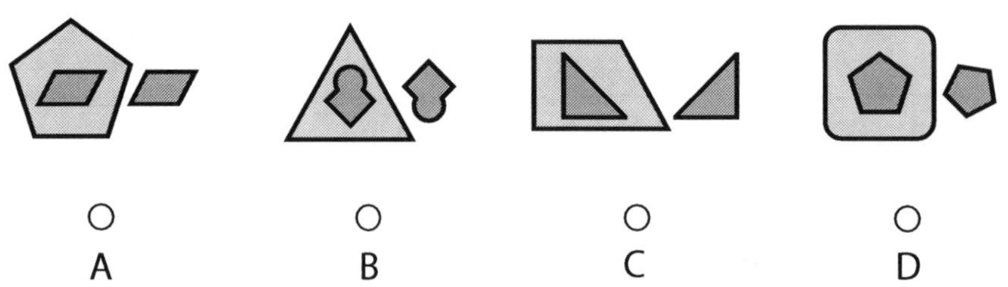

○ A ○ B ○ C ○ D

Question 12

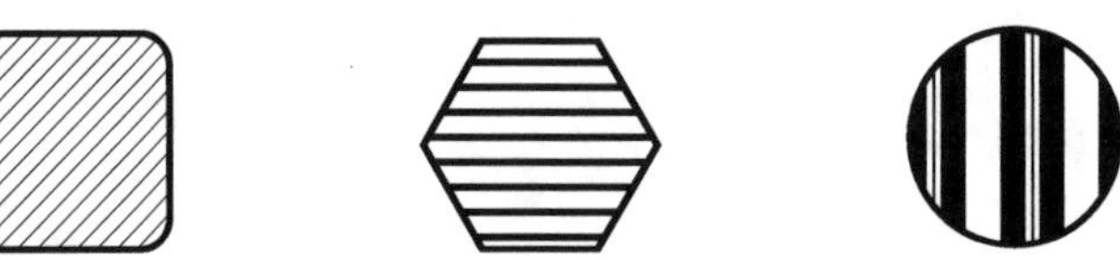

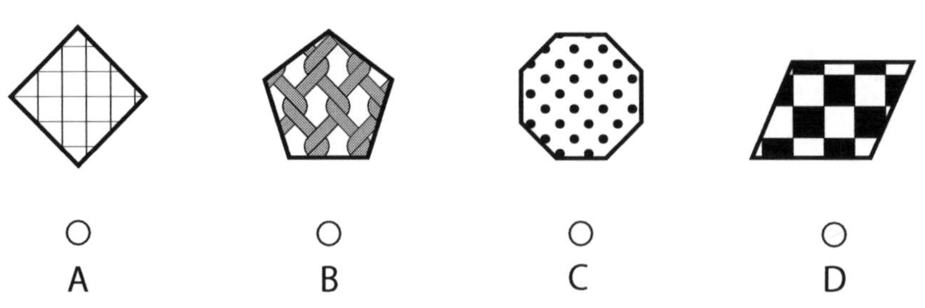

○ A ○ B ○ C ○ D

Question 13

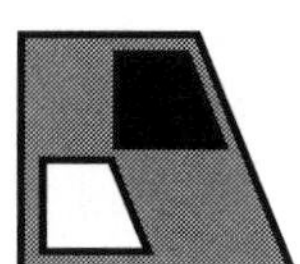  

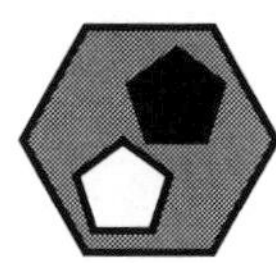
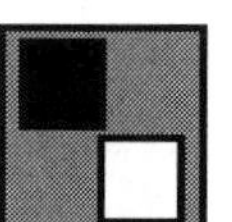

○ A ○ B ○ C ○ D

Question 14

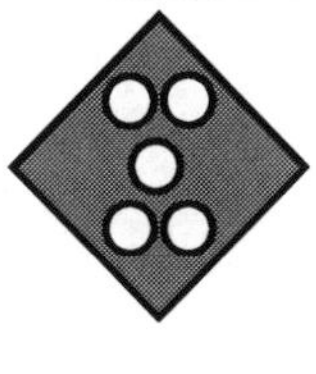
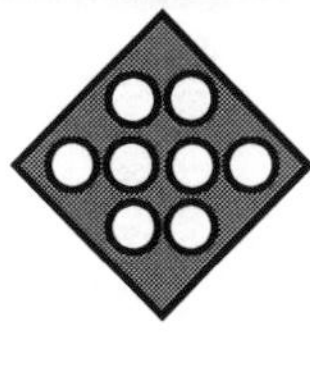
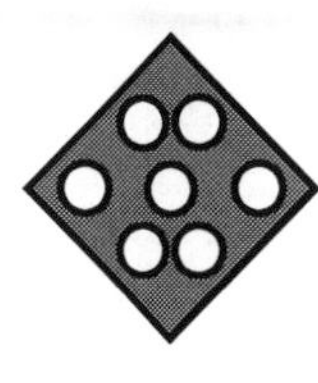

○ A ○ B ○ C ○ D

Question 15

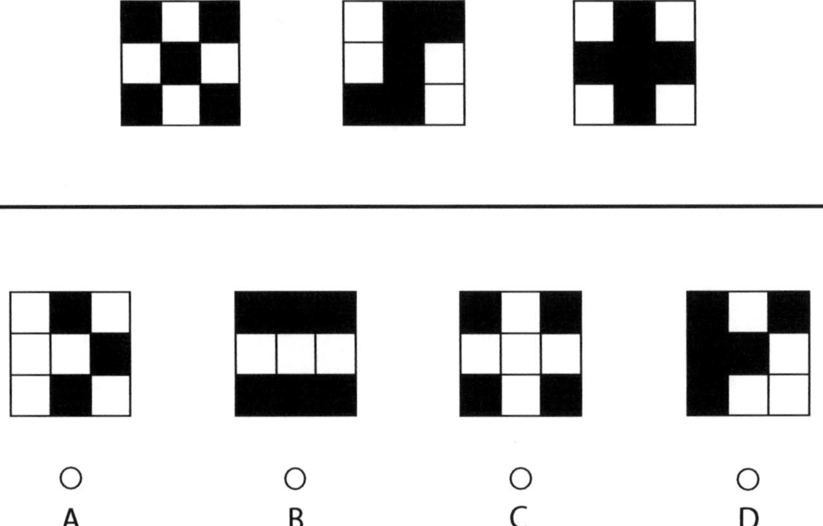

Question 16

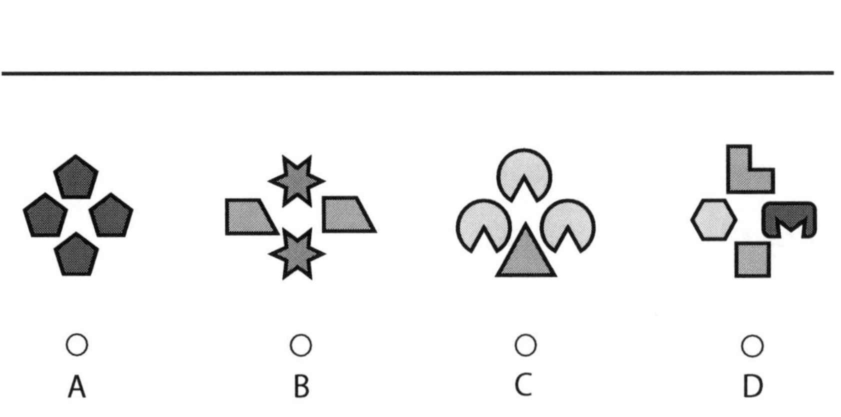

Question 17

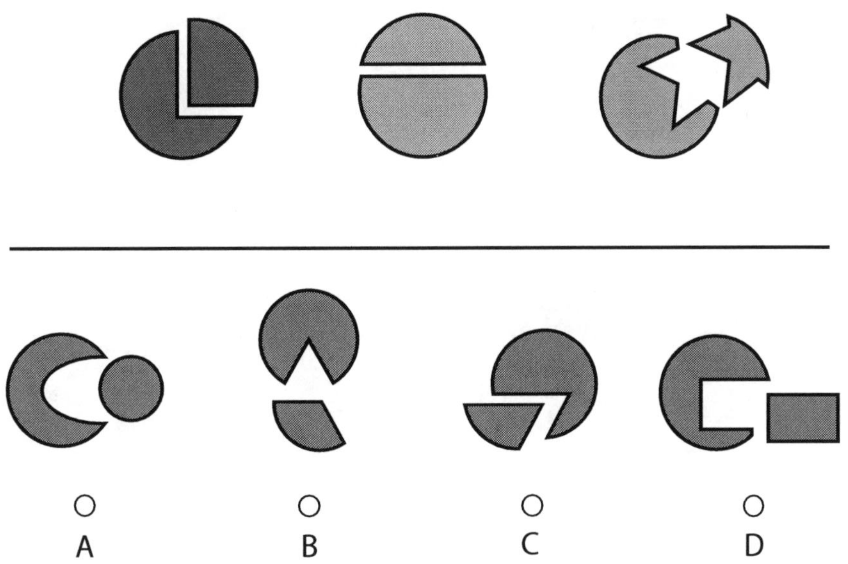

Question 18

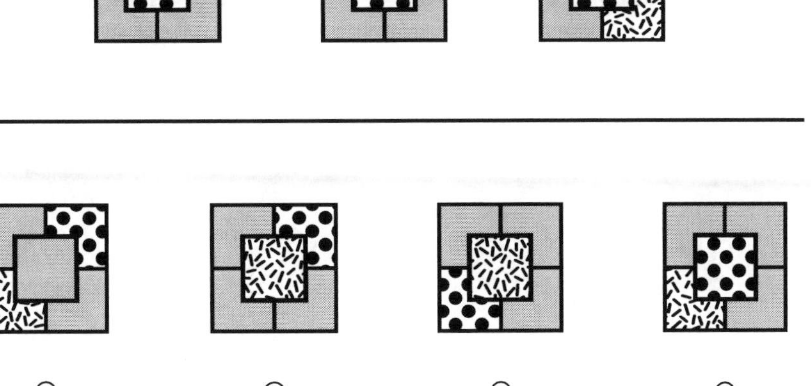

○ A ○ B ○ C ○ D

Question 19

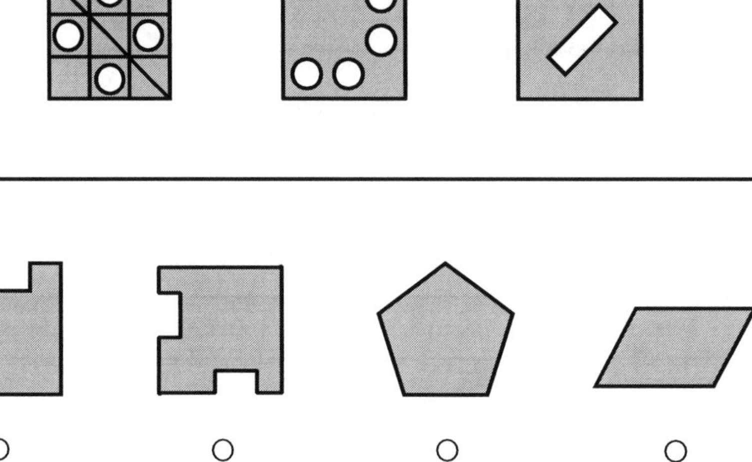

Question 20

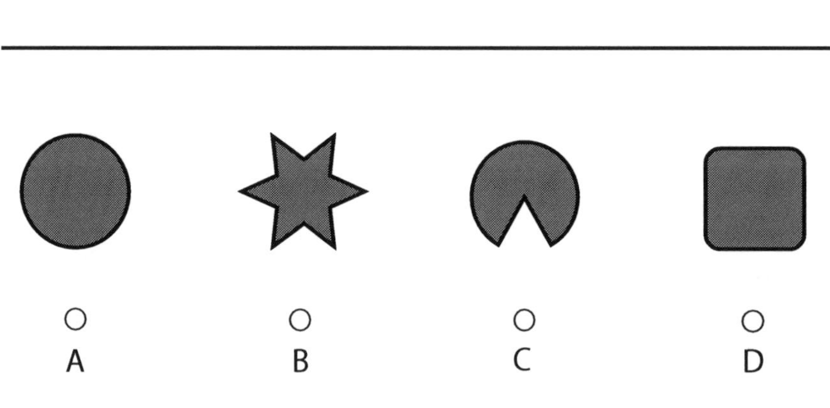

PRACTICE TEST 1

ANSWERS

&

EXPLANATIONS

CogAT Verbal Analogies

Answers and Explanations

Answers

1. B	6. E	11. C	16. D	21. A
2. C	7. D	12. B	17. E	22. A
3. A	8. B	13. E	18. B	
4. C	9. A	14. E	19. C	
5. C	10. E	15. D	20. C	

Explanations

1. (B)

   The opposite of bright is dark and the opposite of easy is difficult. Therefore, (B) is the correct answer.

2. (C)

   The color of a banana is yellow and the color of a strawberry is red. Therefore, (C) is the correct answer.

3. (A)

   A bakery is a place where baked goods including cakes are sold. A restaurant is a place where food including steaks are sold. Therefore, (A) is the correct answer.

4. (C)

   Spring is a season and Sunday is a part of week. Therefore, (C) is the correct answer.

5. (C)

   A referee is an official who regulates the rules of soccer game. An umpire is an official who regulates the rules of baseball game. Therefore, (C) is the correct answer.

6. (E)

   A reward is a thing given in recognition of one's good services or achievements. Whereas a penalty is a punishment imposed for bad behaviors or breaking rules. Therefore, (E) is the correct answer.

7. (D)

   Gloves are a covering for the hands worn for protection against cold or dirt. Socks are a garment for the feet. Therefore, (D) is the correct answer.

8. (B)

   A driver is a person who drives a car. A pilot is a person who operates the flying controls of an airplane. Therefore, (B) is the correct answer.

9. (A)

   You use legs to run and use arms to throw an object. Therefore, (A) is the correct answer.

10. (E)

    California is a western state out of 50 US states. English is a type of language out of many languages in the world. Therefore, (E) is the correct answer.

11. (C)

    A nurse works in a hospital and a teacher works in a school. Therefore, (C) is the correct answer.

12. (B)

    Receive is the opposite of give. Spend is the opposite of save. Therefore, (B) is the correct answer.

13. (E)

    A boat travels on water. Skis glide on snow. Therefore, (E) is the correct answer.

14. (E)

    Glue used for sticking objects or materials together is sticky. Icy road which produces much less friction than the dry road does is slippery. Therefore, (E) is the correct answer.

15. (D)

    A film director makes movies. A poet is a person who write poems. Therefore, (D) is the correct answer.

16. (D)

 Above is the opposite of below. After is the opposite of before. Therefore, (D) is the correct answer.

17. (E)

 A chef is a person who cooks food in a restaurant. A waiter in a restaurant is a person who serves customers at a table. Therefore, (E) is the correct answer.

18. (B)

 Cotton candy is a form of spun sugar. Cheese is a diary product derived from milk. Therefore, (B) is the correct answer.

19. (C)

 A party is a social gathering of invited guests to celebrate one's achievements. A race is a competition between runners or horses or vehicles to see which is the fastest in covering a set course. Therefore, (C) is the correct answer.

20. (C)

 A square is a four-sided figure. Whereas a pentagon a five-sided figure. Therefore, (C) is the correct answer.

21. (A)

 You use a pen to write, while you use a brush to paint. Therefore, (A) is the correct answer.

22. (A)

 The president is a head officer of the United States, while a governor is a head officer of the Florida state. Therefore, (A) is the correct answer.

CogAT Sentence Completion

Answers and Explanations

Answers

1. C	6. B	11. C	16. D
2. C	7. E	12. E	17. D
3. A	8. A	13. C	18. C
4. C	9. B	14. C	19. E
5. A	10. B	15. D	20. A

Explanations

1. (C)

   A chef is a professional who makes tasty food. The word "even though" means that two things are related in opposite way. So, you should look for a word that is the opposite of good. Since the word "terrible" means extremely bad, (C) is the correct answer.

2. (C)

   My uncle is proud <u>of</u> being a firefighter. Therefore, (C) is the correct answer.

3. (A)

   A doctor is a qualified practitioner of medicine who treat people medically. Therefore, (A) is the correct answer.

4. (C)

   Since Jason uses a calculator everyday, he always brings the calculator to school. Therefore, (C) is the correct answer.

5. (A)

   Venom, a poisonous substance that is typically injected into prey or aggressors by biting or stinging, is harmful. The word "lethal" means extremely harmful. Therefore, (A) is the correct answer.

6. (B)

   A comedian is an entertainer whose act is designed to make an audience laugh. Therefore, (B) is the correct answer.

7. (E)

   Since the weather and skies can affect everyone's mood, (E) is the correct answer.

8. (A)

   The word "plant" means that place a flower or tree in the ground so that it can grow. Therefore, (A) is the correct answer.

9. (B)

   The word "remain" means to stay in the place that one has been occupying. The soldiers were ordered to <u>remain</u> at their posts makes the most sense. Therefore, (B) is the correct answer.

10. (B)

    The word "nervous" means to be easily agitated or tending to be anxious. His <u>nervous</u> mom is always worrying that something terrible will happen to him makes the most sense. Therefore, (B) is the correct answer.

11. (C)

    Daniel is the second <u>tallest</u> boy in his school. Therefore, (C) is the correct answer.

12. (E)

    The word "recover" means to return to a normal state of health. Therefore, (E) is the correct answer.

13. (C)

    The word "extinct" means to no longer exist. Therefore, (C) is the correct answer.

14. (C)

    The cat meowed and the dog barked. Therefore, (C) is the correct answer.

15. (D)

    The word "rinse" means to wash something with clean water to remove soap or dirt. I <u>rinse</u> my dog off with fresh water whenever he swims in the ocean makes the most sense. Therefore, (D) is the correct answer.

16. (D)

    A leash is a strap or cord for restraining and guiding a dog or other animal. Therefore, (D) is the correct answer.

17. (D)

    A trailer is a vacation home pulled by a truck or a car. Therefore, (D) is the correct answer.

18. (C)

    The word "hover" means to remain in one place in the air. Pelicans continually <u>hover</u> near the water and dive for fish makes the most sense. Therefore, (C) is the correct answer.

19. (E)

    The word "knit" means to make sweaters by interlocking loops of wool or other yarn with knitting needles or on a machine. Therefore, (E) is the correct answer.

20. (A)

    A college is an educational institution that students go after graduating from high schools. My brother graduated from a high school. He worked painting houses to earn money for <u>college</u> makes the most sense. Therefore, (A) is the correct answer.

CogAT Verbal Classification

Answers and Explanations

Answers

1. A	6. D	11. D	16. C
2. C	7. C	12. A	17. E
3. E	8. C	13. C	18. E
4. C	9. D	14. B	19. E
5. A	10. C	15. A	20. D

Explanations

1. (A)

   A Lion, a cheetah, and a tiger are part of the cat family. Therefore, (A) is the correct answer.

2. (C)

   An apartment, a hut, a shelter, and a cabin are dwelling places. Therefore, (C) is the correct answer.

3. (E)

   Venus, Mars, Jupiter, and Earth are planets. However, the Moon is an astronomical satellite that orbits planet Earth. Therefore, (E) is the correct answer.

4. (C)

   An adjective is a word or phrase that modifies or describes a noun. The words tall, beautiful, soft, and loud are adjectives. Therefore, (C) is the correct answer.

5. (A)

   A vessel is a craft for traveling on water. A boat, a paddle steamer, a ship, and a yacht are vessels. Therefore, (A) is the correct answer.

6. (D)

   Swiss, Mozzarella, Cheddar, and Feta are names of cheese. Therefore, (D) is the correct answer.

7. (C)

   Coal, wood, gas, and diesel are different types of fuels. Therefore, (C) is the correct answer.

8. (C)

   Bark, trunk, branch, and roots are parts of a tree. Therefore, (C) is the correct answer.

9. (D)

   Puddings, cakes, ice creams, and pies are types of desserts. Therefore, (D) is the correct answer.

10. (C)

    Fear, joy, disgust, and surprise are emotions. Therefore, (C) is the correct answer.

11. (D)

    The words "CD", "NO", "ST", and "XY" consist of two consecutive letters. Therefore, (D) is the correct answer.

12. (A)

    A square, a circle, a triangle, and a rectangle are all shapes. Therefore, (A) is the correct answer.

13. (C)

    Lilac, lily, and daffodil are names of flowers. Therefore, (C) is the correct answer.

14. (B)

    Tumble, topple, and collapse are ways of falling down. Therefore, (B) is the correct answer.

15. (A)

    Condiments are substances such as ketchup, mustard, and mayonnaise that are used to add flavor to food. Therefore, (A) is the correct answer.

16. (C)

    Brass, aluminum, and copper are types of metals. Therefore, (C) is the correct answer.

17. (E)

    Maple, palm, and oak are types of trees. Therefore, (E) is the correct answer.

18. (E)

    A bat, a cat, a rat, and a goat are animals that end with a letter T. Therefore, (E) is the correct answer.

19. (E)

    History, math, literature, and science are all school subjects. Therefore, (E) is the correct answer.

20. (D)

    A bench, a chair, a couch, and a sofa are all furniture that you can sit on. Therefore, (D) is the correct answer.

CogAT Number Analogies

Answers and Explanations

Answers

1. E	6. E	11. A	16. C
2. D	7. D	12. A	17. D
3. E	8. A	13. D	18. B
4. E	9. A	14. E	
5. C	10. C	15. B	

Explanations

1. (E)
   The second number of each pair is 5 more than the first number; that is, $5+5=10$, $3+5=8$, and $7+5=12$. Therefore, (E) is the correct answer.

2. (D)
   The second number of each pair is obtained by multiplying the first number by 2; that is, $2\times 2=4$, $4\times 2=8$, and $8\times 2=16$. Therefore, (D) is the correct answer.

3. (E)
   The second number of each pair is 3 less than the first number; that is, $9-3=6$, $7-3=4$, and $11-3=8$. Therefore, (E) is the correct answer.

4. (E)
   The second number of each pair is 11 more than the first number; that is, $3+11=14$, $7+11=18$, and $11+11=22$. Therefore, (E) is the correct answer.

5. (C)
   The second number of each pair is obtained by dividing the first number by 2; that is, $26\div 2=13$, $24\div 2=12$, and $22\div 2=11$. Therefore, (C) is the correct answer.

6. (E)

   The second number of each pair is obtained by multiplying the first number by itself; that is, $2 \times 2 = 4$, $3 \times 3 = 9$, and $4 \times 4 = 16$. Therefore, (E) is the correct answer.

7. (D)

   The second number of each pair is the units digit of the first number; that is, 2 is the units digit of 12, 6 is the units digit of 56, and 9 is the units digit of 79. Therefore, (D) is the correct answer.

8. (A)

   The second number of each pair is 15 minutes more than the first number; that is, 15 minutes after 1:15 is 1:30, 15 minutes after 3:25 is 3:40, and 15 minutes after 5:40 is 5:55. Therefore, (A) is the correct answer.

9. (A)

   The second number of each pair is 9 less than the first number; that is, $13 - 9 = 4$, $17 - 9 = 8$, and $24 - 9 = 15$. Therefore, (A) is the correct answer.

10. (C)

    The second number of each pair is 25 more than the first number; that is, $25 + 25 = 50$, $40 + 25 = 65$, and $53 + 25 = 78$. Therefore, (C) is the correct answer.

11. (A)

    The second number of each pair is obtained by multiplying the first number by 3; that is, $2 \times 3 = 6$, $4 \times 3 = 12$, and $5 \times 3 = 15$. Therefore, (A) is the correct answer.

12. (A)

    The second number of each pair is the tens digit of the first number; that is, 3 is the tens digit of 234, 5 is the tens digit of 156, and 7 is the tens digit of 471. Therefore, (A) is the correct answer.

13. (D)

    The second number of each pair is 1 more than twice the first number; that is, $2 \times 2 + 1 = 5$, $3 \times 2 + 1 = 7$, and $6 \times 2 + 1 = 13$. Therefore, (D) is the correct answer.

14. (E)

    The second number of each pair is obtained by dividing the first number by 3; that is, $9 \div 3 = 3$, $12 \div 3 = 4$, and $18 \div 3 = 6$. Therefore, (E) is the correct answer.

15. (B)

    The second number of each pair is 20 minutes before the first number; that is, 20 minutes before 1:25 is 1:05, 20 minutes before 3:40 is 3:20, and 20 minutes before 8:00 is 7:40. Therefore, (B) is the correct answer.

16. (C)

    The second number of each pair is 1 less than half the first number; that is, $8 \div 2 - 1 = 3$, $12 \div 2 - 1 = 5$, and $20 \div 2 - 1 = 9$. Therefore, (C) is the correct answer.

17. (D)

    The second number of each pair is obtained by multiplying the first number by 111; that is, $3 \times 111 = 333$, $5 \times 111 = 555$, and $8 \times 111 = 888$. Therefore, (D) is the correct answer.

18. (B)

    The second number of each pair is one day after the first number; that is, the day after March 9 is March 10, the day after October 15 is October 16. Since May has 31 days, the day after May 31 is June 1. Therefore, (B) is the correct answer.

CogAT Number Puzzles

Answers and Explanations

Answers

1. C	6. C	11. A	16. E
2. D	7. B	12. B	
3. C	8. D	13. C	
4. E	9. B	14. A	
5. A	10. E	15. C	

Explanations

1. (C)

   $\boxed{8} + 8 + 9 = 25$. Therefore, (C) is the correct answer.

2. (D)

   $17 = \boxed{14} - 2 + 5$. Therefore, (D) is the correct answer.

3. (C)

   $2 \times \boxed{5} = 2 + 3 + 5$. Therefore, (C) is the correct answer.

4. (E)

   $14 + 15 = 17 - 6 + \boxed{18}$. Therefore, (E) is the correct answer.

5. (A)

   $9 + \boxed{7} - 6 = 20 - 10$. Therefore, (A) is the correct answer.

6. (C)

   $\boxed{33} - 6 - 15 = 4 + 8$. Therefore, (C) is the correct answer.

7. (B)

   $1+2+3+4=2\times\boxed{5}$. Therefore, (B) is the correct answer.

8. (D)

   $13+9-8=21-\boxed{13}+6$. Therefore, (D) is the correct answer.

9. (B)

   $2\times2\times2=\boxed{2}+6$ Therefore, (B) is the correct answer.

10. (E)

    $\boxed{10}>2+3+4$. Therefore, (E) is the correct answer.

11. (A)

    $17+\boxed{19}=12+9+15$. Therefore, (A) is the correct answer.

12. (B)

    $31+26=\boxed{22}+13+22$ Therefore, (B) is the correct answer.

13. (C)

    $33+\boxed{55}+44=44+55+33$. Therefore, (C) is the correct answer.

14. (A)

    $\boxed{12}+2<3+5+7$. Therefore, (A) is the correct answer.

15. (C)

    $14+23-31=\boxed{32}-11-15$. Therefore, (C) is the correct answer.

16. (E)

    $\boxed{6}\times4=2\times3\times4$. Therefore, (E) is the correct answer.

CogAT Number Series

Answers and Explanations

Answers

1. C	6. B	11. D	16. D
2. C	7. D	12. C	17. C
3. A	8. E	13. E	18. C
4. B	9. C	14. A	
5. C	10. E	15. C	

Explanations

1. (C)

   The numbers are decreasing by 3. So, the number that replaces the question mark is $13 - 3 = 10$. Therefore, (C) is the correct answer.

2. (C)

   The numbers are doubled. So, the number that replaces the question mark is $16 \times 2 = 32$. Therefore, (C) is the correct answer.

3. (A)

   The numbers are increasing by 10. So, the first number that replaces the question mark is 4. Therefore, (A) is the correct answer.

4. (B)

   The numbers are formed by adding one, two, three, four, five, and six; that is $1+\mathbf{1} = 2$, $2+\mathbf{2} = 4$, $4+\mathbf{3} = 7$, $7+\mathbf{4} = 11$, $11+\mathbf{5} = 16$, and $16+\mathbf{6} = 22$. Therefore, (B) is the correct answer.

5. (C)

   The numbers are decreasing by 5. So, the number that replaces the question mark is $54 - 5 = 49$. Therefore, (C) is the correct answer.

6. (B)

   The numbers 23, 41, and 55 are repeating. So, the number that replaces the question mark is 41. Therefore, (B) is the correct answer.

7. (D)

   The numbers are increasing by 7 and are repeating twice except the last number. So, the number that replaces the question mark is 19. Therefore, (D) is the correct answer.

8. (E)

   The numbers are decreasing by half. The complete pattern is $\{320, 160, 80, 40, 20, 10, 5\}$. So, the number that replaces the question mark is 320. Therefore, (E) is the correct answer.

9. (C)

   There are two patterns in this question. The numbers in the first, the third, the fifth, and the seventh are increasing by 1. The numbers in the second, the fourth, and the sixth are decreasing by 1. So, the number that replaces the question mark is 11. Therefore, (C) is the correct answer.

10. (E)

    The numbers are formed by multiplying the previous term by 3. The complete pattern is $\{1, 3, 9, 27, 81, 243, 729\}$. So, the number that replaces the question mark is 243. Therefore, (E) is the correct answer.

11. (D)

    The numbers are increasing by 15. So, the number that replaces the question mark is $105 + 15 = 120$. Therefore, (D) is the correct answer.

12. (C)

    The numbers are formed by a pattern: subtract 1 and add 3. $10 - \mathbf{1} = 9$, $9 + \mathbf{3} = 12$, $12 - \mathbf{1} = 11$, $11 + \mathbf{3} = 14$, $14 - \mathbf{1} = 13$, and $13 + \mathbf{3} = 16$. Therefore, (C) is the correct answer.

13. (E)

    The numbers are decreasing by 11. So, the number that replaces the question mark is $45 - 11 = 34$. Therefore, (E) is the correct answer.

14. (A)

    The consecutive odd-numbered terms are decreasing by 10: 50, 40, 30, and 20. The consecutive even-numbered terms are increasing by 5: 5, 10, and 15. So, the number that replaces the question mark is 20. Therefore, (A) is the correct answer.

15. (C)

    The numbers are formed by a pattern: Multiply by 3 and divide by 2. $8 \times \mathbf{3} = 24$, $24 \div \mathbf{2} = 12$, $12 \times \mathbf{3} = 36$, $36 \div \mathbf{2} = 18$, $18 \times \mathbf{3} = 54$, and $54 \div \mathbf{2} = 27$. Therefore, (C) is the correct answer.

16. (D)

    There is one 1, followed by two 2's, followed by three 3's. So, the next number that replaces the question mark is 4. Therefore, (D) is the correct answer.

17. (C)

    Each term is 1 more than twice the previous term. The complete pattern is $\{2, 5, 11, 23, 47, 95, 191\}$. So, the number that replaces the question mark is 191. Therefore, (C) is the correct answer.

18. (C)

    The numbers are the first seven perfect squares; that is, the first term is $1 \times 1 = 1$, the second term is $2 \times 2 = 4$, the third term is $3 \times 3 = 9$, and so on and so forth. The complete pattern is $\{1, 4, 9, 16, 25, 36, 49\}$. So, the number that replaces the question mark is 49. Therefore, (C) is the correct answer.

CogAT Figure Matrices

Answers and Explanations

Answers

1. A	6. E	11. C	16. C
2. A	7. D	12. C	17. E
3. E	8. C	13. A	18. C
4. E	9. B	14. C	19. D
5. D	10. B	15. B	20. B

Explanations

1. (A)

   The second figure is a larger image of the first figure and is rotated counterclockwise 180°. The figure in (A) is a larger image of the third figure and is rotated counterclockwise 180°. Therefore, (A) is the correct answer.

2. (A)

   In the first figure, two squares intersect. The second figure shows an overlapping region of the two squares. In the third figure, two circles intersect. The figure in (A) shows an overlapping region of two circles. Therefore, (A) is the correct answer.

3. (E)

   In the first figure, there is a circle inside a square. If you put a square inside a circle, you get the second figure. In the third figure, there is a triangle inside a circle. If you put a circle inside a triangle, you get the figure in (E). Therefore, (E) is the correct answer.

4. (E)

   If you rotate two stars 90° clockwise in the first figure, you get the second figure. If you rotate two stars 90° clockwise in the third figure, you get the figure in (E). Therefore, (E) is the correct answer.

5. (D)

   The number of sides of a figure inside increases by 1. In the top row, a triangle (3-sided figure) becomes a square (4-sided figure). In the bottom row, a pentagon (5-sided figure) becomes a hexagon (6-sided figure). Therefore, (D) is the correct answer.

6. (E)

   If you rotate the first figure 90° clockwise, you get the second figure. If you rotate the third figure 90° clockwise, you get the figure in (E). Therefore, (E) is the correct answer.

7. (D)

   The second figure is obtained by rotating a letter A 90° counterclockwise. The answer is obtained by rotating a letter Z 90° counterclockwise. Therefore, (D) is the correct answer.

8. (C)

   In order to get the second figure, rearrange three circles in the first figure in the following pattern. Put the middle circle at the top, the third circle in the middle, and the first circle at the bottom. The third figure has a triangle at the top, a circle in the middle, and a square at the bottom. So, the answer should have the circle at the top, the square in the middle, and the triangle at the bottom. Therefore, (C) is the correct answer.

9. (B)

   If you merge a triangle and a circle in the first figure, you get the second figure. If you merge two rectangles in the third figure, you get the figure in (B). Therefore, (B) is the correct answer.

10. (B)

    If you combine two shaded triangular regions in the first figure, you get a diamond shape in the second figure. If you combine four shaded quarter circles, you get the figure in (B). Therefore, (B) is the correct answer.

11. (C)

    The first figure has one straight line and one curved line. The second figure has two straight lines and one curved line. So, the number of straight lines in the top row increases by one. The third figure has two straight lines and one curved line. So, the answer should have three straight lines and one curved line. Therefore, (C) is the correct answer.

12. (C)

    The first figure has 9 squares which are either shaded or unshaded. The second figure is obtained by changing shaded squares to unshaded squares and vice versa. Do the same thing for the third figure to get the answer. Therefore, (C) is the correct answer.

13. (A)

    The first figure consists of two parts: a white circle with a smaller shaded square inside and a letter D. The second figure is obtained by putting a small white circle inside a large shaded square and reflecting the letter D vertically. The third figure consists of two parts: a shaded triangle with a small white circle inside and a letter R. The answer should have a small shaded triangle inside a large white circle and a vertically reflected letter R. Therefore, (A) is the correct answer.

14. (C)

    The second figure is obtained by rotating the first figure 45° clockwise. If you rotate the third figure 45° clockwise, you get the figure in (C). Therefore, (C) is the correct answer.

15. (B)

    The first figure has a shaded triangle at the top and a white circle at the bottom. The second figure is obtained by putting two shaded circles at the top and a white triangle at the bottom. The third figure has a shaded square at the top and a white diamond at the bottom. The answer should have two shaded diamonds at the top and a white square at the bottom. Therefore, (B) is the correct answer.

16. (C)

    The second figure is obtained by switching patterns of the first figure diagonally. If you switch patterns of the third figure diagonally, you get the figure in (C). Therefore, (C) is the correct answer.

17. (E)

    The second figure is obtained by reflecting the first figure horizontally. If you reflect the third figure horizontally, you get the figure in (E). Therefore, (E) is the correct answer.

18. (C)

    As you move across the row from the left to right, reflect the figure to the left horizontally and add one circle. Therefore, (C) is the correct answer.

19. (D)

    In each row, the second figure is a 90° clockwise rotation of the first figure and the third figure is a 90° clockwise rotation of the second figure. In addition, the colors of three figures in the second column are all white. Therefore, (D) is the correct answer.

20. (B)

    The first figure in each row is the inner shape in the third figure and its color changes from back to white or white to black. The second figure in each row is the outer shape in the third figure and its color changes from back to white or white to black. In addition, the colors alternates from black to white as you move across each column. Therefore, (B) is the correct answer.

CogAT Paper Folding

Answers and Explanations

Answers

1. D	6. D	11. B	16. A
2. B	7. C	12. D	
3. C	8. C	13. B	
4. D	9. B	14. D	
5. B	10. A	15. C	

Explanations

1. (D)

   The paper is folded vertically once. So, there will be 4 holes if it is unfolded completely as shown below.

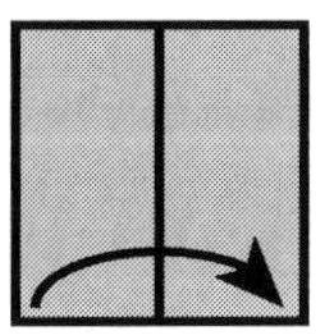

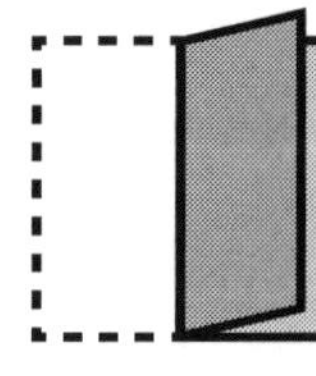
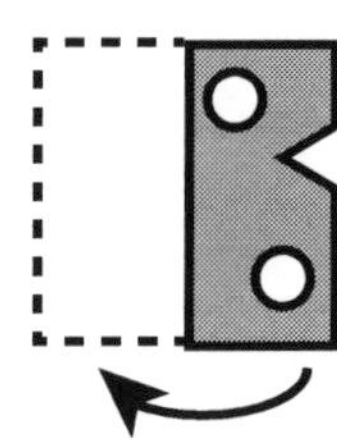
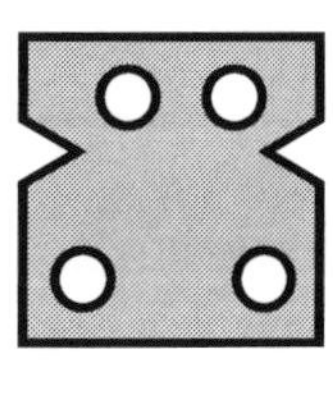

Therefore, (D) is the correct answer.

2. (B)

   The paper is folded horizontally once. So, there will be 2 rectangles, 2 stars, and 4 holes if it is unfolded completely as shown below.

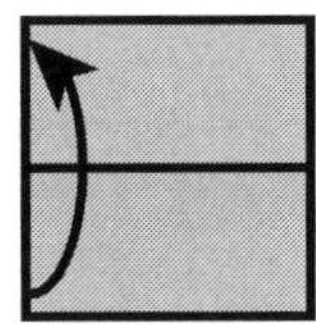
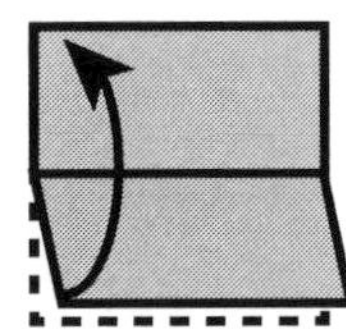
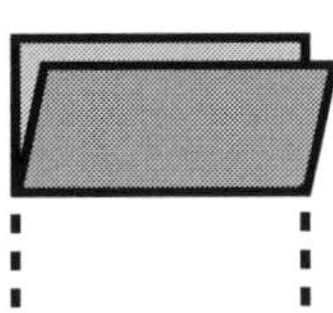
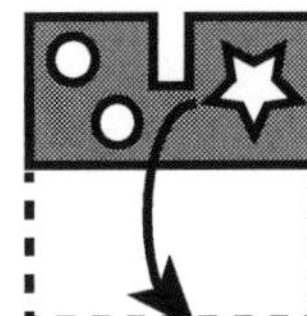
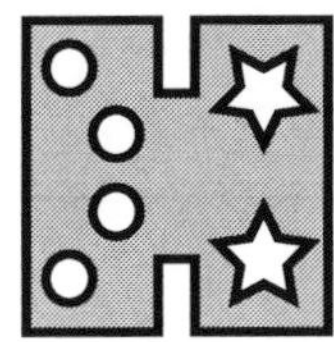

   Therefore, (B) is the correct answer.

3. (C)

   The paper is folded diagonally once. So, there will be 2 large holes and 4 squares if it is unfolded completely as shown below.

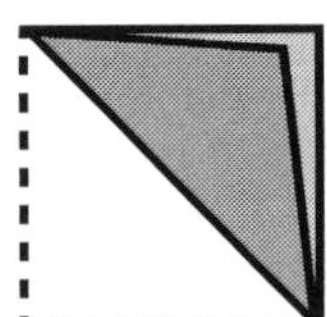

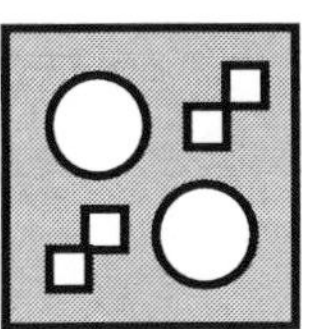

   Therefore, (C) is the correct answer.

4. (D)

   The paper is folded diagonally once. So, there will be 4 large holes and a rectangle if it is unfolded completely as shown below.

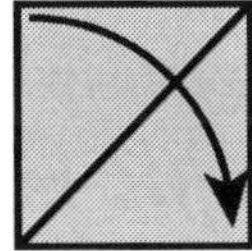

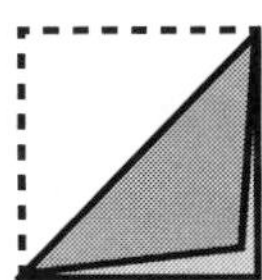

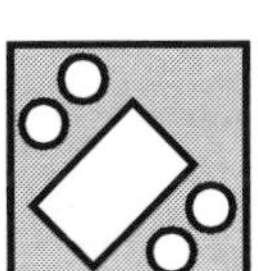

   Therefore, (D) is the correct answer.

5. (B)

The paper is folded vertically and then folded horizontally. So, there will be 4 holes near the center of the paper and 4 diamonds near the corner of the paper if it is unfolded completely as shown below.

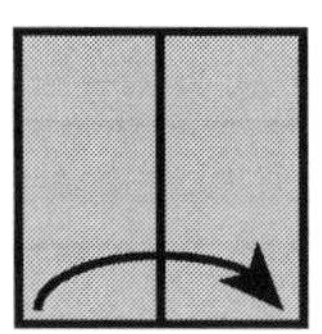 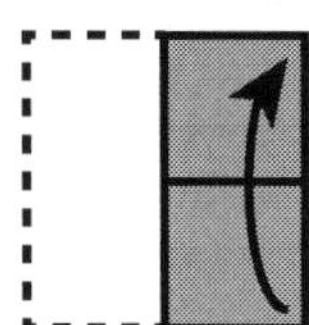  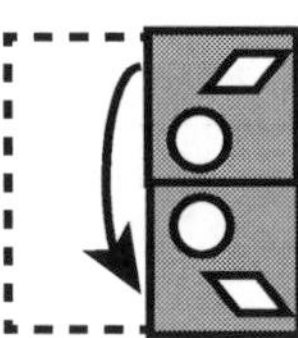 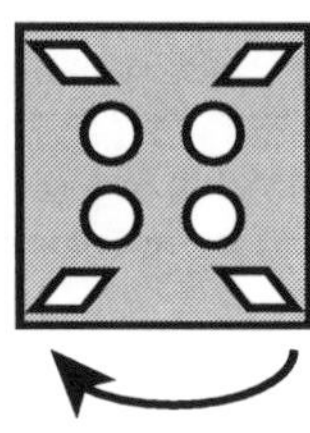

Therefore, (B) is the correct answer.

6. (D)

The paper is folded horizontally and then folded vertically. So, you will get the figure if it is unfolded completely as shown below.

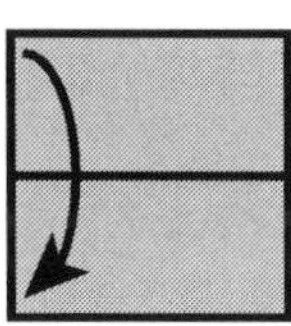 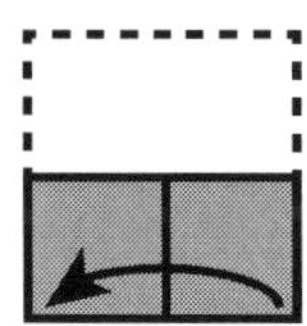 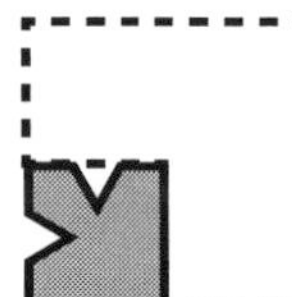 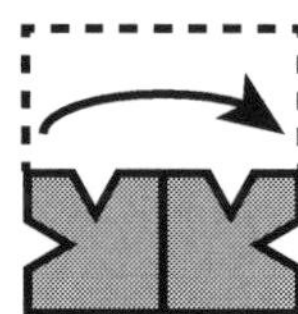 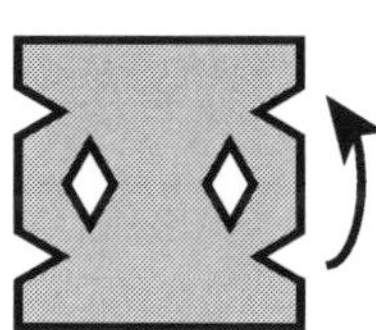

Therefore, (D) is the correct answer.

7. (C)

The paper is folded diagonally twice. So, there will be 12 holes if it is unfolded completely as shown below.

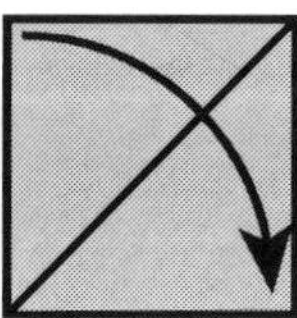   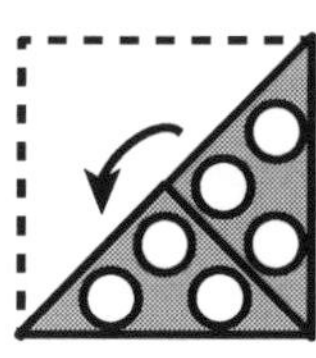 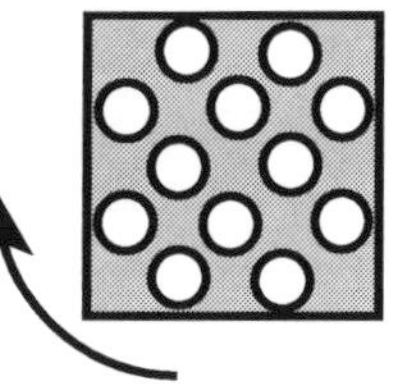

Therefore, (C) is the correct answer.

8. (C)

The paper is folded diagonally twice and then folded vertically. So, you will get the figure if it is unfolded completely as shown below.

 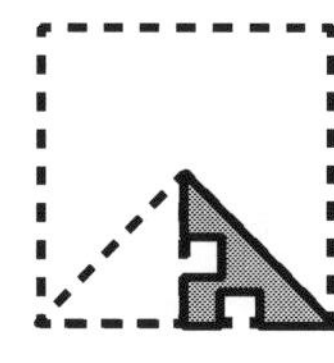  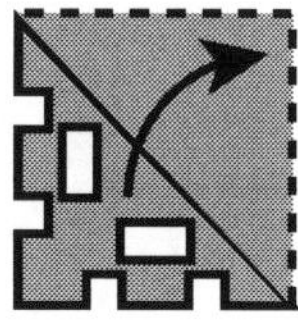 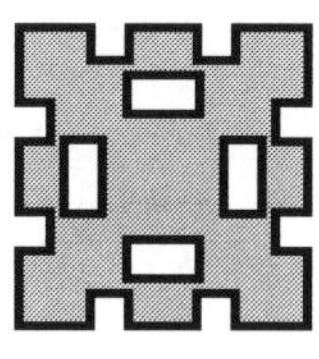

Therefore, (C) is the correct answer.

9. (B)

The paper is folded vertically and then folded horizontally. So, there will be 12 holes if it is unfolded completely as shown below.

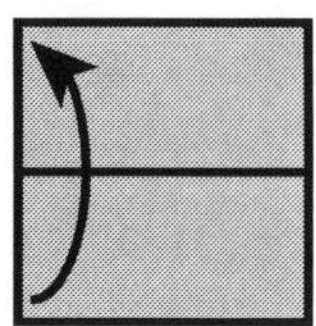 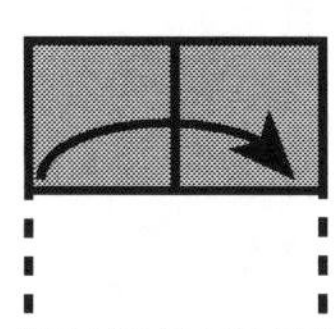 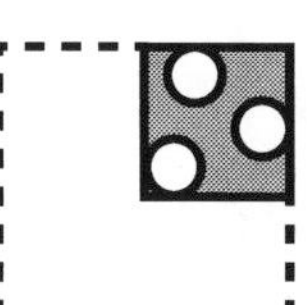 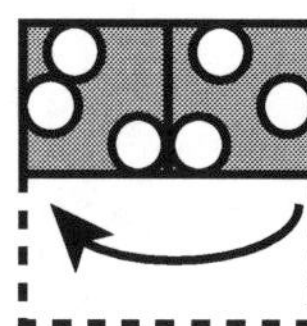 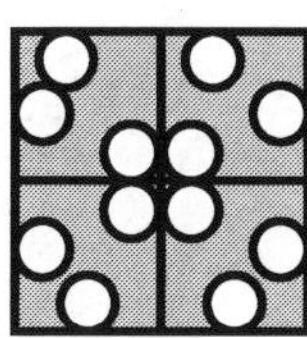

Therefore, (B) is the correct answer.

10. (A)

The paper is folded vertically and folded horizontally twice. So, you will get the figure if it is unfolded completely as shown below.

 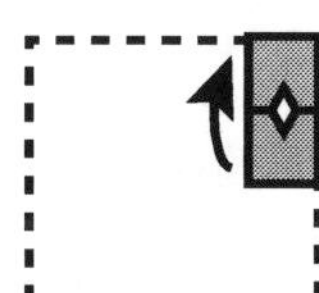 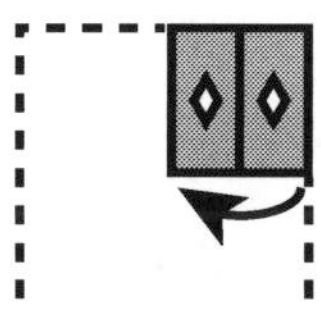 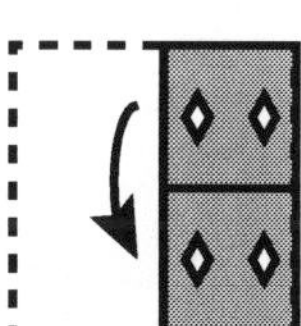 

Therefore, (A) is the correct answer.

11. (B)

The paper is folded horizontally once and then folded vertically twice. So, you will get the figure if it is unfolded completely as shown below.

   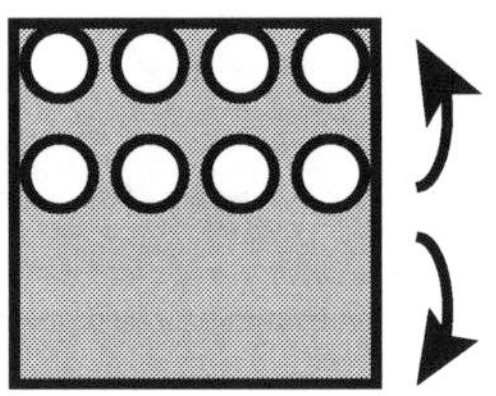

Therefore, (B) is the correct answer.

12. (D)

The paper is folded vertically and horizontally, and then folded diagonally. So, you will get the figure if it is unfolded completely as shown below.

  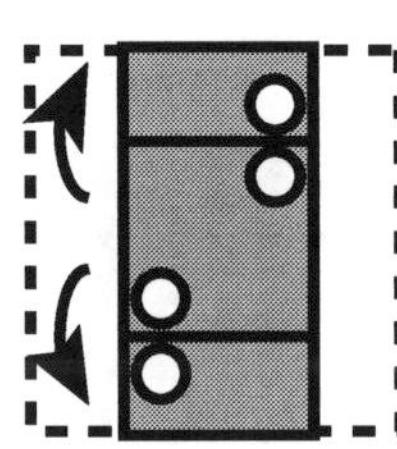 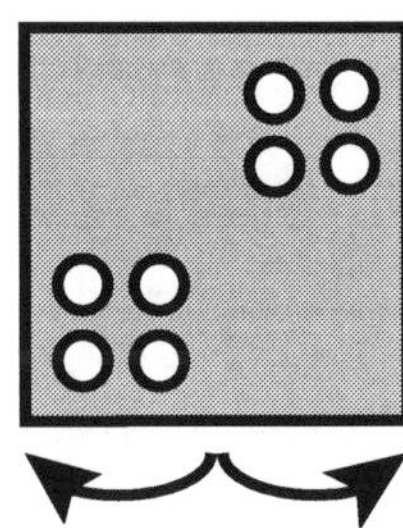

Therefore, (D) is the correct answer.

13. (B)

The paper is folded diagonally twice and then folded horizontally. So, you will get the figure if it is unfolded completely as shown below.

    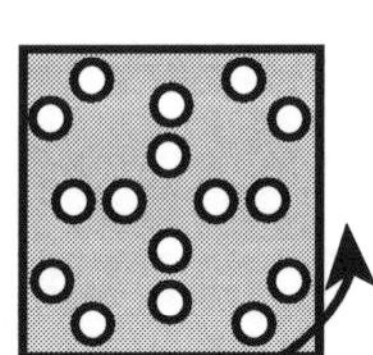

Therefore, (B) is the correct answer.

14. (D)

The paper is folded vertically and horizontally, and then folded diagonally. So, you will get the figure if it is unfolded completely as shown below.

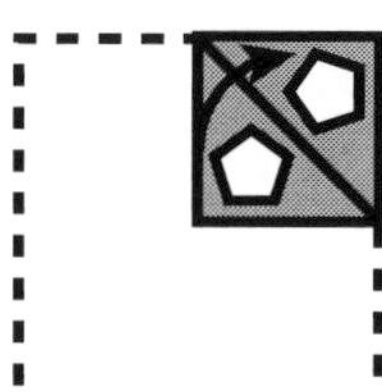
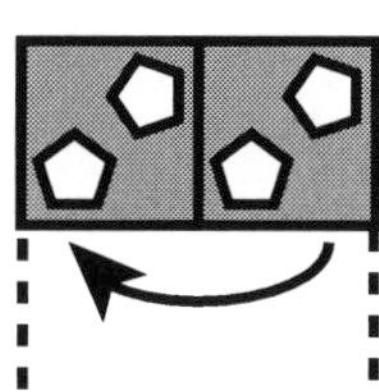
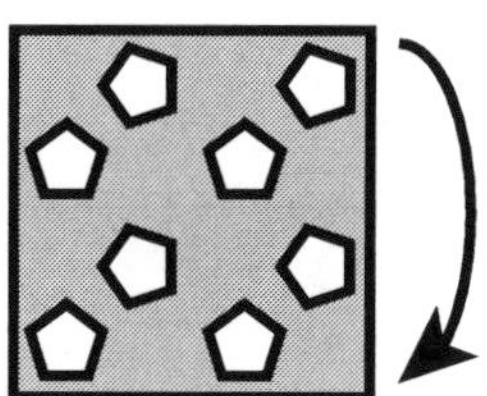

Therefore, (D) is the correct answer.

15. (C)

The paper is folded horizontally and vertically, and then folded diagonally. So, you will get the figure if it is unfolded completely as shown below.

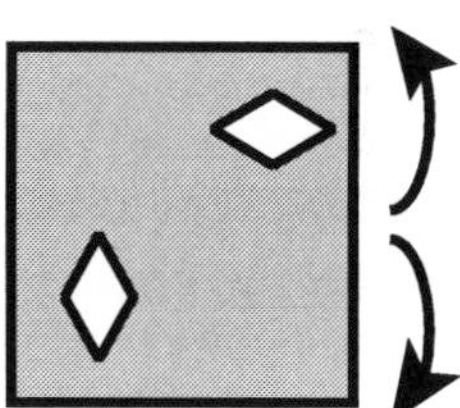

Therefore, (C) is the correct answer.

16. (A)

The paper is folded vertically and horizontally, and then folded diagonally. So, you will get the figure if it is unfolded completely as shown below.

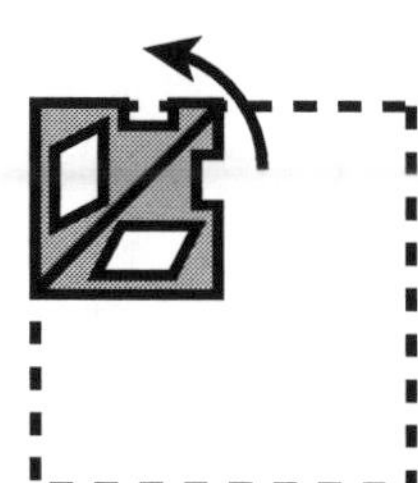
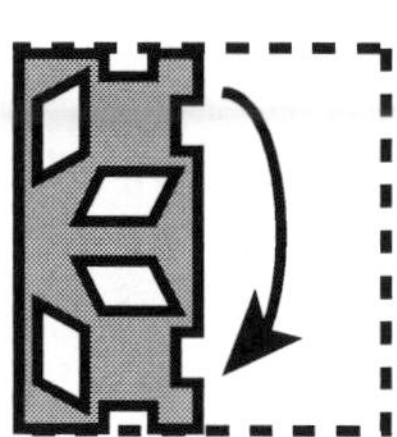
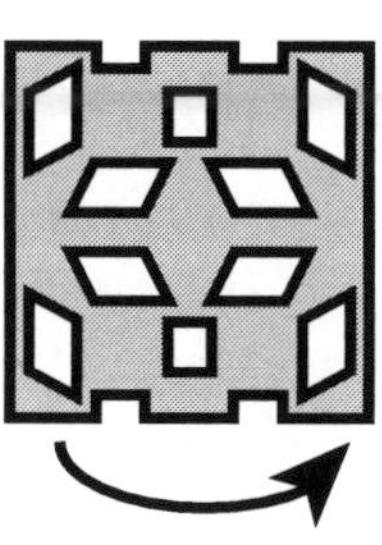

Therefore, (A) is the correct answer.

CogAT Figure Classification

Answers and Explanations

Answers

1. C	6. D	11. B	16. D
2. A	7. B	12. C	17. A
3. A	8. D	13. D	18. B
4. C	9. D	14. B	19. A
5. A	10. A	15. B	20. C

Explanations

1. (C)

   The figures in the top row have a gray circle and a black circle which touch inside of a large circle. Therefore, (C) is the correct answer.

2. (A)

   The figures in the top row have six sides. Therefore, (A) is the correct answer.

3. (A)

   The figures in the top row have two shapes. An outer shape has a horizontal stripes pattern and an inner shape has a vertical stripes pattern. Therefore, (A) is the correct answer.

4. (C)

   The figures in the top row have three different shapes. Therefore, (C) is the correct answer.

5. (A)

   Each figure in the top row has two shapes: The right shape is a horizontal reflection of the left shape. Therefore, (A) is the correct answer.

6. (D)

The figures in the top row consist of 2 black squares and 2 white squares. Therefore, (D) is the correct answer.

7. (B)

The figures in the top row have circles at two corners. Therefore, (B) is the correct answer.

8. (D)

Each figure in the top row is divided into 4 equal regions, and the three regions are shaded. Therefore, (D) is the correct answer.

9. (D)

Each figure in the top row consists two shapes. The shape in the right side is a horizontal reflection of the shape that lies inside of the left side. Therefore, (D) is the correct answer.

10. (A)

Each figure in the top row has 4 shapes. The only shapes in the top and bottom are the same. Therefore, (A) is the correct answer.

11. (B)

The figures in the top row have patterns that consist of straight lines. Therefore, (B) is the correct answer.

12. (C)

The figures in the top row have four-sided shapes inside. Therefore, (C) is the correct answer.

13. (D)

The figures in the top row have 9 squares, of which only four squares are shaded. Therefore, (D) is the correct answer.

14. (B)

The figures in the top row have odd-number of circles inside. The figure in (B) has 7 circles inside. Therefore, (B) is the correct answer.

15. (B)

The figures in the top row consist of 4 different shapes. Therefore, (B) is the correct answer.

16. (D)

The figures in the top row have three similar shapes. The colors of the two similar shapes inside are white and black. Therefore, (D) is the correct answer.

17. (A)

The figures in the top row are symmetric about the line that passes through the left lower corner to right upper corner of the figures. Therefore, (A) is the correct answer.

18. (B)

Each figure in the top row has five squares: two shaded squares and two squares with dots and horizontal lines, which are located opposite side of each other. A black square is on the top of the four squares. The figures in the top row are the rotational images of each other. Therefore, (B) is the correct answer.

19. (A)

The figures in the top row have one line of symmetry which is the vertical line. Therefore, (A) is the correct answer.

20. (C)

The figures in the top row have two shapes, which create a square if the two shapes are combined. Therefore, (C) is the correct answer.

PRACTICE TEST 2

ANSWERS

&

EXPLANATIONS

CogAT Verbal Analogies

Answers and Explanations

Answers

1. E	6. B	11. C	16. A	21. B
2. E	7. B	12. E	17. E	22. D
3. A	8. D	13. C	18. E	
4. B	9. A	14. C	19. E	
5. B	10. D	15. A	20. D	

Explanations

1. (E)

   A baby cat is called a kitten and a baby bear is called a cub. Therefore, (E) is the correct answer.

2. (E)

   A scale is used to measure weight of an object. A saw is used to cut wood or other materials. Therefore, (E) is the correct answer.

3. (A)

   A letter is a part of the alphabet and a steering wheel is a part of a car. Therefore, (A) is the correct answer.

4. (B)

   A characteristic of fire is hot and a characteristic of candy is sweet. Therefore, (B) is the correct answer.

5. (B)

   An ignition key is used to start a car and a match is used to start a fire. Therefore, (B) is the correct answer.

6. (B)

   The two words "difficult" and "complicated" have the same meaning, while the two words funny and hilarious have the same meaning. Therefore, (B) is the correct answer.

7. (B)

   A farmer's main goal is to produce good crops or healthy animals in a farm. A teacher's main goal is to educate students in a school. Therefore, (B) is the correct answer.

8. (D)

   The opposite of talk is listen and the opposite of laugh is cry. Therefore, (D) is the correct answer.

9. (A)

   A cup is used for a drink and a chair is used to seat a single person. Therefore, (A) is the correct answer.

10. (D)

    A finger is a part of a hand and a leaf is a part of a tree. Therefore, (D) is the correct answer.

11. (C)

    A jaguar lives in a mountain and a whale lives in the ocean. Therefore, (C) is the correct answer.

12. (E)

    Sweet is the opposite of bitter. Strong is the opposite of weak. Therefore, (E) is the correct answer.

13. (C)

    Something that is big is huge, while something that is little is tiny. Therefore, (C) is the correct answer.

14. (C)

    A piano is a kind of instrument and a female is a gender(male or female). Therefore, (C) is the correct answer.

15. (A)

    Traffic lights are devices positioned at road intersections to control flows of traffic. A password is a string of characters used to protect access to resources. Therefore, (A) is the correct answer.

16. (A)

    Noisy is the opposite of silent. Dangerous is the opposite of safe. Therefore, (A) is the correct answer.

17. (E)

    A wrench is a kind of tool and an apple is a type of fruit. Therefore, (E) is the correct answer.

18. (E)

    The past tense of run is ran. The past tense of sing is sang. Therefore, (E) is the correct answer.

19. (E)

    A lens is a part of a camera. Pedals are parts of a bicycle. Therefore, (E) is the correct answer.

20. (D)

    Students are in a school and juries are in a court. Therefore, (D) is the correct answer.

21. (B)

    A necklace is a type of jewelry worn around the neck. A bracelet is a type of jewelry worn around the wrist. Therefore, (B) is the correct answer.

22. (D)

    The outer case of a bean is called a pod, while the outer case of a nut is called a shell. Therefore, (D) is the correct answer.

CogAT Sentence Completion

Answers and Explanations

Answers

1. B	6. C	11. D	16. E
2. B	7. C	12. D	17. E
3. C	8. E	13. C	18. B
4. A	9. A	14. A	19. C
5. B	10. A	15. E	20. B

Explanations

1. (B)

   Each time I travel, I learn about what to bring to be prepared makes the most sense. Therefore, (B) is the correct answer.

2. (B)

   The word "spread" means to extend over a certain area. After I spread ketchup and mustard on meat, I eat my sandwich makes the most sense. Therefore, (B) is the correct answer.

3. (C)

   The word "fill" means to put something into a container so that it is completely or almost completely full. Thus, I fill containers with potting soil to plant flowers makes the most sense. Therefore, (C) is the correct answer.

4. (A)

   My vacation was fun. Hopefully we can go back to the same place next year makes the most sense. Therefore, (A) is the correct answer.

5. (B)

   Jenny wakes up late every morning. She doesn't have time to make her bed. Thus, she often leaves her bed unmade. Therefore, (B) is the correct answer.

6. (C)

   A life jacket is a sleeveless inflatable jacket for keeping a person afloat in water to save s/he from drowning. Therefore, (C) is the correct answer.

7. (C)

   Crabs are sea creatures which live on the ocean floor. Thus, The blue crab is found deep in the Atlantic ocean makes the most sense. Therefore, (C) is the correct answer.

8. (E)

   Ben is excited about moving from Texas to New York makes the most sense. Therefore, (E) is the correct answer.

9. (A)

   Dumpsters are large trash receptacles designed to be emptied into a truck. Thus, as dumpsters are almost full, our environment is getting dirty makes the most sense. Therefore, (A) is the correct answer.

10. (A)

    A rainstorm is a storm with heavy rain. Thus, we had to go home early. There was a sudden rainstorm makes the most sense. Therefore, (A) is the correct answer.

11. (D)

    My family went on vacation last month. Therefore, (D) is the correct answer.

12. (D)

    A mess is a dirty state of a place. Thus, My cat made a mess on the floor. I had to clean it up makes the most sense. Therefore, (D) is the correct answer.

13. (C)

    The word "lay" means to put down gently or carefully. Thus, a full-grown salmon is ready to lay eggs makes the most sense. Therefore, (C) is the correct answer.

14. (A)

    Beavers are large rodents that build dams with sticks and mud. Therefore, (A) is the correct answer.

15. (E)

    As soon as we arrive at the campsite, we will set up the tent makes the most sense. Therefore, (E) is the correct answer.

16. (E)

    When the rain hit the roof, it makes plunking noises. Therefore, (E) is the correct answer.

17. (E)

    The word "pat" means to touch quickly and gently with the flat of the hand. Joshua saw a dog walking down the street. He wanted to pat the dog makes the most sense. Therefore, (E) is the correct answer.

18. (B)

    The English class ended. So students packed up their bags makes the most sense. Therefore, (B) is the correct answer.

19. (C)

    "Please move out of my way! Let me through!" makes the most sense. Therefore, (C) is the correct answer.

20. (B)

    Hopping is a movement by jumping on one foot. Thus, squirrels love hopping from tree to tree makes the most sense. Therefore, (B) is the correct answer.

CogAT Verbal Classification

Answers and Explanations

Answers

1. B	6. E	11. A	16. B
2. A	7. E	12. A	17. B
3. D	8. B	13. A	18. C
4. A	9. E	14. E	19. C
5. E	10. B	15. A	20. C

Explanations

1. (B)
   Thanksgiving, Independence day, and Labor day are national holidays. Therefore, (B) is the correct answer.

2. (A)
   Blue, yellow, and red are colors. Therefore, (A) is the correct answer.

3. (D)
   Rain, snow, hail, and sleet are types of precipitation that drop in the earth. Therefore, (D) is the correct answer.

4. (A)
   Group, assembly, crowd, and regiment are words that describe a number of people. Therefore, (A) is the correct answer.

5. (E)
   Trust, belief, confidence, and faith are words that have the same meaning. Therefore, (E) is the correct answer.

6. (E)

   Sweden, France, Canada, and South Korea are names of countries in the world. Therefore, (E) is the correct answer.

7. (E)

   Pork, lamb, chicken, and beef are types of meat. Therefore, (E) is the correct answer.

8. (B)

   Heavy-eyed, tired, sleepy, and drowsy are words that have similar meanings. Therefore, (B) is the correct answer.

9. (E)

   Parsley, sage, dill, and basil are types of herbs. Therefore, (E) is the correct answer.

10. (B)

    An inch, a yard, a mile, and a foot measure length. Therefore, (B) is the correct answer.

11. (A)

    A sourdough, a biscuit, and a baguette are types of bread. Therefore, (A) is the correct answer.

12. (A)

    A stock pot, a skillet, and a roasting pan are essential tools used in the kitchen. Therefore, (A) is the correct answer.

13. (A)

    Talent, capability, skill, and expertise are words that describe the ability to do something well. Therefore, (A) is the correct answer.

14. (E)

    Hip hop, rap, and rock are types of music. Therefore, (E) is the correct answer.

15. (A)

    Copy, imitation, reproduction, and impression are words that describe an imitation of a person or thing. Therefore, (A) is the correct answer.

16. (B)

    Literature is any type of writings on any subject. Novel, poetry, and nonfiction are types of literature. Therefore, (B) is the correct answer.

17. (B)

    Lodging, accommodation, housing, and residence are words that describe a room, or building in which someone may live or stay. Therefore, (B) is the correct answer.

18. (C)

    Shape, structure, and form are words that describe external appearance of someone or something. Therefore, (C) is the correct answer.

19. (C)

    Ear, apple, ice, and umbrella are words that start with a vowel (a, e i, o, u). Therefore, (C) is the correct answer.

20. (C)

    Applaud, admire, honor, and congratulate are words that are used to express warm approval or admiration for someone or something. Therefore, (C) is the correct answer.

CogAT Number Analogies

Answers and Explanations

Answers

1. B	6. C	11. B	16. C
2. A	7. B	12. E	17. D
3. B	8. D	13. C	18. B
4. E	9. A	14. D	
5. D	10. B	15. D	

Explanations

1. (B)
   The second number of each pair is 2 less than the first number; that is, $8 - 2 = 6$, $11 - 2 = 9$, and $24 - 2 = 22$. Therefore, (B) is the correct answer.

2. (A)
   The second number of each pair is 50 more than the first number; that is, $5 + 50 = 55$, $50 + 50 = 100$, and $36 + 50 = 86$. Therefore, (A) is the correct answer.

3. (B)
   The second number of each pair is obtained by dividing the first number by 2; that is, $40 \div 2 = 20$, $60 \div 2 = 30$, and $90 \div 2 = 45$. Therefore, (B) is the correct answer.

4. (E)
   The second number of each pair is 15 less than the first number; that is, $30 - 15 = 15$, $25 - 15 = 10$, and $56 - 15 = 41$. Therefore, (E) is the correct answer.

5. (D)
   The second number of each pair is obtained by multiplying the first number by 3; that is, $10 \times 3 = 30$, $20 \times 3 = 60$, and $30 \times 3 = 90$. Therefore, (D) is the correct answer.

6. (C)

   The second number of each pair is the last two digits of the first number; that is, the last two digits of 134 is 34, the last two digits of 362 is 62, and the last two digits of 783 is 83. Therefore, (C) is the correct answer.

7. (B)

   The second number of each pair is obtained by multiplying the first number by 10; that is, $10 \times 10 = 100$, $50 \times 10 = 500$, and $100 \times 10 = 1000$. Therefore, (B) is the correct answer.

8. (D)

   The second number of each pair is the hundreds digit of the first number; that is, 6 is the hundreds digit of 618, 5 is the hundreds digit of 539, and 8 is the hundreds digit of 895. Therefore, (D) is the correct answer.

9. (A)

   The second number of each pair is 10 minutes less than the first number; that is, 10 minutes before 3:25 is 3:15, 10 minutes before 9:40 is 9:30, and 10 minutes before 7:05 is 6:55. Therefore, (A) is the correct answer.

10. (B)

    The second number of each pair is obtained by multiplying the first number by itself; that is, $5 \times 5 = 25$, $6 \times 6 = 36$, and $9 \times 9 = 81$. Therefore, (B) is the correct answer.

11. (B)

    The second number of each pair is 1 more than three times the first number; that is, $3 \times 3 + 1 = 10$, $4 \times 3 + 1 = 13$, and $7 \times 3 + 1 = 22$. Therefore, (B) is the correct answer.

12. (E)

    The second number of each pair is the hundreds digit and units digit of the first number; that is, 39 is the hundreds digit and units digit of 319, 13 is the hundreds digit and units digit of 193, and 29 is the hundreds digit and units digit of 279. Therefore, (E) is the correct answer.

13. (C)

    The second number of each pair is 30 minutes more than the first number; that is, 30 minutes after 3:00 is 3:30, 30 minutes after 6:15 is 6:45, and 30 minutes after 8:30 is 9:00. Therefore, (C) is the correct answer.

14. (D)

    The second number of each pair is obtained by writing the first number backwards. Writing 234, 637, and 517 backwards, you will get 432, 736, and 715, respectively. Therefore, (D) is the correct answer.

15. (D)

    The second number of each pair is 25 cents less than the first number; that is, 25 cents less than \$1.25 is \$1.00, 25 cents less than \$2.50 is \$2.25, and 25 cents less than \$4.00 is \$3.75. Therefore, (D) is the correct answer.

16. (C)

    The second number of each pair is 17 less than the first number; that is, $33-17=16$, $45-17=28$, and $56-17=39$. Therefore, (C) is the correct answer.

17. (D)

    The second number of each pair is obtained by dividing the first number by 2; that is, $5 \div 2 = \frac{5}{2}$, $7 \div 2 = \frac{7}{2}$, and $9 \div 2 = \frac{9}{2}$. Therefore, (D) is the correct answer.

18. (B)

    The second number of each pair is 1 less than three times the first number; that is, $10 \times 3 - 1 = 29$, $20 \times 3 - 1 = 59$, and $30 \times 3 - 1 = 89$. Therefore, (B) is the correct answer.

CogAT Number Puzzles

Answers and Explanations

Answers

1. D	6. C	11. D	16. D
2. B	7. C	12. E	
3. E	8. C	13. C	
4. D	9. A	14. A	
5. E	10. B	15. D	

Explanations

1. (D)

   $\boxed{20} = 3 + 8 + 9$. Therefore, (D) is the correct answer.

2. (B)

   $3 \times \boxed{4} = 3 + 3 + 3 + 3$. Therefore, (B) is the correct answer.

3. (E)

   $8 + 7 - 3 < \boxed{13}$. Therefore, (E) is the correct answer.

4. (D)

   $7 - \boxed{3} = 12 - 10 + 14 - 12$. Therefore, (D) is the correct answer.

5. (E)

   $5 + 3 + 4 = 19 - 2 - \boxed{5}$. Therefore, (E) is the correct answer.

6. (C)

   $14 - 10 + 15 - 9 = \boxed{4} + 6$. Therefore, (C) is the correct answer.

7. (C)

   $25 + \boxed{14} + 37 = 37 + 14 + 25$. Therefore, (C) is the correct answer.

8. (C)

   $\boxed{25} - 9 + 8 = 9 + 8 + 7$. Therefore, (C) is the correct answer.

9. (A)

   $27 + 13 = \boxed{10} \times 4$. Therefore, (A) is the correct answer.

10. (B)

    $19 + 17 - 22 = 2 + \boxed{4} + 8$. Therefore, (B) is the correct answer.

11. (D)

    $6 \times 5 = 15 + 8 + \boxed{9} - 2$. Therefore, (D) is the correct answer.

12. (E)

    $16 + \boxed{12} > 8 + 9 + 10$. Therefore, (E) is the correct answer.

13. (C)

    $40 - 14 - 17 - 5 = \boxed{4}$. Therefore, (C) is the correct answer.

14. (A)

    $7 \times 4 = 7 + \boxed{7} + 7 + 7$. Therefore, (A) is the correct answer.

15. (D)

    $4 \times 7 \times 6 = \boxed{7} \times 4 \times 6$. Therefore, (D) is the correct answer.

16. (D)

    $6 + 9 + \boxed{7} + 5 = 3 \times 3 \times 3$. Therefore, (D) is the correct answer.

CogAT Number Series

Answers and Explanations

Answers

1. B	6. C	11. E	16. B
2. A	7. E	12. B	17. D
3. A	8. C	13. A	18. B
4. E	9. E	14. A	
5. C	10. B	15. D	

Explanations

1. (B)

   The numbers are increasing by 4. So the number that replaces the question mark is $24 + 4 = 28$. Therefore, (B) is the correct answer.

2. (A)

   The numbers are decreasing by 10. So the first number that replaces the question mark is 110. Therefore, (A) is the correct answer.

3. (A)

   The numbers are increasing by 13. The complete pattern is $\{2, 15, 28, 41, 54, 67, 80\}$. So the number that replaces the question mark is 54. Therefore, (A) is the correct answer.

4. (E)

   The numbers are decreasing by half. So the number that replaces the question mark is $128 \div 2 = 64$. The complete pattern is $\{256, 128, 64, 32, 16, 8, 4\}$. Therefore, (E) is the correct answer.

5. (C)

   The numbers are decreasing by 8. So the number that replaces the question mark is 52. The complete pattern is $\{76, 68, 60, 52, 44, 36, 28\}$. Therefore, (C) is the correct answer.

6. (C)

   The numbers 17 and 33 are repeating. So the number that replaces the question mark is 33. Therefore, (C) is the correct answer.

7. (E)

   The numbers are formed by adding one, two, three, four, five, and six; that is $9+\mathbf{1}=10$, $10+\mathbf{2}=12$, $12+\mathbf{3}=15$, $15+\mathbf{4}=19$, $19+\mathbf{5}=24$, and $24+\mathbf{6}=30$. Therefore, (E) is the correct answer.

8. (C)

   The consecutive odd-numbered terms are decreasing by 3: 25, 22, 19, and 16. The consecutive even-numbered terms are increasing by 1: 3, 4, and 5. So the number that replaces the question mark is 16. Therefore, (C) is the correct answer.

9. (E)

   The numbers are formed by subtracting nine, eight, seven, six, five, and four; that is $99-\mathbf{9}=90$, $90-\mathbf{8}=82$, $82-\mathbf{7}=75$, $75-\mathbf{6}=69$, $69-\mathbf{5}=64$, and $64-\mathbf{4}=60$. Therefore, (E) is the correct answer.

10. (B)

    The numbers are increasing by 17. So the number that replaces the question mark is $57+17=74$. The complete pattern is $\{6,23,40,57,74,91,108\}$. Therefore, (B) is the correct answer.

11. (E)

    The numbers are formed by multiplying the previous term by 3. The complete pattern is $\{\frac{2}{3},2,6,18,54,162,486\}$. So the number that replaces the question mark is 162. Therefore, (E) is the correct answer.

12. (B)

    The consecutive odd-numbered terms are increasing by 8: 21, 29, 37, and 45. The consecutive even-numbered terms are all one. So the number that replaces the question mark is 45. Therefore, (B) is the correct answer.

13. (A)

    The numbers are formed by a pattern: add 10 and subtract 6. The complete pattern is $\{34,44,38,48,42,52,46\}$. So the number that replaces the question mark is 46. Therefore, (A) is the correct answer.

14. (A)

The numbers are decreasing by 22. So the number that replaces the question mark is $144 - 22 = 122$. Therefore, (A) is the correct answer.

15. (D)

Each term is 1 less than three times the previous term. The complete pattern is $\{1, 2, 5, 14, 41, 122, 365\}$. So the number that replaces the question mark is $122 \times 3 - 1 = 365$. Therefore, (D) is the correct answer.

16. (B)

The numbers are formed by a pattern: Add 2 and multiply by 2. The complete pattern is $\{1, 3, 6, 8, 16, 18, 36\}$. Therefore, (B) is the correct answer.

17. (D)

The consecutive odd-numbered terms are multiplied by $4:$ 1, 4, 16, and 64. The consecutive even-numbered terms are decreasing by half: 40, 20, and 10. So the number that replaces the question mark is 64. Therefore, (D) is the correct answer.

18. (B)

The number of zeros between the first digit and the last digit of each number is increasing by 1. The number of zero in the first number is 0, the number of zero in the second number is 1, the number of zero in the third number is 2, and so on and so forth. The complete pattern is $\{11, 101, 1001, 10001, 100001, 1000001, 10000001\}$. So the number that replaces the question mark is 10001. Therefore, (B) is the correct answer.

CogAT Figure Matrices

Answers and Explanations

Answers

1. A	6. B	11. E	16. C
2. D	7. A	12. E	17. A
3. D	8. E	13. B	18. B
4. B	9. C	14. B	19. D
5. C	10. A	15. A	20. D

Explanations

1. (A)

   The first figure has 4 squares which are either shaded or unshaded. The second figure is obtained by changing shaded squares to unshaded squares and vice versa. Do the same thing for the third figure to get the answer. Therefore, (A) is the correct answer.

2. (D)

   The first figure has one white circle to the left side of an arrow. The second figure is obtained by putting two black circles to the right side of the arrow. The third figure has one white square at the top side of an arrow. The answer should have two black squares at the bottom side of the arrow. Therefore, (D) is the correct answer.

3. (D)

   The first figure has two smaller shapes and a larger shape. The second figure is obtained by putting two smaller shapes inside the larger shape. The answer should have two smaller shapes inside the larger shape in the third figure. Therefore, (D) is the correct answer.

4. (B)

   The first and the second figures has one horizontal line. However, the second figure has one more vertical lines than the first figure has. The third figure has 2 horizontal lines and 2 vertical lines. So, the answer should have 2 horizontal lines and 3 vertical lines. Therefore, (B) is the correct answer.

5. (C)

   The colors of the first figure are gray, white, and black from outside to inside. The colors of the second figure are black, gray, and white from outside to inside. The colors of the third figure are black, gray, and white from outside to inside. The answer should have white, black, and gray from outside to inside. Therefore, (C) is the correct answer.

6. (B)

   The second figure is obtained by rotating the first figure 90° clockwise. If you rotate the third figure 90° clockwise, you get the figure in (B). Therefore, (B) is the correct answer.

7. (A)

   The second figure is obtained by rotating the first figure 90° counterclockwise and putting two black small circles inside the larger circle. The answer should be a 90° counterclockwise rotation of the third figure and has two black squares inside the larger square. Therefore, (A) is the correct answer.

8. (E)

   The second figure represents the remaining shape after removing 4 white small circles from the large circle in the middle. If you remove 4 smaller circles from the rounded rectangle in the middle, you get the remaining shape in (E). Therefore, (E) is the correct answer.

9. (C)

   The second figure is a mirror image(Vertical reflection) of the first figure. The mirror image of the third figure is the figure in (C). Therefore, (C) is the correct answer.

10. (A)

    The second figure is an outline of a shape obtained by merging three circles in the first figure. An outline of a shape obtained by merging three shapes in the third figure is the figure in (A). Therefore, (A) is the correct answer.

11. (E)

    The second figure is a 45° clockwise rotation of the first figure. The answer should be a 45° clockwise rotation of the third figure. Therefore, (E) is the correct answer.

12. (E)

    The second figure is obtained by rotating the first figure 45° counterclockwise and swapping the colors. If you rotate the third figure 45° counterclockwise and swap the colors, you get the figure in (E). Therefore, (E) is the correct answer.

13. (B)

    The second figure is obtained by rotating the first figure 180° clockwise. If you rotate the third figure 180° clockwise, you get the figure in (B). Therefore, (B) is the correct answer.

14. (B)

    The second figure is obtained by enlarging the first figure and rotating 45° clockwise. If you enlarge the third figure and rotate 45° clockwise, you get the figure in (B). Therefore, (B) is the correct answer.

15. (A)

    The second figure is obtained by making the first figure smaller and rotating 90° counterclockwise from the center of the first figure. If you make the third figure smaller and rotate 90° counterclockwise from the center of the third figure, you get the figure in (A). Therefore, (A) is the correct answer.

16. (C)

    If you combine two shaded regions in the first figure, you get the second figure. If you combine three shaded regions, you get the figure in (C). Therefore, (C) is the correct answer.

17. (A)

    The second figure is obtained by swapping the outer shape and the middle shape in the first figure and keeping their patterns. In addition, change color of the inner shape from white to black. If you swap the outer shape and the middle shape in the third figure, keep their patterns, and change color of the inner shape from white to black, you get the figure in (A). Therefore, (A) is the correct answer.

18. (B)

    The first figure in each row is obtained by putting the second figure on top of the third figure. Therefore, (B) is the correct answer.

19. (D)

    Each row has three shapes: a star, a part of a circle, a hexagon with a circle inside. They are arranged differently in each row. Therefore, (D) is the correct answer.

20. (D)

    Colors change from black to white or black to white as moving across rows and columns. Figures in each row are reflected horizontally as moving from left to right. Therefore, (D) is the correct answer.

CogAT Paper Folding

Answers and Explanations

Answers

1. C	6. B	11. A	16. C
2. C	7. A	12. B	
3. C	8. D	13. A	
4. D	9. C	14. B	
5. A	10. D	15. D	

Explanations

1. (C)

   The paper is folded diagonally. So, there will be 2 squares and 2 triangles if it is unfolded completely as shown below.

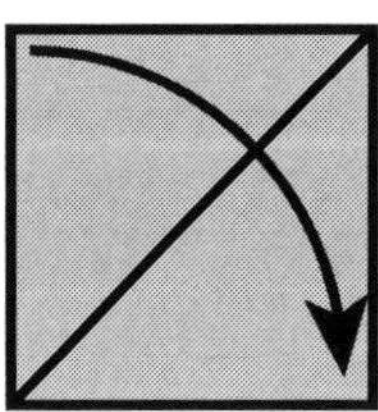

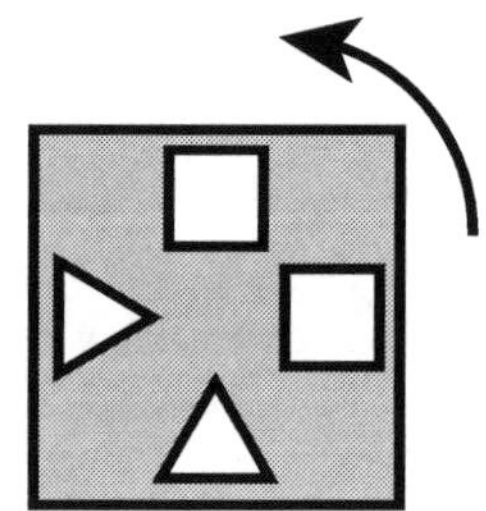

Therefore, (C) is the correct answer.

2. (C)

   The paper is folded vertically. So, you will get the figure if it is unfolded completely as shown below.

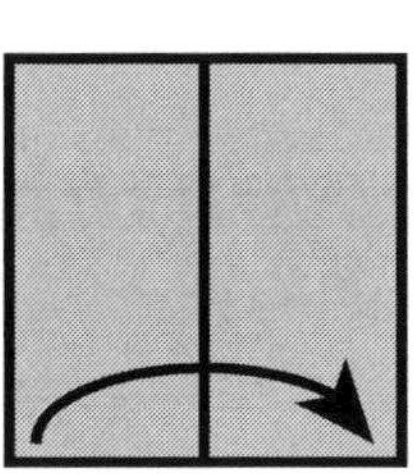 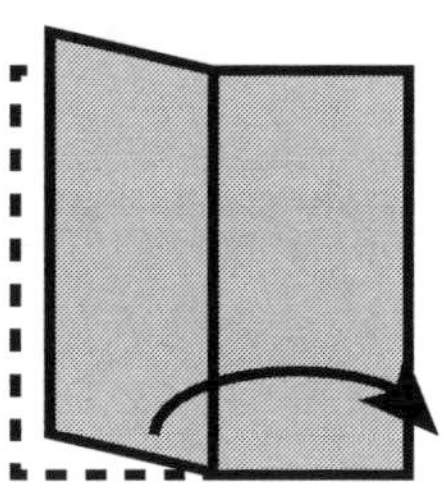 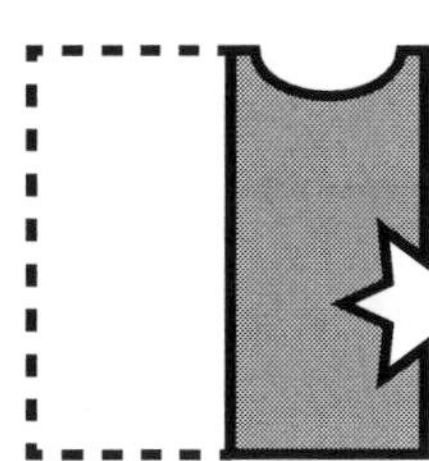 

   Therefore, (C) is the correct answer.

3. (C)

   The paper is folded horizontally. So, you will get the figure if it is unfolded completely as shown below.

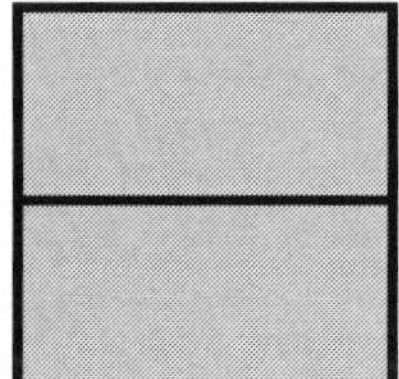 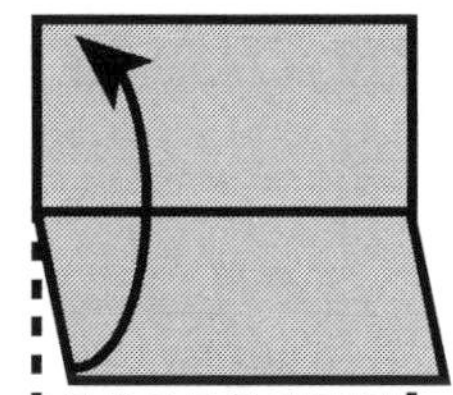 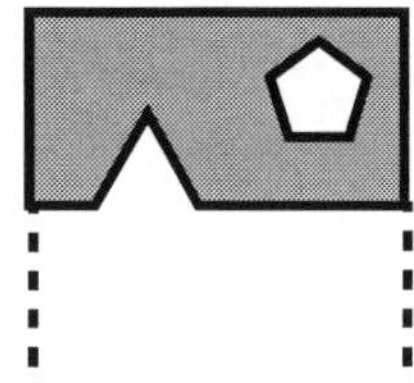 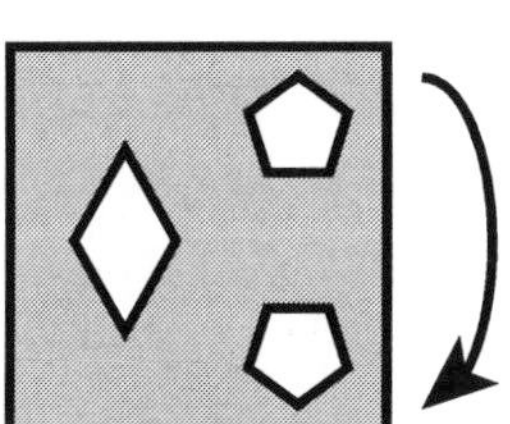

   Therefore, (C) is the correct answer.

4. (D)

   The paper is folded diagonally. So, you will get the figure if it is unfolded completely as shown below.

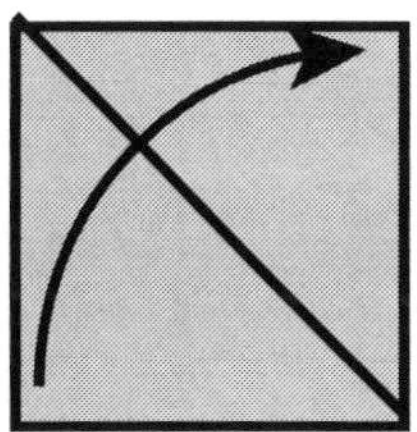  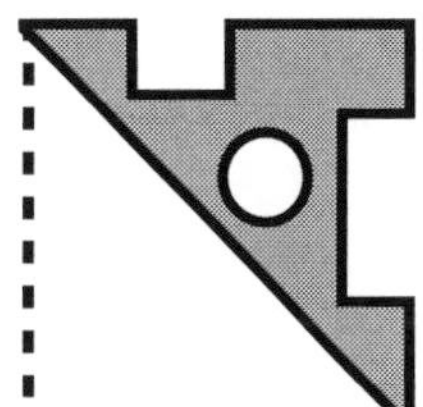 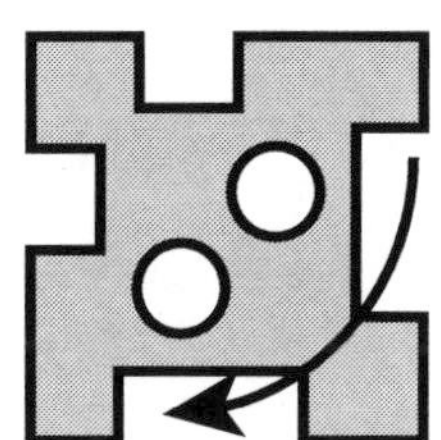

   Therefore, (D) is the correct answer.

5. (A)

The paper is folded diagonally twice and then folded vertically. So, you will get the figure if it is unfolded completely as shown below.

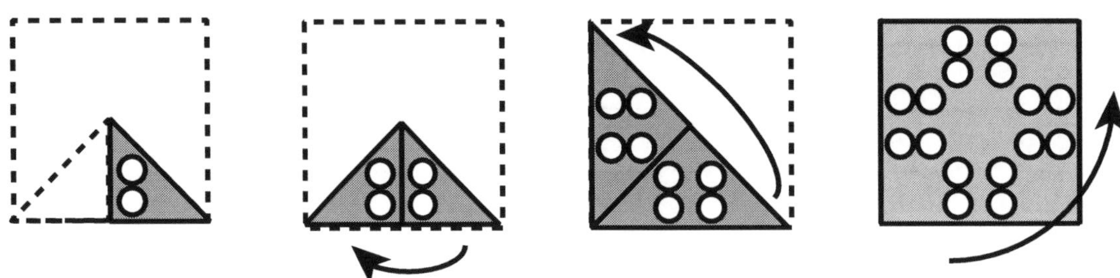

Therefore, (A) is the correct answer.

6. (B)

The paper is folded vertically and then folded horizontally. So, you will get the figure if it is unfolded completely as shown below.

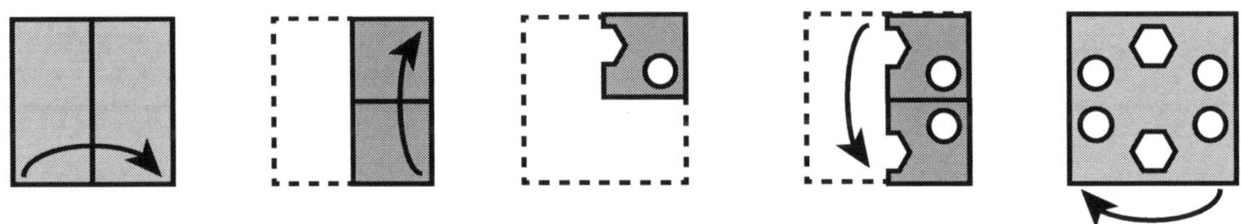

Therefore, (B) is the correct answer.

7. (A)

The paper is folded diagonally twice. So, you will get the figure if it is unfolded completely as shown below.

Therefore, (A) is the correct answer.

8. (D)

The paper is folded vertically and then folded horizontally. So, you will get the figure if it is unfolded completely as shown below.

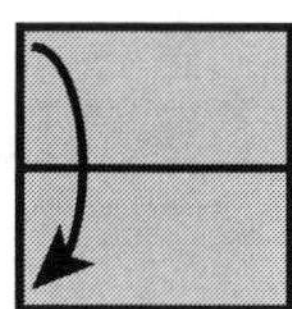
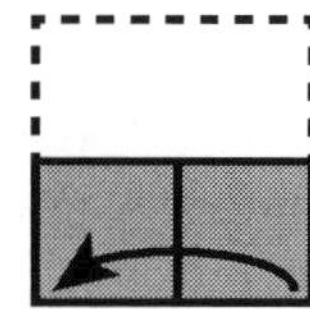
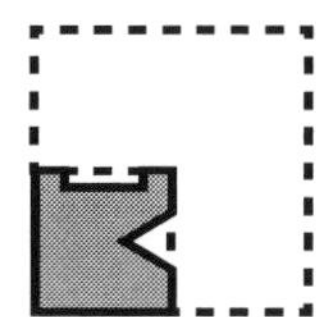
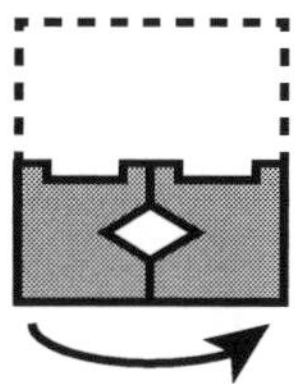
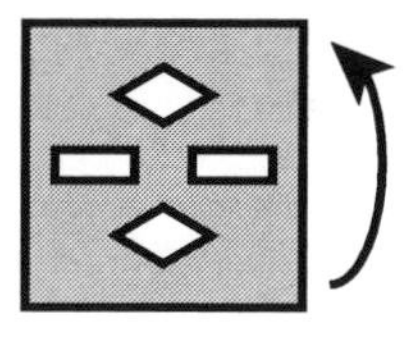

Therefore, (D) is the correct answer.

9. (C)

The paper is folded vertically and horizontally, and then folded diagonally. So, you will get the figure if it is unfolded completely as shown below.

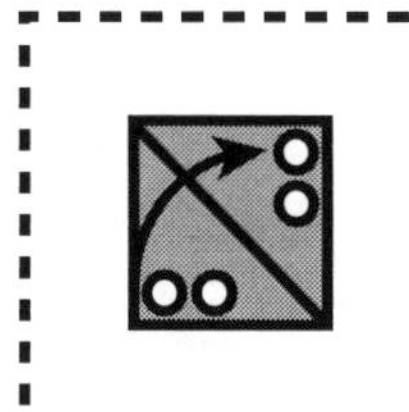
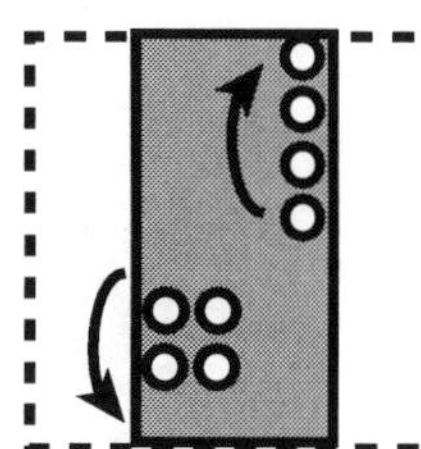
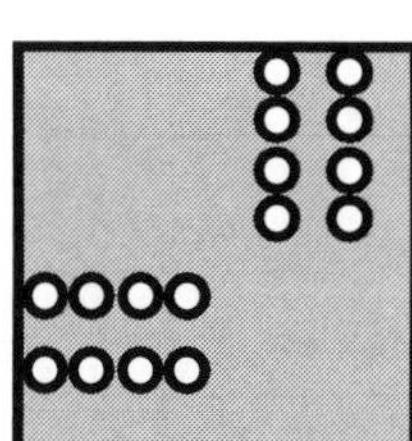

Therefore, (C) is the correct answer.

10. (D)

The paper is folded vertically and then folded horizontally. So, you will get the figure if it is unfolded completely as shown below.

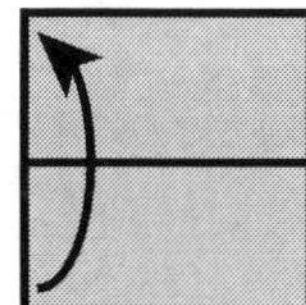
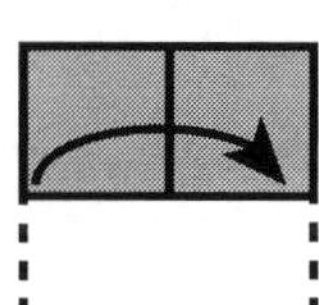
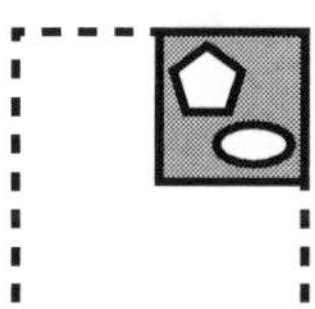

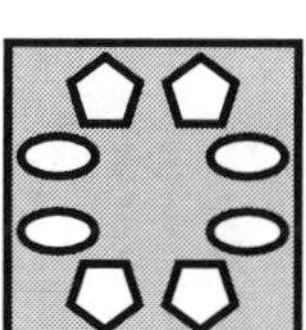

Therefore, (D) is the correct answer.

11. (A)

The paper is folded vertically and folded horizontally twice. So, you will get the figure if it is unfolded completely as shown below.

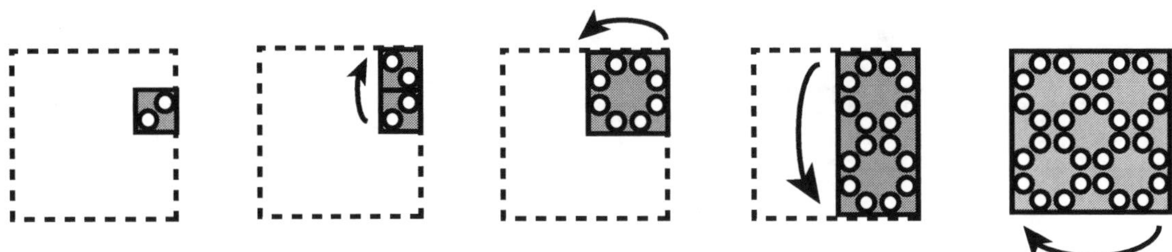

Therefore, (A) is the correct answer.

12. (B)

The paper is folded horizontally once and then folded vertically twice. So, you will get the figure if it is unfolded completely as shown below.

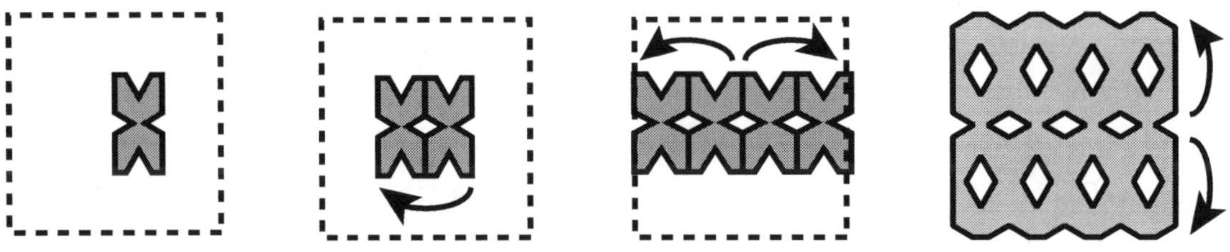

Therefore, (B) is the correct answer.

13. (A)

The paper is folded vertically and horizontally, and then folded diagonally. So, you will get the figure if it is unfolded completely as shown below.

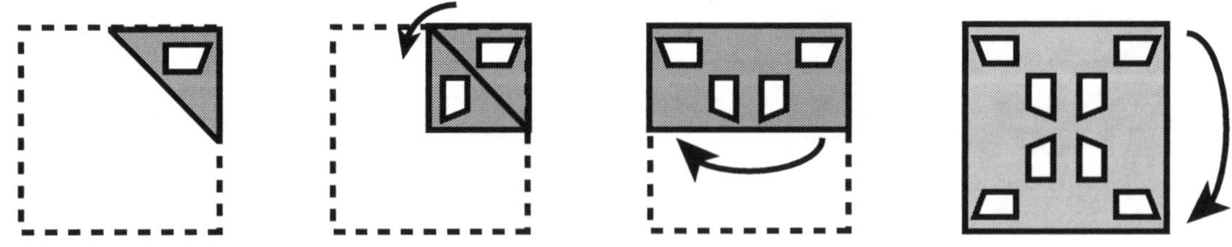

Therefore, (A) is the correct answer.

14. (B)

The paper is folded diagonally twice and then folded horizontally. So, you will get the figure if it is unfolded completely as shown below.

    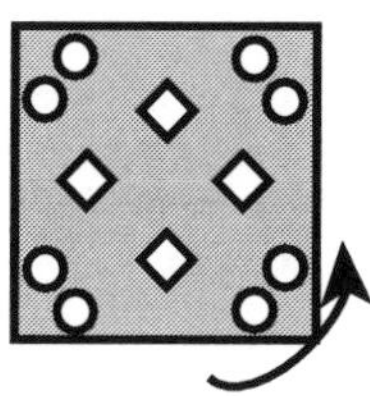

Therefore, (B) is the correct answer.

15. (D)

The paper is folded vertically and horizontally, and then folded diagonally. So, you will get the figure if it is unfolded completely as shown below.

 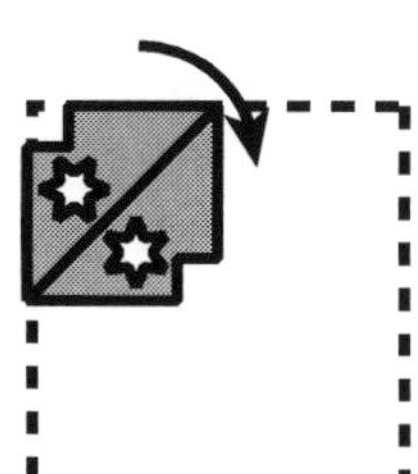  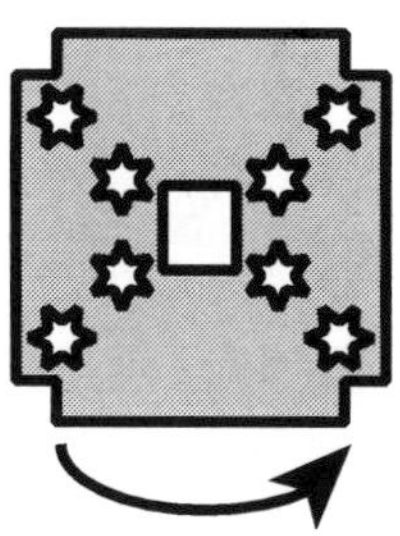

Therefore, (D) is the correct answer.

16. (C)

The paper is folded horizontally and vertically, and then folded diagonally. So, you will get the figure if it is unfolded completely as shown below.

  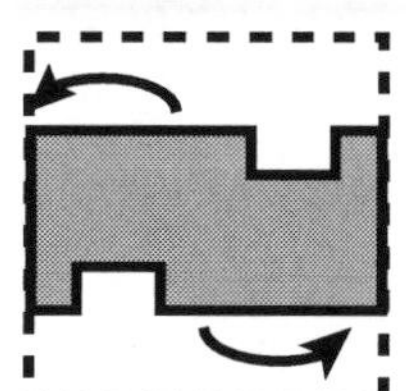 

Therefore, (C) is the correct answer.

CogAT Figure Classification

Answers and Explanations

Answers

1. D	6. D	11. C	16. B
2. C	7. D	12. A	17. C
3. C	8. B	13. D	18. D
4. A	9. B	14. C	19. A
5. B	10. C	15. D	20. B

Explanations

1. (D)

   The figures in the top row have 2 same shapes with the color white and 1 different shape with black color inside. Therefore, (D) is the correct answer.

2. (C)

   The figures in the top row have four sides. Therefore, (C) is the correct answer.

3. (C)

   The figures in the top row have two circles: a white circle which touches the larger circle inside and a black circle which touches the larger circle outside. Therefore, (C) is the correct answer.

4. (A)

   The figures in the top row have two shapes. An outer shape is shaded and an inner shape has a dotted pattern. Therefore, (A) is the correct answer.

5. (B)

   The figures in the top row are divided into 4 equal regions, of which only one region is shaded. Therefore, (B) is the correct answer.

6. (D)

   The figures in the top row consist of 5 squares: 3 black squares and 2 white squares. Therefore, (D) is the correct answer.

7. (D)

   Each figure in the top row has two shapes: The right shape is a vertical reflection of the left shape. Therefore, (A) is the correct answer. Therefore, (D) is the correct answer.

8. (B)

   Each figure in the top row has a circle inside at one of its corners. Therefore, (B) is the correct answer.

9. (B)

   The figures in the top row have a three-sided and a four-sided shapes inside. Therefore, (B) is the correct answer.

10. (C)

    The figures in the top row have four different images. Therefore, (C) is the correct answer.

11. (C)

    Each figure in the top row consists two shapes. The shape in the right side is a vertical reflection of the shape that lies inside of the left side. Therefore, (C) is the correct answer.

12. (A)

    The figures in the top row have patterns that consist of straight lines. Therefore, (A) is the correct answer.

13. (D)

    The figures in the top row consists of three similar four-sided shapes. The colors of the two similar shapes inside are white and black. Therefore, (D) is the correct answer.

14. (C)

    The figures in the top row have even-number of circles inside. The figure in (C) has 8 circles inside. Therefore, (C) is the correct answer.

15. (D)

    The figures in the top row have 9 squares, of which five squares are shaded. Therefore, (D) is the correct answer.

16. (B)

    The figures in the top row consist of 2 pairs of similar shapes. Therefore, (B) is the correct answer.

17. (C)

    The figures in the top row have two shapes, which create a circle if the two shapes are combined. Therefore, (C) is the correct answer.

18. (D)

    The figures in the top row and the figure in (D) are obtained by rotating counter-clockwise $90°$. Therefore, (D) is the correct answer.

19. (A)

    The figures in the top row are symmetric about the line that passes through the left upper corner to right lower corner of the figures. Therefore, (A) is the correct answer.

20. (B)

    The figures in the top row have all sharp corners. Therefore, (B) is the correct answer.

Made in the USA
Middletown, DE
16 August 2019